STORIES IN THE SEAMS

STORIES IN THE SEAMS

A PEOPLE'S HISTORY OF BLACK QUILTS AND THEIR MAKERS

SHARBREON PLUMMER, PHD

CHRONICLE BOOKS
SAN FRANCISCO

Library of Congress Cataloging-in-Publication Data
Names: Plummer, Sharbreon author
Title: Stories in the seams : a people's history of Black quilts and their makers / Dr. Sharbreon Plummer.
Description: San Francisco : Chronicle Books, [2026] | Includes bibliographical references.
Identifiers: LCCN 2026003879 | ISBN 9781797231570 hardcover
Subjects: LCSH: African American quilts | African American quiltmakers--Biography | Art and society--United States | LCGFT: Biographies
Classification: LCC NK9112 .P58 2026
LC record available at https://lccn.loc.gov/2026003879

Manufactured in China.

MIX
Paper | Supporting responsible forestry
FSC™ C169962
FSC www.fsc.org

Design by Allison Weiner.
Typesetting by Frank Brayton.
Typeset in Sabon, Avenir, and Canicule Display.

10 9 8 7 6 5 4 3 2 1

Chronicle books and gifts are available at special quantity discounts to corporations, professional associations, literacy programs, and other organizations. For details and discount information, please contact our premiums department at corporategifts@chroniclebooks.com or at 1-800-759-0190.

Chronicle Books is represented in the UK and Europe by Abrams & Chronicle Books, 22 Ely Place, London EC1N 6TE, abramsandchronicle.co.uk, and Média-Participations, 57 rue Gaston Tessier, 75166 Paris CEDEX 19, media-participations.com.

Chronicle Books LLC
680 Second Street
San Francisco, California 94107
chroniclebooks.com

This book is dedicated to our ancestors,
whose creativity could not be confined to a page.
May the seeds you've planted for us bloom free in every lifetime.

CONTENTS

INTRODUCTION

Why Black Quilts?

This book begins with a simple belief: Black quilting traditions matter and it is always the right time to give them the attention they deserve. When we are searching for ways to heal, reconnect with history, and build community, Black quilters offer important lessons. Their work shows us how creativity can be a tool for survival, a way to care for ourselves and others, and a method for keeping culture alive. Quilting has long been a part of Black life in the United States, a practice that has been passed down through families, churches, and communities. Some quilts were made out of necessity, using whatever fabric was available to keep loved ones warm. Others were made to mark special events or to tell stories that might otherwise be forgotten. Today, Black quilters are still making, preserving, and innovating. They continue to build something meaningful from seemingly disparate pieces.

Despite quilting's deep roots in Black culture and American history, it has often been overlooked and misunderstood. Across time, the variety within Black quilting has been flattened into a single style or story. This book pushes against those limiting beliefs. It highlights the many reasons Black people quilt: to honor ancestors, to express political beliefs, to process grief, to find peace, or simply to create beauty. It also shows how many different styles and approaches exist—some grounded in tradition, others more experimental. At the heart of this book is the belief that, for Black people, the quilters' voices and lived experiences are just as important as the quilts themselves. Even when working in distinct ways, Black quilters have collectively cared both for the self and for the community. When Black quilters sit down to sew, they're doing more than making an object. They're creating space to reflect, to rest, and to resist. Whether done in the solitude of a personal studio or within a collective setting, quilting allows us to make meaning in a world that often feels chaotic or overwhelming.

This book doesn't try to tell the whole story of Black quilting—no single book could. Instead, it brings together different voices, histories, and examples to show just how rich and varied this tradition is. Whether you're new to quilting or have a long relationship with it, you'll find something here that speaks to the "why" of Black quiltmaking and how quilts will continue to inspire generations. At a time when many are trying to make sense of their place in the world, Black quilts remind us that healing, connection, and creativity are still possible, and that through their assembly, quilts put us back together as well.

PART I

MEMORY

Memory lives in fabric.

It is tucked between the seams of worn clothes and in the DNA embedded within the cloth—from both the material and its maker. Within Black quilting traditions, memory is a driving force for creation, reclaiming cultural histories and resisting social erasure. This section traces the ways Black quilters have engaged memory as both a material and a practice: how memory is preserved, translated, and reimagined through cloth. Across the following chapters, we follow quilts not only as objects, but as living records.

We begin with an origin story in "Homecoming," a chapter that excavates quilting's foundations in the South. Rather than seeing quilts solely as utilitarian responses to oppression, I think of them as early proof of self-definition. Through quilting gatherings and the resulting creations, enslaved women cultivated space for beauty. Making was a form of becoming that was shaped by togetherness. As women gathered around a quilting frame, they also developed their individual creativity and a network of support. As generations moved from plantation quarters to resettlement communities during the Depression, quilts bore witness to upheaval while carrying the weight and warmth of home. Stories like those of Harriet Powers and Chany Scot Black offer a look at the skill and variety that existed across the region. "Homecoming" also explores how quilts were carried beyond the South while tethering Black communities back to their homes.

"Quilts as a Muse" expands this conversation by moving into the realm of cultural reflection and artistic citation, exploring how citation can extend beyond a quote or text as a reference in written work. Black artists working outside of textiles have incorporated—or cited—quilt pattern motifs within their works for decades. In this case, the quilt pivots from private keepsake to public symbol. We see how artists, writers, and makers across time and across disciplines have turned to quilts not just for inspiration, but for visual language that connects back to their cultural communities. In the hands of Jacob Lawrence, quilts illuminate the isolation of migration. In Romare Bearden's collages, they signal a return to heritage. For writers like Alice Walker, the quilt becomes a metaphor of inheritance. Contemporary artists, from Alison Saar to Sedrick Huckaby, build on this legacy by intertwining personal and cultural memory into material form, exploring the importance of quilting to Black life and history. Through their work, we come to understand that quilting's influence stretches far beyond the meeting of the seams.

Finally, "A League of Their Own" offers an account of those who have made memory their life's work. The scholars, organizers, and cultural stewards profiled here have not only preserved quilts but have also fought for the stories embedded within them. Cuesta Benberry, Roland L. Freeman, and Dr. Carolyn Mazloomi are presented as architects of a more just archive, shaped by the multitudes of Black quilt practices. Their efforts remind us that memory must be actively protected or it risks being erased. They remind us that the documentation of Black quilting is not a singular act of preservation but an ongoing intervention against forgetting.

Together, these three chapters affirm that Black quilting is a vessel for memory shaped by centuries of collective effort.

Home-
coming

To trace the lineage of quilting in America is to follow a thread interwoven into Black Southern life. Although needle and cloth have ancient histories across continents, the story of quilting in the United States cannot be told without acknowledging Black women in the South. Under the weight of bondage, quilting became more than a domestic chore. It became a practice of memory, a vessel for resistance, and a quiet act of care passed from hand to hand, from generation to generation.

Enslaved women stitched out of necessity, making covers to shield themselves and their families against the cold night air that seeped through thin walls. Quilting, even under watchful eyes and brutal conditions, offered a rare space where a creative spirit could grow. Without a pen, they wrote with thread. With diminished voices, they spoke through pattern and texture. In the American South, quilting grew roots in red clay and cotton fields. It thrived in living quarters, kitchens, and eventually in living rooms and church basements, adapting with time but never severed from its original home. To understand the depth of Black quilting is to reckon with the realities of enslavement and to witness the brilliance that emerged in spite of (and because of) it. It is a tradition born of utility, yes, but also of imagination, survival, and grace.

Black women in the antebellum period were faced with two forms of labor. In addition to the grueling work of crop cultivation alongside men and children, they were also responsible for many of the textile-related tasks on plantations such as harvesting indigo and processing cotton. Early crops like indigo had to be kept free of weeds, then harvested and fermented through a process that took anywhere from twelve to fifteen hours.[1] It was a skilled process that demanded a great deal of beating and stirring to produce the dye that would later be sold and used both locally and nationally. At plantations in states like the Carolinas and Virginia, workspaces for spinning and weaving were created to lessen cloth costs and produce clothing for those who were enslaved.[2] At Thomas Jefferson's plantation, Monticello, it was estimated that over a hundred enslaved people were clothed with thousands of yards of cloth by the early nineteenth century, which was often made possible by the dual labor and skills of Black women.[3]

The introduction of Eli Whitney's cotton gin in 1790 shifted cotton production and the institution of slavery as a whole. The textile industry in Great Britain was growing rapidly, and the demand for cotton garments was also growing internationally. In order to keep up with production demands, there needed to be an increase in slave labor. As a result, the number of enslaved people in the United States grew by over three million between 1790 and 1860.[4] With labor yielding nearly two hundred pounds per day, the price of cotton clothing dropped by nearly 90 percent.[5]

The gin's development led to cotton becoming a booming US export in the nineteenth century. This allowed American-manufactured fabrics to become more popular and more readily available for domestic use as well. As a result, quilting became more easily accessible. Early quilts had been made with imported fabric or handspun materials crafted by enslaved women, but as the availability of fabrics increased, so did the possibilities for creating more decorative quilts for plantation homes.

An elaborate appliqué quilt—such as the one on page 17—is an example of what would have been created by enslaved women for use inside the plantation home. Appliqué involves hand sewing fabric, often cut into a specific shape or embellishment, onto a background fabric. The *Flower Basket Quilt* is said to have been made on the Wilson and Lucinda Lewis plantation in Copiah County, Mississippi, around 1860. The detail of the design signals a deep technical skill. The motifs were appliquéd to the white background, and ruching was used to gather and create flower petals at the end of each stem. The quilters also stuffed

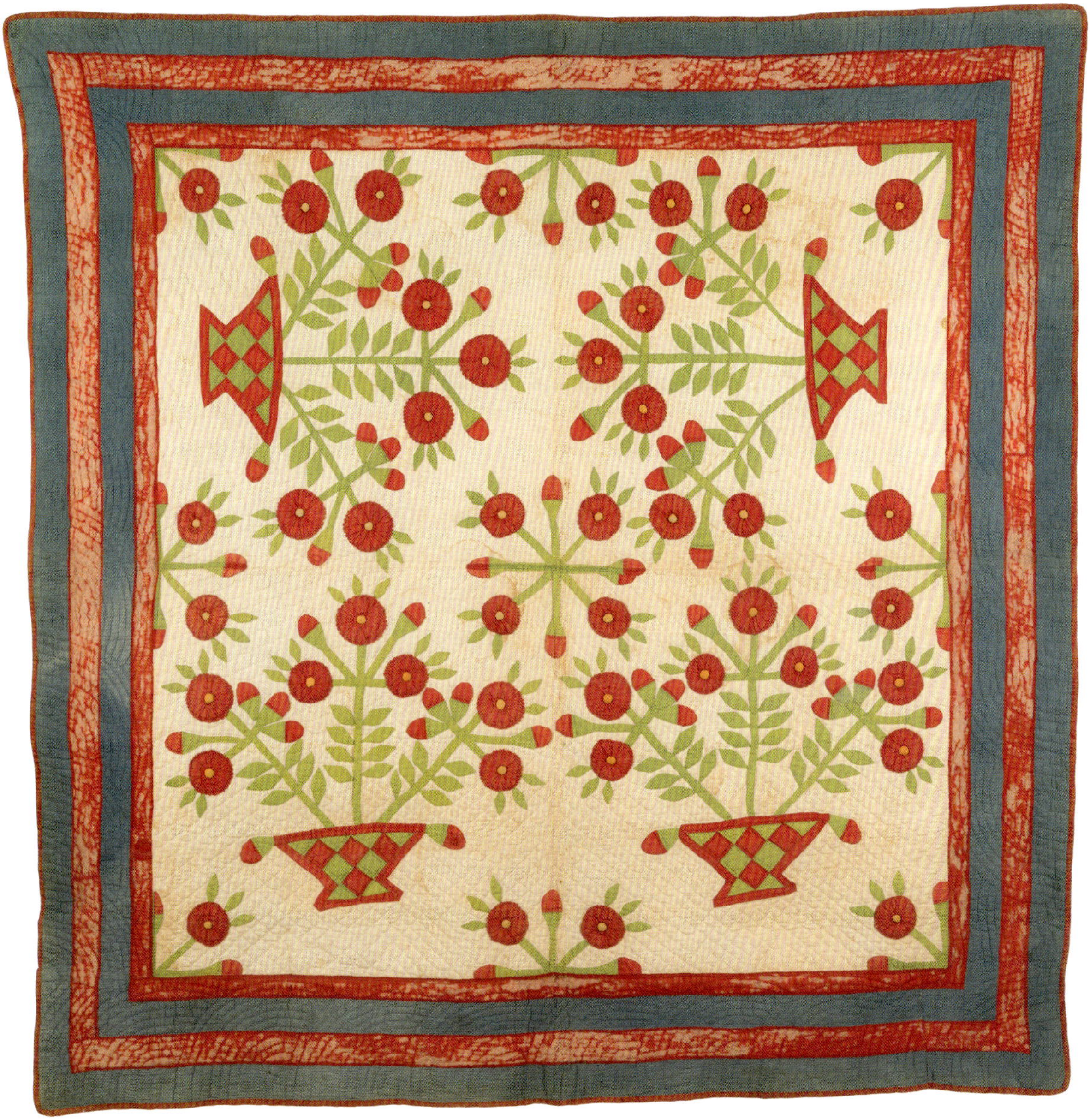

Bedcover–Quilt, Bed, made by an enslaved person or persons, 1860

the yellow center of each flower to add dimension and finished the piece with elaborate hand quilting.[6]

In the face of inhumane circumstances, enslaved women established the early foundation for individual creativity through their work on quilts and in textile production. When they weren't creating quilts and other goods for the plantation by day, they were spending nights and free moments creating quilts for their own families' use. With the remnants and scraps made available to them, Black quilters were able to create personal quilts free from supervision or outside direction.

Quilting parties—also known as quiltings, bees, or frolics—also became a way to build social connections while completing multiple quilts over the course of one evening. Women and men would gather together, typically on their only free day, to eat, dance, and quilt. As scholar Gladys-Marie Fry describes, two types of quiltings were

An African American Woman Seated Indoors Beside a Large Quilt, in or near Richmond County, Georgia, in the Late 19th Century, Robert E. Williams, 1872/1898

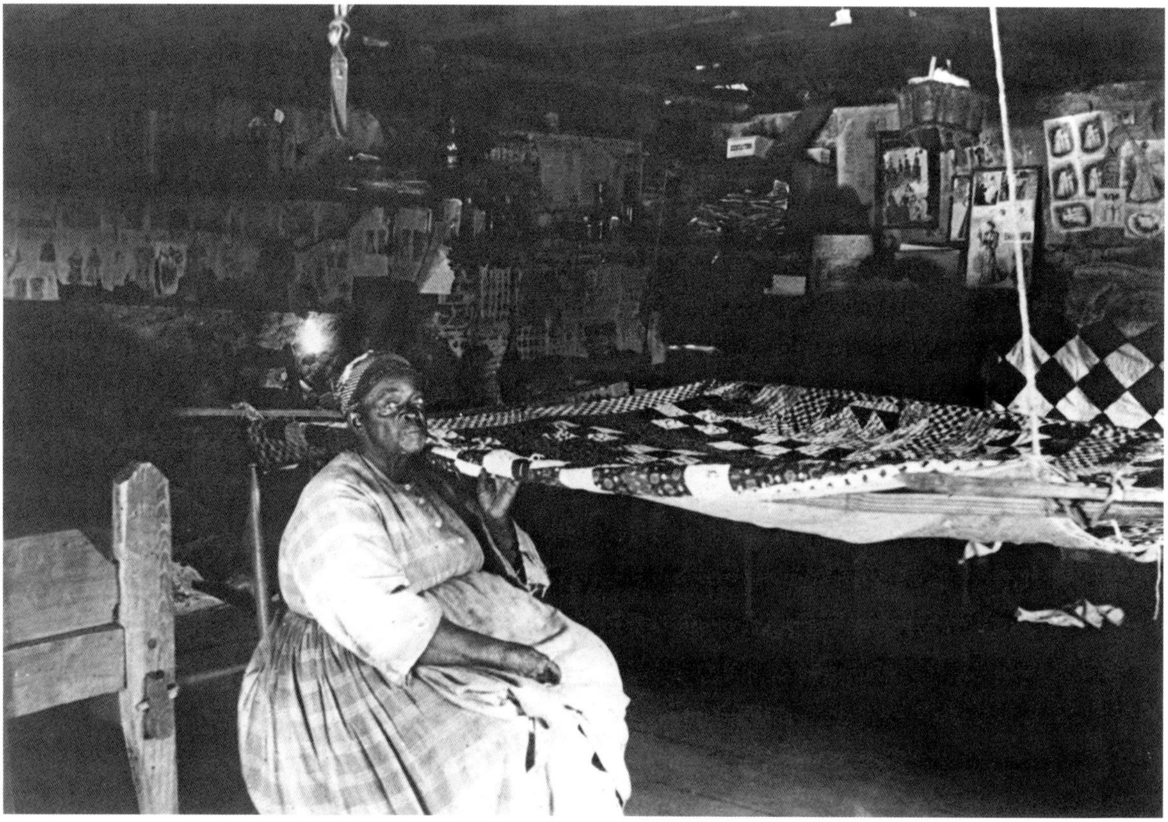

common on plantations. Some were "elaborate affairs in which each phase of the events was orchestrated," and others were "more impromptu scaled-down affairs that rotated nightly from cabin to cabin."[7] She continues by discussing how the format of the parties varied depending on the season or time of week. Enslaved people even used the gatherings as a form of community care. For example, there is a record of women in South Carolina hosting a quilting for a man who was raising his children alone and needed support.[8] The WPA Slave Narrative Project recorded several examples of formerly enslaved interviewees who recalled quiltings as a central part of their life on plantations:

One of the most enjoyable affairs in those days was the quilting party. Every night they would assemble at some particular house and help that person to finish her quilts. The next night, a visit would be made to someone else's home and so on, until everyone had a sufficient amount of bed clothing made for the winter. Besides, this was an excellent chance to get together for a pleasant time and discuss the latest gossip.

—Camilla Jackson, Georgia[9]

Mother said they had cornshuckings, quiltings and cotton pickings on the plantation. She told me a good deal about the cornshuckings: about how they selected a general, whose job was to get up on top of the corn pile and holler at the top of his voice, leading the cornshucking song, while the others all shucked the corn and sang. After the corn was all shucked there were always fine eats. I can remember the quiltings myself. The women went from one house to another and quilted as many as 12 quilts in one night sometimes. After the quilts were all finished they had a big spread of good food too. Now it takes a whole month to quilt one quilt and nothing to eat.

—Mary Colbert, Georgia[10]

Through quilting bees, enslaved communities deepened their bonds with one another, and the act of quilting became an intergenerational act. Quilters could be liberated in their expression and refine their skill through guidance and observations. Quilting spaces were

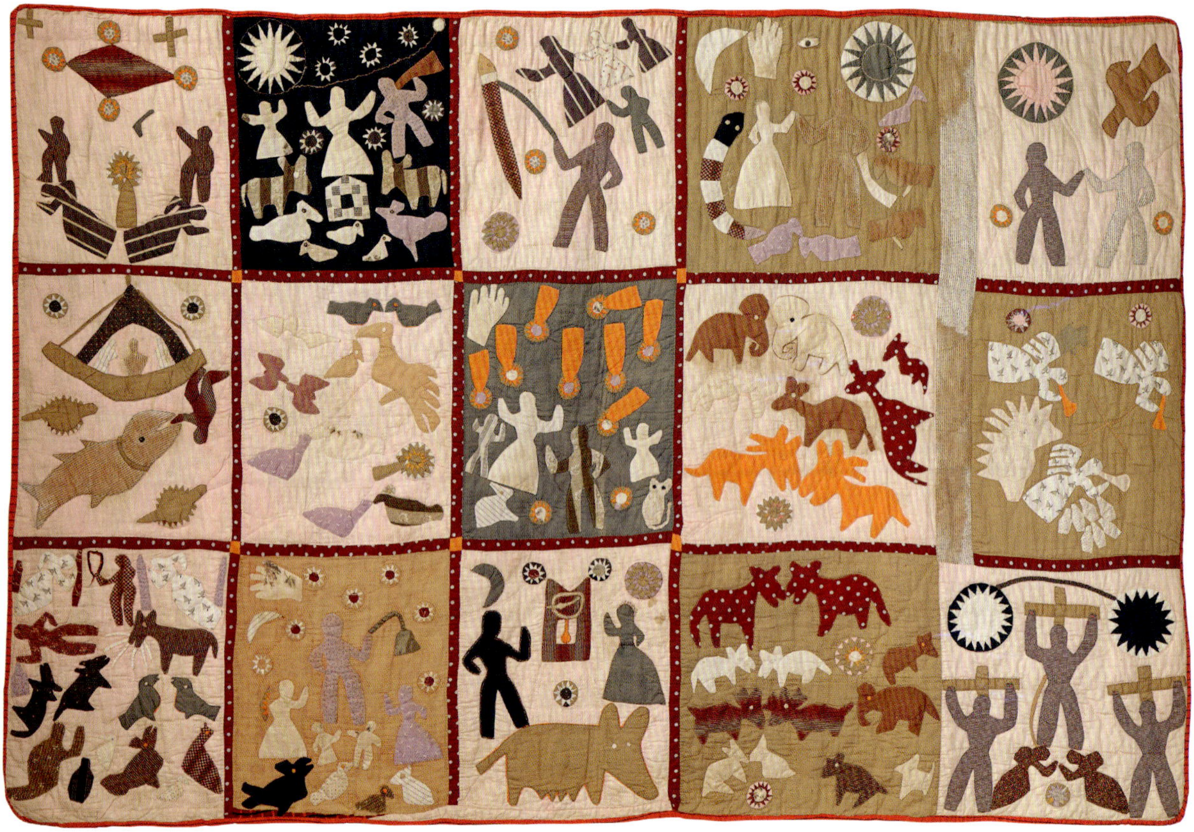

Pictorial Quilt, Harriet Powers, 1895–98

integral to plantation life and everyday existence, offering some sense of community and connection in the midst of otherwise unthinkable circumstances.

Harriet Powers, who was born into slavery and lived through emancipation, is one of the most notable Black quilters of the nineteenth century. Her style of narrative quilting was both ahead of its time and in direct opposition to what early scholars assumed Black quiltmakers were capable of. Her *Bible Quilt* and *Pictorial Quilt* are evidence of a woman who took great pride in her artistry and chose fabric as the medium to capture her memories and experiences in the Deep South. Powers's *Bible Quilt* was shown at the 1886 Georgia Fair, capturing the eye of a woman named Jennie Smith. Smith, a white art teacher at a local girls' school, was intrigued by the quilt and eventually purchased it for five dollars (roughly two hundred dollars today). With the exchange, she also received a detailed account of Powers's illustrations. The eleven appliquéd squares captured well-known Bible stories that Powers had committed to memory, such as those about Cain and Abel, the Last Supper, and the crucifixion of Jesus Christ.[11] In 1895, the *Bible Quilt* was shown at the Cotton States and International Exposition in Atlanta, Georgia. Inside the expo's "Negro Building," viewers were able to see the quilt, which was also admired in newspaper reports of the event.[12]

Using the same style of figurative appliqué, Powers's *Pictorial Quilt* blends biblical references with hyperlocal events. According to her account, two of the blocks recall falling stars (the 1833 Leonid meteor shower) and "the dark day of May 19, 1780," during which smoke from a forest fire blocked the sun.[13] Both quilts, now housed respectively in the Smithsonian and the Museum of Fine Arts, Boston, tell a story of a deeply self-aware artist who refused to be limited by perceptions of what a formerly enslaved Black woman could do.

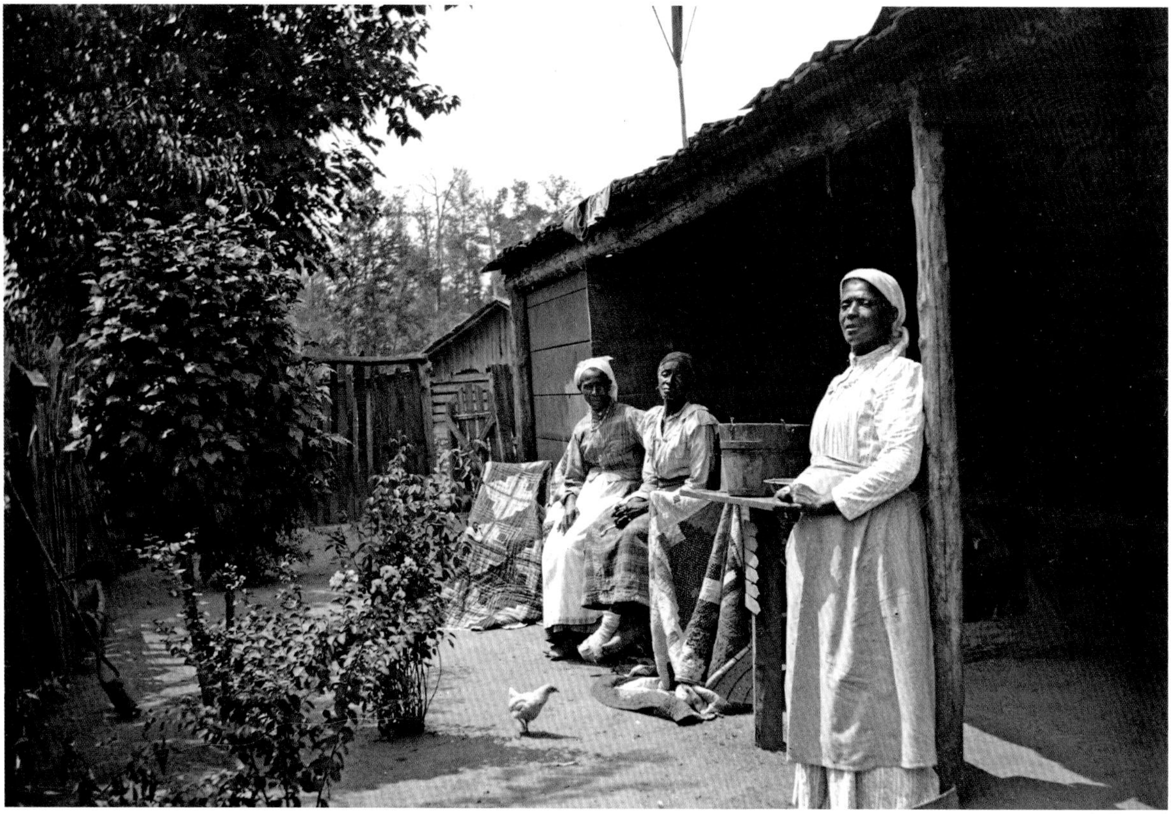

Three African American Women with Quilts Outside a Cabin in Rural Wilcox County, Alabama, Mary Lee Simpson, 1910–19

In the years following emancipation, Black quilters in the South navigated a rapidly shifting social and economic landscape. No longer bound by the laws of chattel slavery, they entered Reconstruction with the promise of freedom but little material support to build new lives. Faced with the uncertainties of labor, land, and citizenship, they relied on their quiltmaking and textile work to generate resources. The postbellum period introduced new layers of economic necessity and creative assertion to their work. During slavery, quilting was often done under the watchful eyes of enslavers, and quilters were limited to the use of scraps from the plantation household and tied to the demands of utility and subservience. Freedwomen brought technical expertise honed under bondage into the fraught era of Reconstruction and beyond.

Bedcover, most likely made by Narcissa L. Erwin Black Johnson and Chany Scot Black, is a unique example of a piece that explicitly

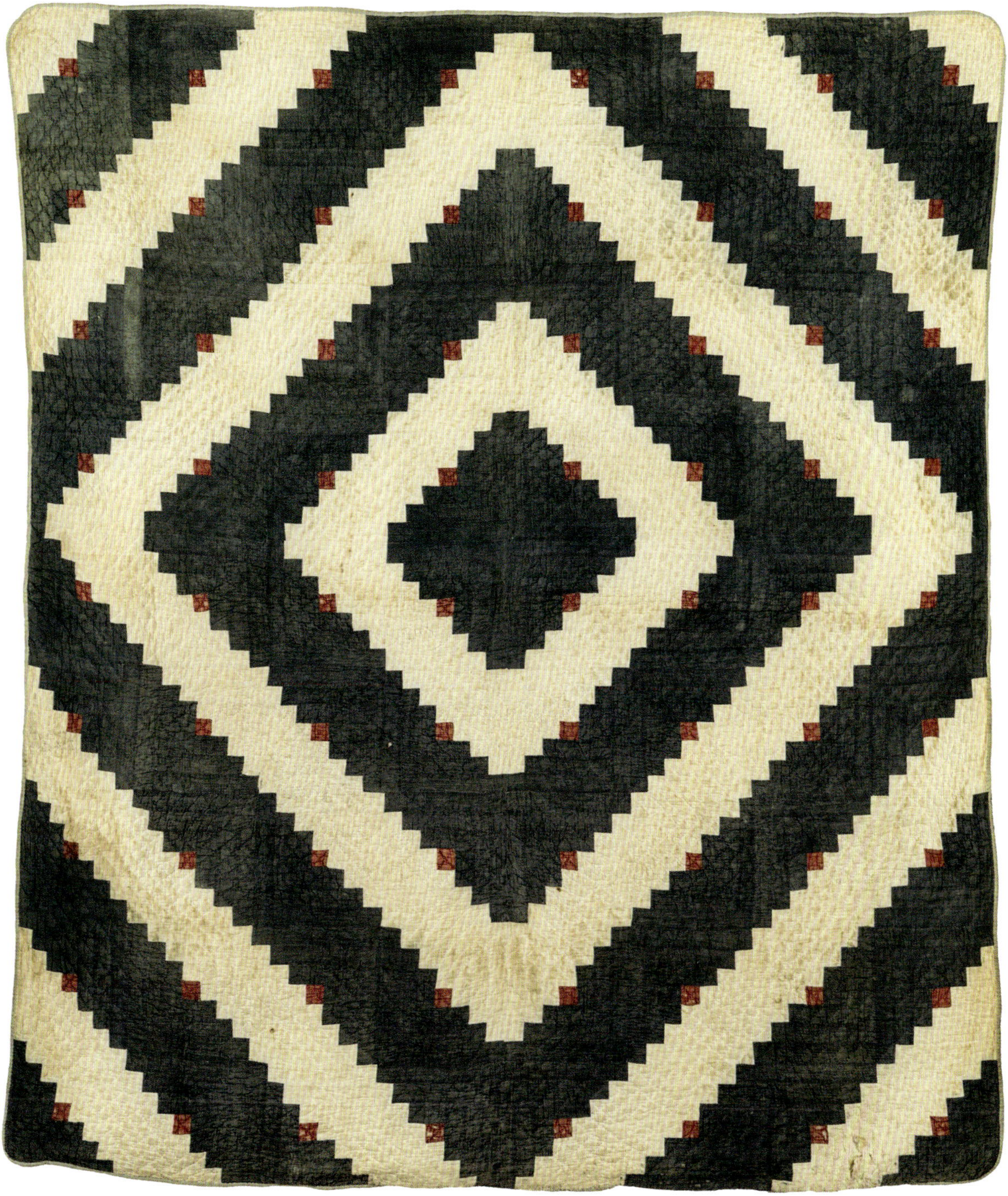

Bedcover–Quilt, Bed, possibly made by Narcissa L. Erwin Black Johnson and Chany Scot Black, circa 1870

named a formerly enslaved maker as a collaborator. Narcissa Black married John Black Jr., who inherited his family's plantation following his father's passing. His inheritance also included four enslaved people, including Chany Scot Black, who was a skilled weaver and seamstress. Narcissa kept diaries of her daily life, chronicling the running of the plantation and life during the Civil War. Her records recounted Chany working closely with her to process wool and cotton, spin and weave cloth, and hand dye materials using natural dyes (like the indigo used to create this quilt). Following her husband's illness and death in 1865, Narcissa had to use her skills as a seamstress, along with Chany's expertise, to maintain the household as a widow. Chany continued to work for Narcissa, and once she became a freedwoman, she was even able to purchase her own loom and start a textile business. Eventually Chany was forced to relocate her family to Illinois due to threats from the Ku Klux Klan. Although Narcissa did explicitly acknowledge Chany's work on the quilt, the conflation of their skills in her writings makes it difficult to know how much of the work was done collectively versus by Chany with Narcissa's input.

At the turn of the twentieth century, racial violence, land theft, and economic exploitation continued to undercut the possibilities of freedom. Sharecropping and tenant farming replaced slavery with new systems of debt and control. Black families had limited access to store-bought cloth, leading many women to rely on feed sacks, worn garments, and salvaged scraps often purchased on credit.

By the 1930s, the economic collapse of the Great Depression had turned the United States upside down. Although its impact was felt nationally, preexisting inequalities were also deepened. Nearly half of Black Americans were unemployed by 1932, with rural agricultural workers—especially in the South—bearing the brunt of the downturn. Quiltmaking remained a domestic necessity and emerged as part of the federal response to the crisis.[14]

In 1935 the US government launched the Works Progress Administration (WPA) as part of President Franklin D. Roosevelt's New Deal, an expansive relief effort designed to combat widespread joblessness. As historian Janneken Smucker writes, its purpose "centered on putting Americans to work on various projects that would benefit the public."[15] The WPA funded public infrastructure, education, the arts,

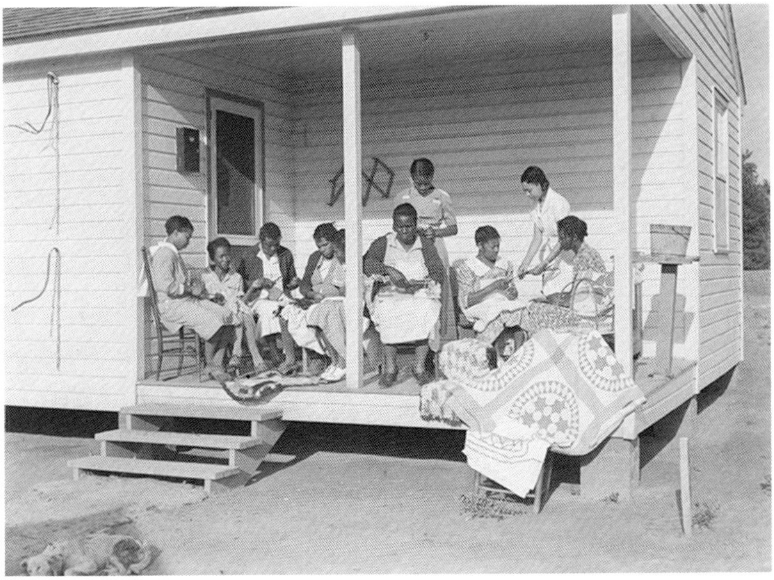

Home Economics and Home Management Class for Adults, Under Supervision of Miss Evelyn M. Driver (Standing in White Uniform). Everything They Make Including the Small Handmade Looms Utilizes Materials of Local Origin Such as Cornshucks, Cane, Flour and Meal and Feed Sacks, Etc. Flint River Farms, Georgia, Marion Post Wolcott, 1939

and—notably—sewing projects. These projects employed thousands of women, including Black women, to produce clothing, bedding, and quilts. In cities like Milwaukee, the WPA's Handicraft Project employed as many as five thousand people, including unskilled workers, elders, and those otherwise excluded from the workforce.[16] These workers were trained to produce textiles for use in schools, hospitals, orphanages, and government institutions.[17]

Whereas the Handicraft Project focused on producing items for wider consumption, the WPA also sponsored sewing rooms that were tailored for families in need. Planned communities and labor camps across the South received training from home economics instructors as part of initiatives developed by the Cooperative Extension Service and the Farm Security Administration (FSA). This led to the establishment of community sewing rooms and the distribution of surplus cotton to make practical goods, including quilts.[18]

For Black quilters in the South, WPA programs provided an opportunity to earn wages while learning

Making a Quilt from Surplus Commodity Cotton in Greensboro, Greene County, Georgia, Jack Delano, 1941

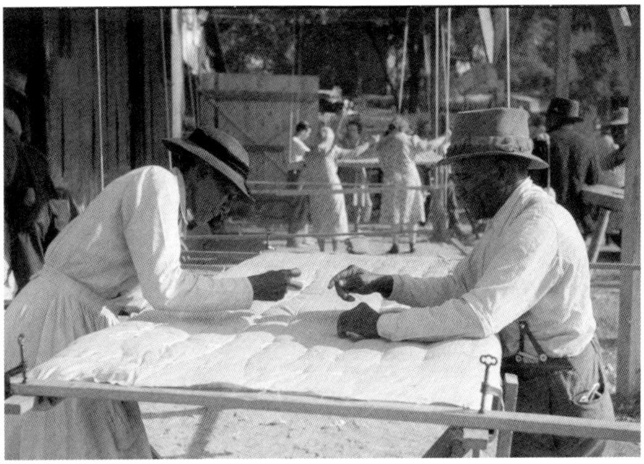

skills and working communally, albeit in segregated conditions. Though local officials often discriminated against Black applicants, many were able to gain access to sewing rooms and other resources. Quilts stitched under federal programs were sometimes required to follow patterns, but Black quilters infused them with regional styles and other distinct touches. Even within the confines of state-regulated templates, they expressed a sense of individuality. The resulting quilts are artifacts of a particular moment in which Black women's domestic labor was momentarily recognized, though never fully valued, through compensation and other means. The WPA's initiatives—especially in tandem with New Deal agricultural and housing reforms—also contributed to the cultural flourishing of communities like Gee's Bend, Alabama. There, federal support for landownership and self-sufficiency created conditions in which Black quiltmaking traditions could deepen and evolve.[19]

Within the larger Depression-era initiatives, there were local projects that reflected the experiences of their particular communities. In the 1930s, within the segregated Tennessee Valley, Ruth Clement Bond worked with women to create works that brought their voices to the forefront. Created around 1937, *Black Power* was one of several quilts designed under Bond's guidance during her time in the Tennessee Valley Authority (TVA) community. The TVA was created to address a range of economic, environmental, and technological challenges in the Tennessee Valley, a region spanning parts of seven Southern states that had been hit hard by the Great Depression. The TVA focused on flood control, electricity generation, reforestation, and economic development through large infrastructure projects—particularly the construction of dams and power plants.[20] Bond's husband, Dr. J. Max Bond Sr., served as the TVA's director of Negro personnel, a rare role for a Black man in a federal program at the time.[21] While he worked to improve labor conditions for Black workers, Ruth Clement Bond turned her attention to the lives of their wives, organizing classes and cultural programs in the resettlement camps.

Out of these efforts emerged a small but visionary quiltmaking group—Black women who combined traditional skills with new visual strategies. Bond, who had studied at Northwestern University and Oberlin, brought a modernist lens to the group's design work. She offered patterns that reflected contemporary ideas about race, labor, and

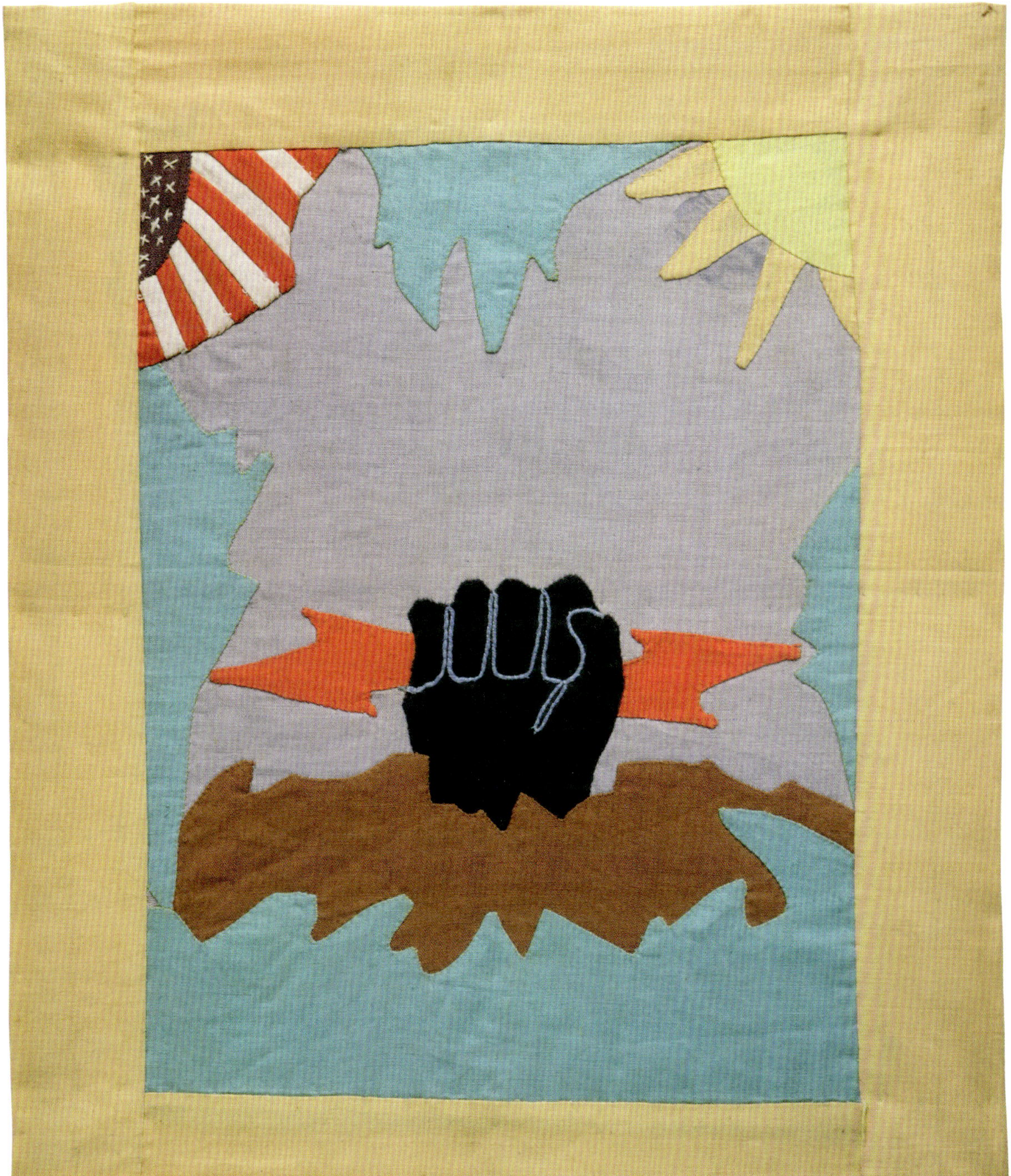

Tennessee Valley Authority Appliqué Quilt Design of a Black Fist, Ruth Clement Bond, 1934

identity, while the women executed the quilts with skill and precision. *Black Power* was one result of this collaboration, manifesting as a bold fabric panel that departed from conventional Southern patterns in favor of a more pictorial format. Though the quilt was based on Bond's drawing, its making was a shared act. The women she worked with brought their own experiences, aesthetics, and sewing skills.

Bond wrote that her design of *Black Power* was intended to reflect the group "pushing up through the obstacles—through objections." She continued, "We were coming up out of the Depression and we were going to live a better life through our efforts. The opposition wasn't going to stop us."[22]

Only a few of the TVA-era quilts survive today, but *Black Power* endures as a testament to the times. It reveals the depth of thought and collaboration that existed within these New Deal–era communities, even under the weight of segregation and discrimination. The quilts made during enslavement, Reconstruction, and later under WPA programs endure as records of persistence. Through war and social neglect, Black quilters created culture and the beginnings of a tradition informed by lived experience, as well as by their individual and collective voices.

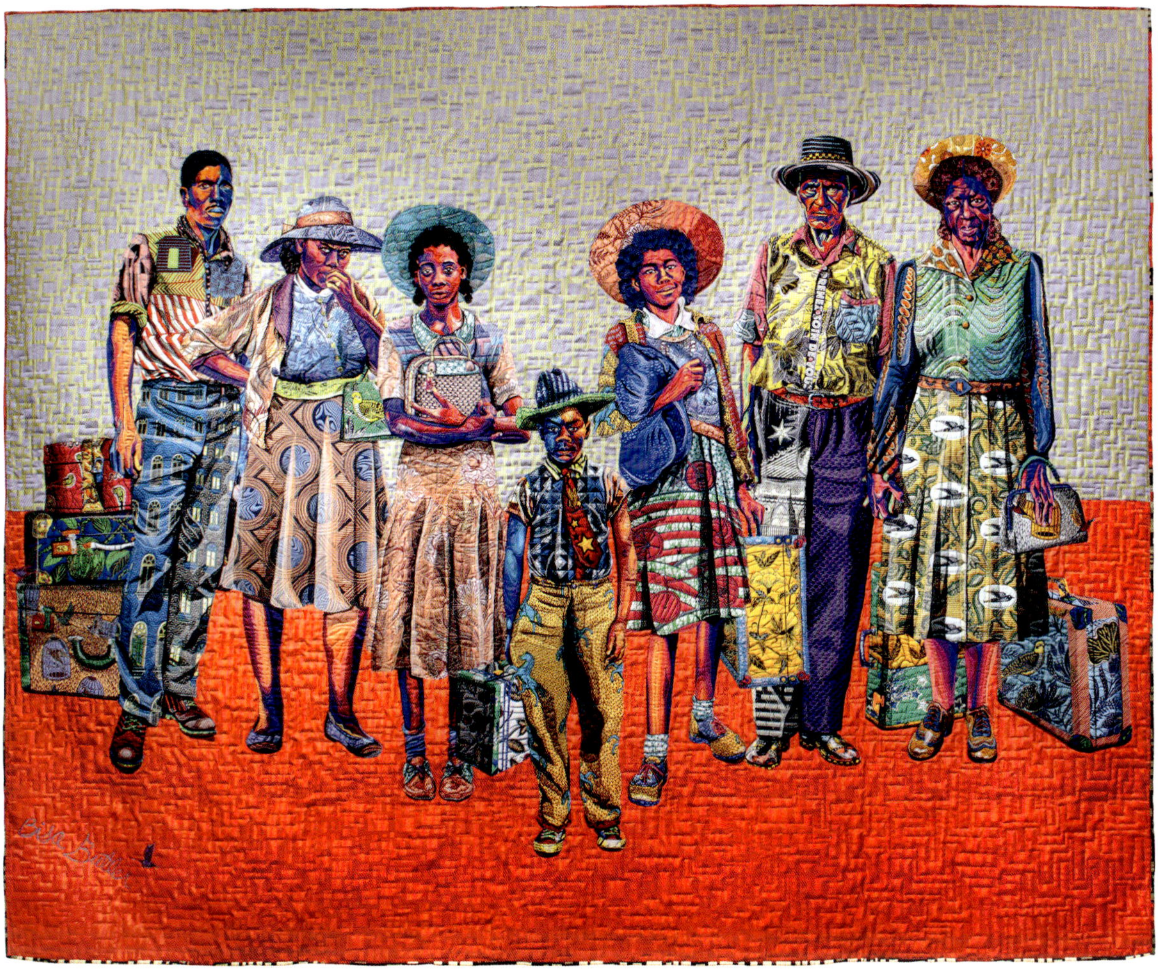

The Warmth of Other Sons, Bisa Butler, 2020

Concurrent with the Great Depression and the decades to follow, Black southerners were relocating in droves, pursuing opportunities to create a new life away from the threats of their region of origin. As captured in Bisa Butler's contemporary quilt *The Warmth of Other Sons*, Black residents gathered what they had and set forward as part of the Great Migration. From 1910 to 1970, roughly six million Black people uprooted their lives, destined for industrial cities in the North, the Midwest, and eventually the West. As James Gregory describes, this collective movement would shape a Black Southern diaspora who "became

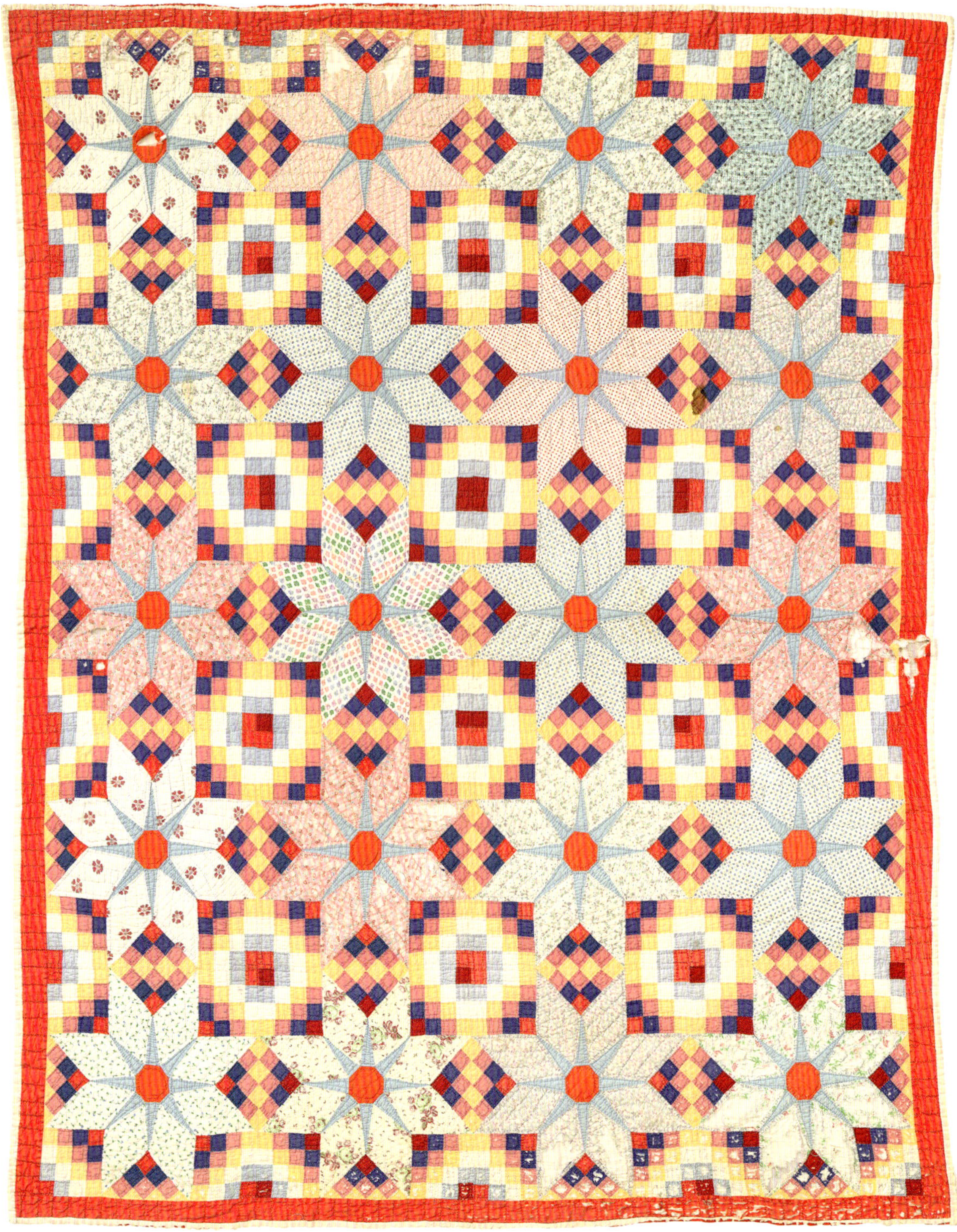

agents of change who used the opportunity of geography to alter the cultural and political landscape of the nation and all its regions."[23] As Southern ways of being became enmeshed with the practices of other regions, cultural traditions like art, literature, and intellectual production underwent a metamorphosis.

What is overdue for discussion is the nuanced relationship of quilts to the Great Migration. They were carried beyond Black homes in the South, ensuring warmth in colder regions and bridging their keepers back to the lives they left behind. For those who quilted, home may have looked different, but the teachings shaped by Southern life were embedded within them. Some Black quilters were eager to leave behind the remnants of the South and the harms it had inflicted. For others, quilts were a tether to memories that couldn't be erased by distance. During this time, quilts also became a record of movement that mapped how family structures and ties to place evolved.

(Untitled) Shadow Star is an example of how quilts transitioned across maternal and state lines. It was created by Bettie Chaffold and Rebecca Smith in Bastrop, Louisiana, right before the start of the Great Depression. The quilt's wear shows that the detailed pattern didn't deter its owners from using it frequently. Chaffold's daughter, Laura Louise Johnson, was the steward of the quilt, later bringing it to California upon relocation. Johnson worked as an antiques dealer, which emphasizes her appreciation for old objects and their value. The quilt would later rotate out of the family and into the hands of Eli Leon, who acquired the quilt for his personal collection.

Grandmother's Quilt stitches together a century of memory, labor, and love across three generations of Black women rooted in Alabama and Anacostia, a historic neighborhood in southeast Washington, DC. The quilt top was pieced by Annie Strong Howard, who arranged chevron shapes into a repeating pattern known as the Virginia Reel. These pinwheel motifs spin in four vertical columns, some set directly against a rich green background, others framed in seven yellow rectangles. Five of these yellow panels begin or end in patchwork squares made from striped and polka-dotted fabrics in deep browns, blues, and blacks—scraps that likely tell a story of life in Alabama.

Untitled (Shadow Star), Rebecca Smith and Bettie Chaffold ,1920s–30s

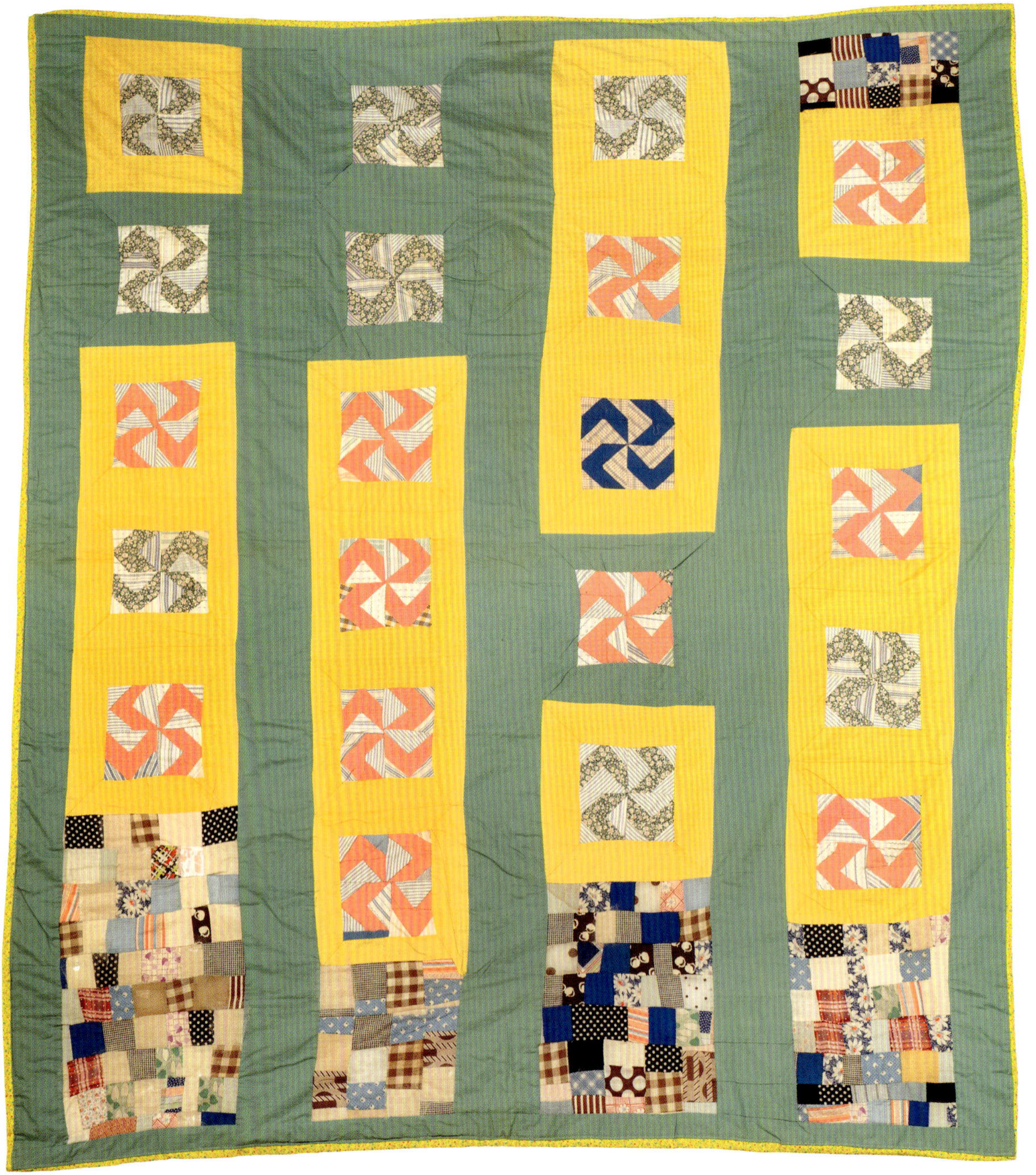

Grandmother's Quilt, Annie Strong Howard and Dianne Dale, 20th century

Annie's daughter, Marie Howard Dale, was born in Montgomery, Alabama, in 1914 and relocated to Anacostia with her husband in the 1940s. Decades later, in 1990, she entrusted the unfinished heirloom quilt to her daughter, Dianne Dale. Dianne carefully restored and completed it by hand, adding batting, repairing fragile sections, and backing it with yellow calico. She returned the finished quilt to her mother in the mid-1990s, and it remained on display in Marie's home until shortly before her death in 2011. Now housed at the Anacostia Community Museum, *Grandmother's Quilt* is part of the Dale-Patterson family collection—a living archive of objects and documents that trace the family's migrations, creativity, and enduring bonds through time and place.[24] While others might have discarded the top or left it incomplete, Marie knew that her daughter understood the importance of the quilt to their family's story and could add her own chapter to it.

The story of Black quilters is one of unstoppable presence. Their ingenuity is a tradition born in bondage, nourished through community, and adapted across generations and geographies. Black quilts function as heirlooms and cultural relics. They point us back to the lives of women who refused erasure, who gathered in circles shaped by love, and who passed on their skills as a means of preserving both dignity and connection. In tracing this lineage, we are not just learning history—we are returning to it. We are reminded that home is not always a fixed location. It can also be found in practice. Thus, Black quiltmaking is a form of homecoming.

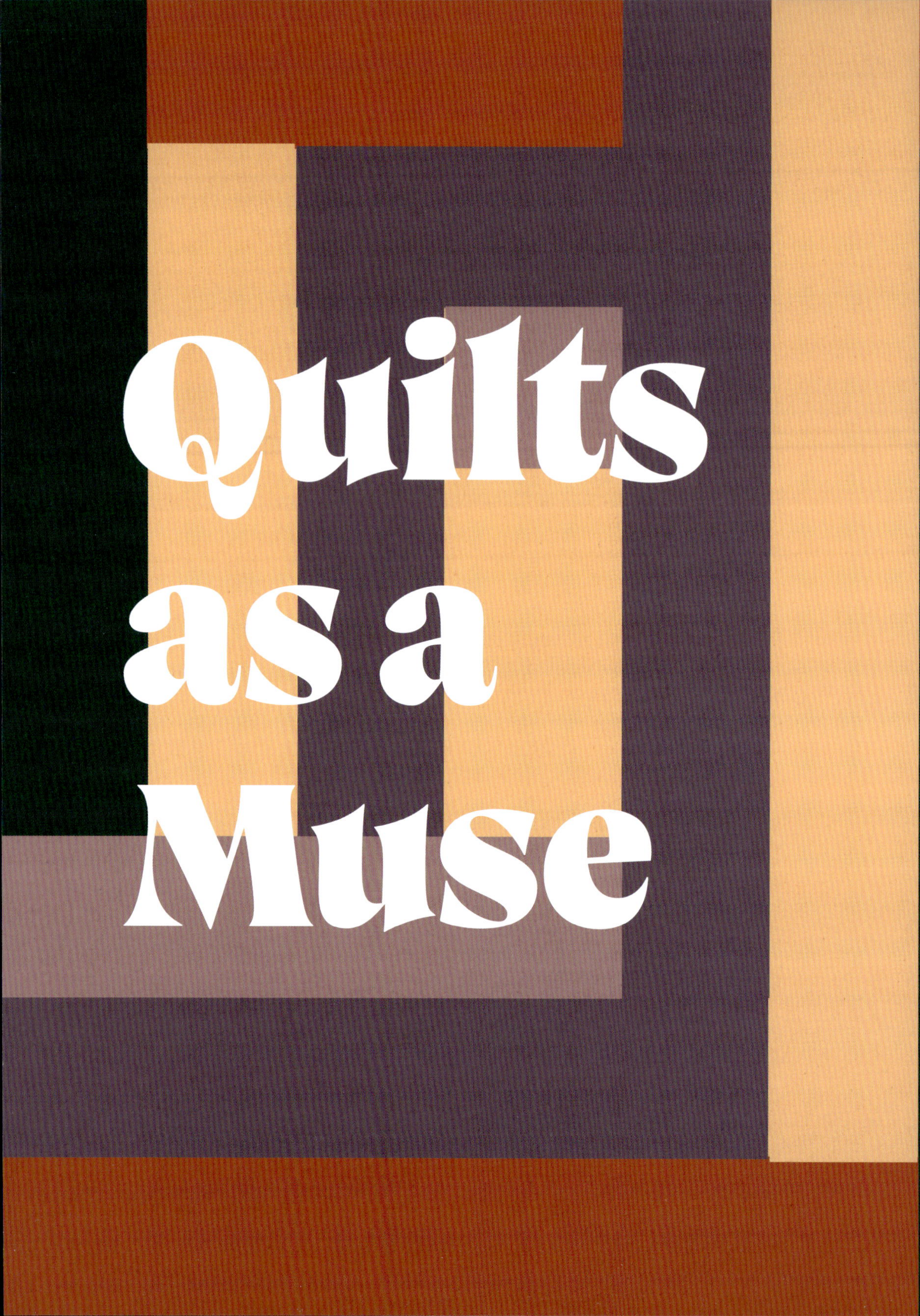

Quilts as a Muse

When we reflect on the larger artistic canon, we may not consider quilting as a central part of it. However, quiltmaking has provided an entry point for artists across many disciplines to explore their creativity and artistic voice. If we look to art history, specifically Black art history, we will find that artists have cited quilts for decades, using them to invoke ties to home, family, and memory. For them, artistic citation has been an act of reference and reverence that illuminates the quilt as an artifact inseparable from Black life. Creators and cultural stewards have used words and images to address the staying power of quilting as a deeply impactful and ancestral practice. While researchers of the 1970s and '80s argued that Black quiltmakers were hidden in obscurity, quilts were always present for those who were truly able to see them. Artists who were dedicated to showcasing the beauty of everyday life in their communities offered quilts a platform. From highlighting the use of quilts to support civil rights to everyday acts like breaking bread at sewing circles, Black artists referenced quilts as an archive of culture.

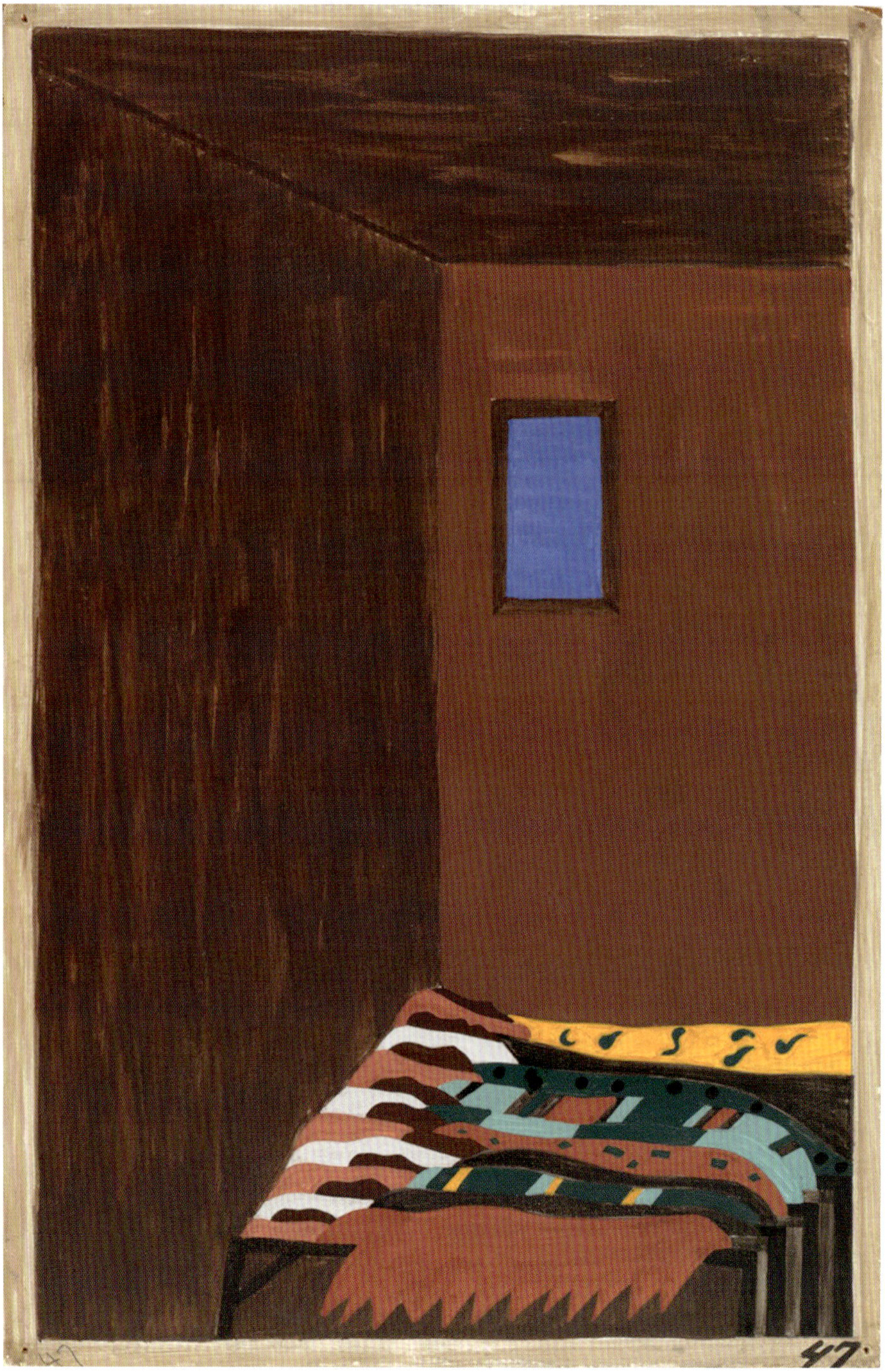

The Migration Series, Panel no. 47: As the Migrant Population Grew, Good Housing Became Scarce, Jacob Lawrence, 1940–41

JACOB LAWRENCE

The Great Migration (1910–70) marked one of the largest movements of people in US history. Nearly six million Black people relocated from the South to states across the North, West, and Midwest. Faced with the violence and economic impact of post-Reconstruction segregation, many Black Southerners packed up the life they knew to seek refuge and opportunity in a new home. Harlem Renaissance painter Jacob Lawrence was witness to this transition. A child of parents who relocated during the early years of the Great Migration, he came of age in Harlem, in New York City, where he observed firsthand the challenges and triumphs faced by new residents. At twenty-three years old, Lawrence set out on a mission to tell the stories of those who had arrived in search of a better life. This led to the development of his acclaimed sixty-panel epic *The Migration Series*. The numbered vignettes capture the conditions that led to relocation and the experiences migrants encountered along their journey.

Panel 47 of the series highlights the importance of quilts, which soothed new residents and provided hope in the midst of despair. A group of tenants are crowded into an empty room where the only pops of color are found in the quilts that keep them warm. In a 1992 interview, Lawrence alluded to how household objects like quilts not only offered comfort but also shaped his definition of art: "We lived in a deep depression. Not only my mother, but the poor people in general. . . . In order to add something to our lives, they decorated their tenements and their homes in all of these colors. . . . My artistic sensibility came from this ambiance. . . . It's only in retrospect that I realized that I was surrounded by art."

Although Lawrence doesn't identify the figures in *Panel 47*, it is clear that they brought along their coverings as an extension of the home they had left but wanted to remember. The quilts could have been made by a loved one left behind, or by the hands that they now kept warm. Regardless of their origin, we know they offered comfort and familiarity in a foreign place and brought beauty to bleak surroundings. They also contributed to a creative approach to homemaking that became part of what Lawrence understood as a Black aesthetic.

ROMARE BEARDEN

Also a child of the Great Migration and celebrated figure of the Harlem Renaissance, Romare Bearden used his artistic practice to document the migration and changes across society at large. Romare was a painter for most of his life, but he shifted to collage late in his career to depict the multifaceted quality of the Black experience. These later works offer a snapshot of life in the North and memories of the South. There are parallels between how Bearden described his collage practice and the assemblage of quiltmaking. He also often explicitly cited quilts in the content and titles of his works. Surrounded by quilts in childhood, he viewed them as an extension of his heritage that allowed him to bridge the past and present, and to honor the humanity found in everyday Black life.

Patchwork Quilt, Romare Bearden, 1970

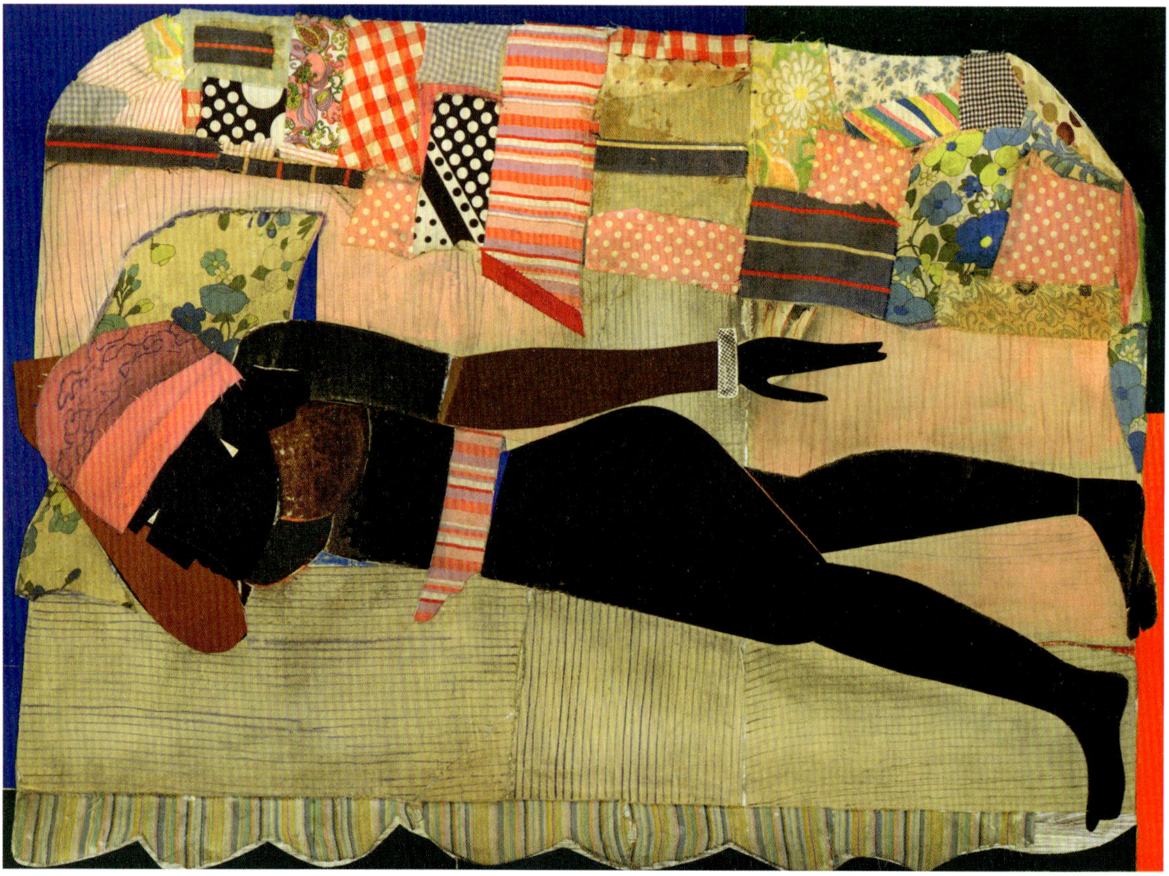

Patchwork Quilt (1970), one of Bearden's best-known collages, is a vivid example of his reverence toward quilts. The figure depicted on the quilt, whose style references both Egyptian relief and Benin sculpture, lies atop a quilt that is reminiscent of one you might find on a clothesline or porch railing. The imperfections of the fabrics and their placement feel familiar. *Patchwork Quilt* could be in conversation with the quilts and other textile-based objects from Black Southern cooperatives that were circulating around the nation at the time. Just a few years earlier, groups such as the Poor People's Corporation Sewing Co-op and the Freedom Quilting Bee had begun as outgrowths of the civil rights movement, using sewing as a source of economic independence. The fabrics and patterns seen in *Patchwork Quilt* resemble many of the motifs that would have been found on tables at bees across the Deep South.

Maquette for Quilting Time, Romare Bearden, 1985

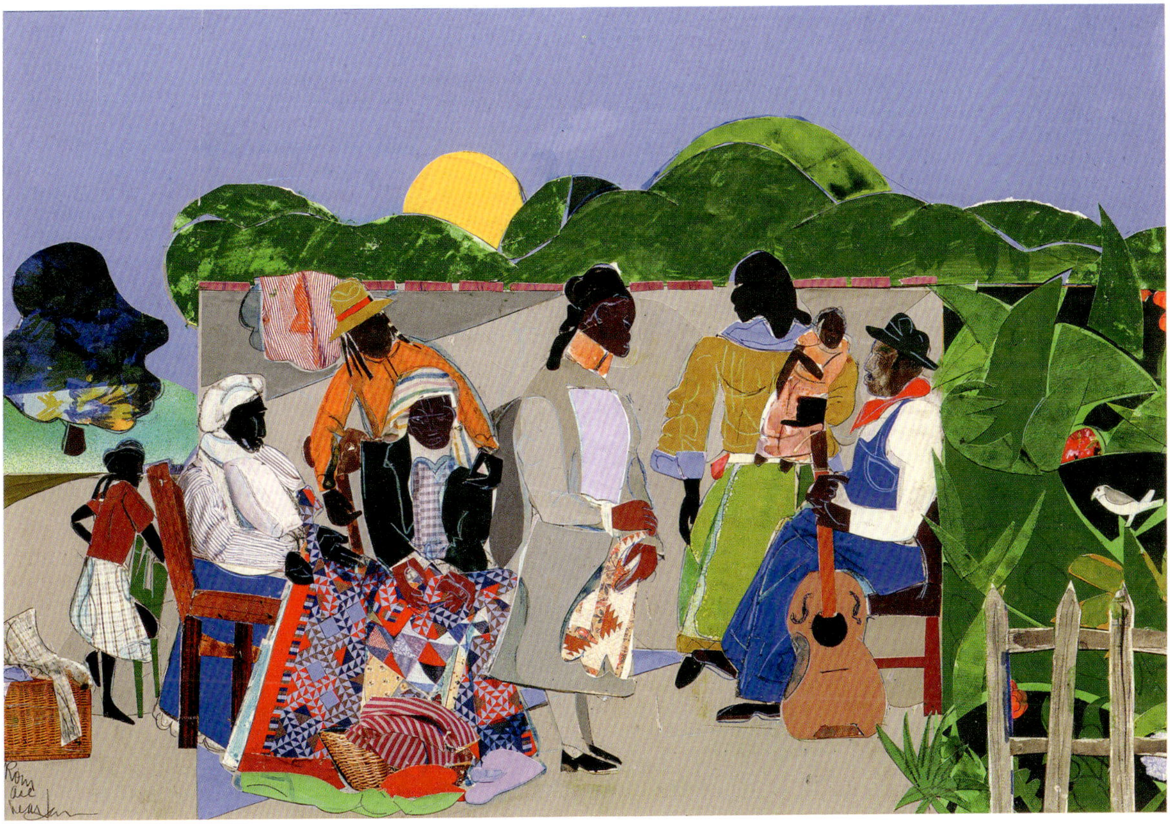

In other works Bearden more explicitly recognized the significance of quilting bees, creating montages that showcased how they anchored relationships and communities. Works like *Maquette for Quilting Time* allow us to see quilting as an act of leisure that holds an intergenerational appeal. Looking closely, we see that elders are depicted as masters of the craft while a young girl in the corner is delightfully engaged with fabric. She represents the story of many whose earliest memories of quilts were of spending time at the feet of their grandmothers, sorting fabric and observing as they worked.

Contemporary Artwork

While twentieth-century artists had a particular relationship to quilts, representations of quilts continue to permeate contemporary artworks, especially as a mode of storytelling.

ALISON SAAR

Alison Saar's *Swing Low* uses sculpture to depict quilt blocks three-dimensionally. The blocks connect to form the foundation of a 13-foot homage to abolitionist Harriet Tubman.

Each element of Tubman's portrait, which is made of bronze and Chinese graphite, is forged with careful consideration of her life and journey through the Underground Railroad. Saar was especially interested in elevating Tubman's post-emancipation impact in a holistic way, including her work as a spy, army nurse, and healer. The base of *Swing Low* uses quilt references as the foundation that Tubman, an unstoppable force, stands upon. When describing the importance of quilts to the work, Saar explains:

I chose to present her with a quilt as a base that shows these stations of her life as a tool for furthering understanding of who she was historically. I did it in pictograms because she herself, being illiterate, wouldn't have been able to read her own history early on. And I like the idea that it's equally understood by children who are too young to read or maybe by people who don't have the vision to be reading anymore since it's also tactile. I also wanted to talk about her spirit, so she has this sort of supernatural component of pulling these roots up out of the ground and tilling the soil and turning it over and uprooting stuff to create space for something new to take root.[25]

The embossed pictograms on the foundation mimic early story quilts, which typically combine appliquéd figures and motifs that recall a personal or historical narrative. During the nineteenth century in particular, story quilts were a way for Black women to use their voices and exercise their agency when the written word may not have been available to them. One might even argue that Saar is citing a school of Black nineteenth-century quilters, such as Harriet Powers and several others whose names have been lost, who were stewards of the imagery that grounds Tubman's footing in *Swing Low*.

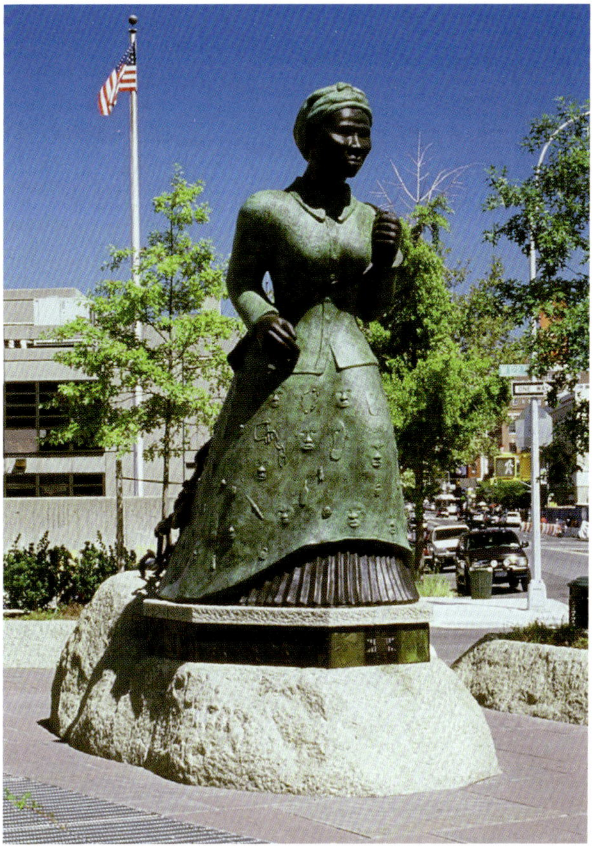

Swing Low: Harriet Tubman Memorial, Alison Saar, 2007

DR. TANEKEYA WORD HARRIS

Dr. Tanekeya Word Harris's prints are rooted in Afrofuturism and Black aesthetics, often focusing on themes such as Black identity, hair, and womanhood. Her work is a visual documentation of the shifts and continuities within these themes, celebrating the past, present, and future of Black women's experiences. She weaves themes of Black interiority, material culture, and nature into what she calls the "everyday fantastical." This approach involves portraying the ordinary lives of Black women and girls infused with elements of the extraordinary. For example, in her linocut triptych *not your great, great grandmother's fairytale*, the three panels thread together memory, speculative storytelling, and reimagination. Explaining the references for her linocuts, Harris writes, "I rummaged through my drawer of ephemeral archives, mostly of vernacular images of Black girls found in varied lots in estate sales, online and photo albums (thrifting and my paternal grandmother's)."[26] The linocuts' imagery references iconography of a Southern

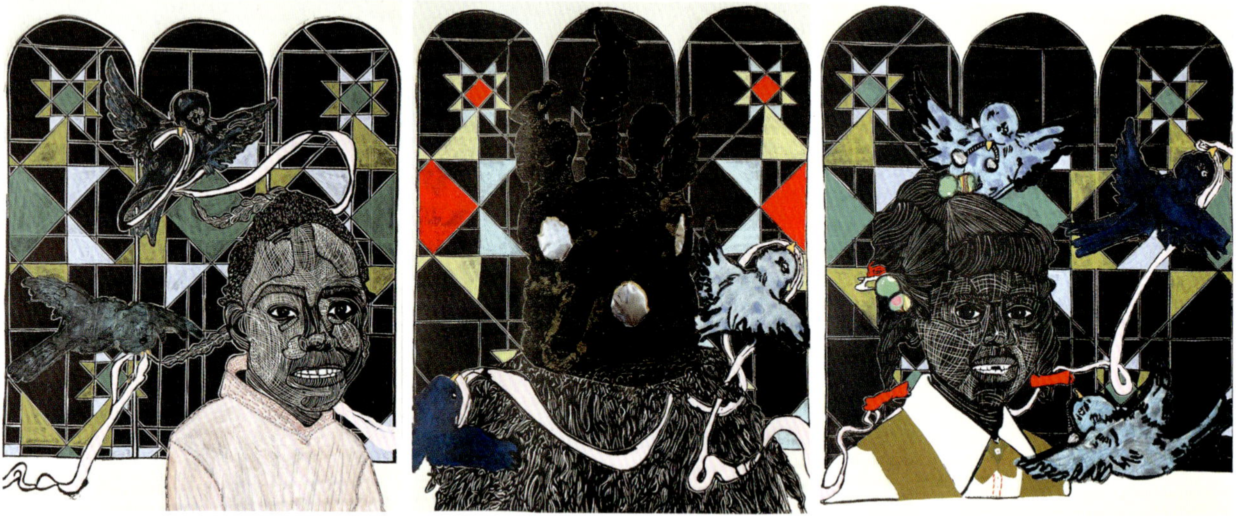

not your great, great grandmother's fairytale, full triptych, Tanekeya Word Harris, 2023

experience and Harris's Mississippi upbringing. She returns to girlhood through this series, using the geography, storytelling, and lessons learned at home to craft her version of a fairy tale whose happy ending is still rooted in the realities of race and gender. Mende masks, bluebirds, and barrettes are coded references to the passage of time, the evolution of culture, femininity, and microaggressions that continue to impact Black girls and women. She also integrates star block patterns into stained glass windows, transporting the viewer to the surroundings of a Sunday service through the eyes of a child. Star block patterns are etched into each panel to pay homage to the visual language of enslaved Africans who birthed foundational quilting practices in the wake of oppression. They appear to watch over each figure as an ancestral reminder that liberation is on the horizon. Through the combination of quiet, yet powerful iconography, she utilizes lore as a means of both remembering and dreaming. The stories gathered at the feet of grandmothers are honored as a guide for the next generation of girls and women to shape their own happy endings.

SEDRICK HUCKABY

Painter Sedrick Huckaby credits his grandmother, Hallie Beatrice Carpenter, for seeding his appreciation of quilts and their possibilities. Quilts were a common fixture in his grandparents' home and a backdrop to his daily life. As he grew as an artist, he came to understand quiltmaking as his grandmother's artistic practice, despite her never explicitly referring to herself as an artist. His desire to "glorify everyday people,"[27] combined with his regard for his grandmother, led Huckaby to develop monumental panels that often depict family members and quilts in conversation with one another.

Through his paintings Huckaby reflects on the importance of families and the ties that keep them connected. His grandmother often serves as a muse in his work and is a representation of the many elders who have anchored their descendants. "I wanted, in my own way, to canonize this figure as a part of the African-American family," he says. "I wanted to historically note this figure of Big Momma, who she was to the family, what she did, and what she meant to our lives."[28] By putting items that are often created by family matriarchs at the center of his work, Huckaby creates a conversation about quilts serving as an extension of love, identity, and inheritance for those who experience their warmth. To Huckaby, quilts are more than just objects; they're monuments to the values and love that transcend time.

A Love Supreme: Spring, Sedrick Huckaby, 2001-09

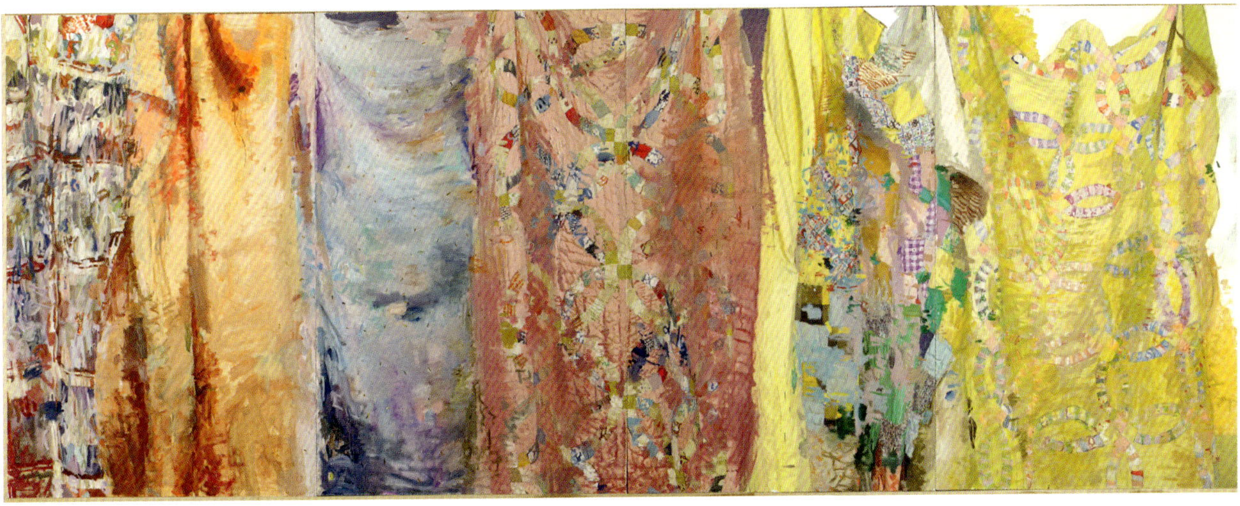

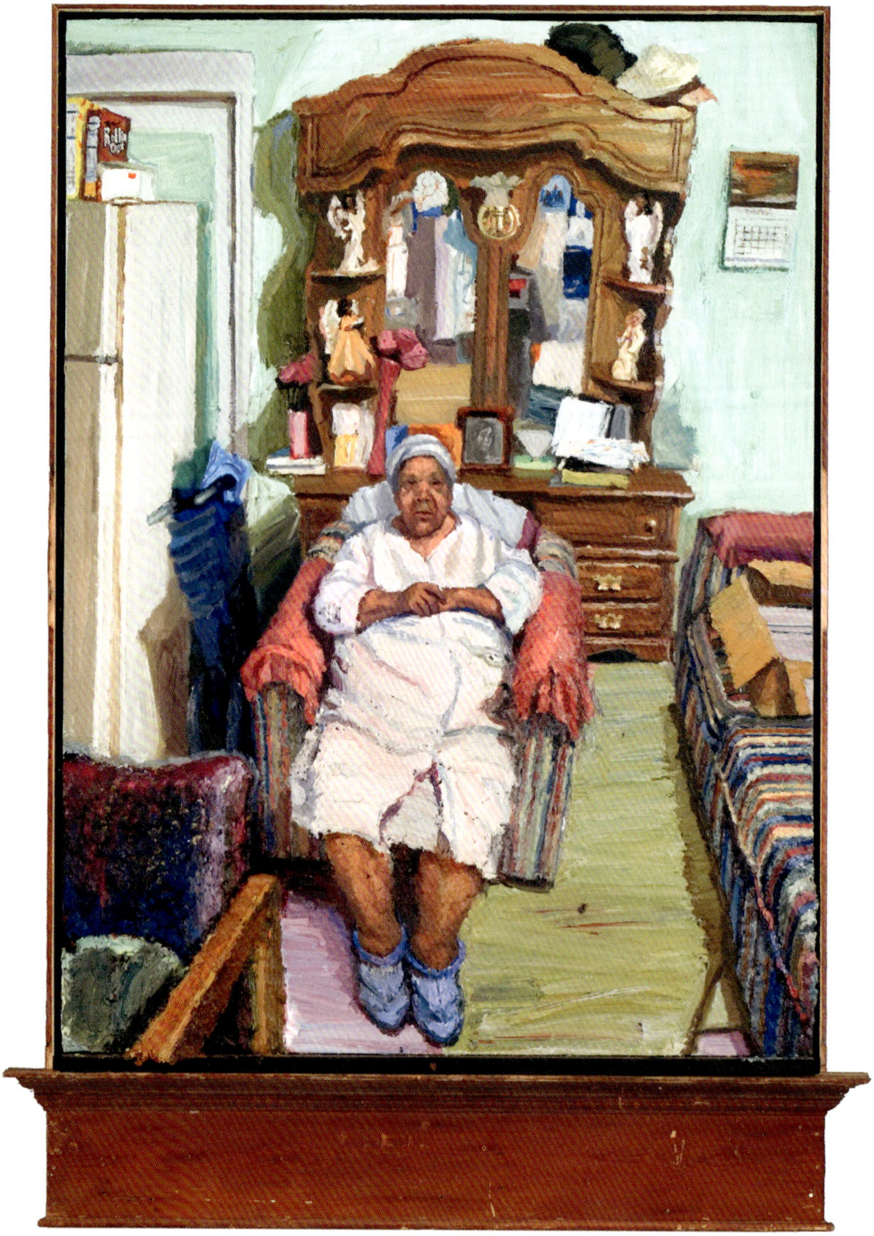

Sitting in Her Room, Sedrick Huckaby, 2008

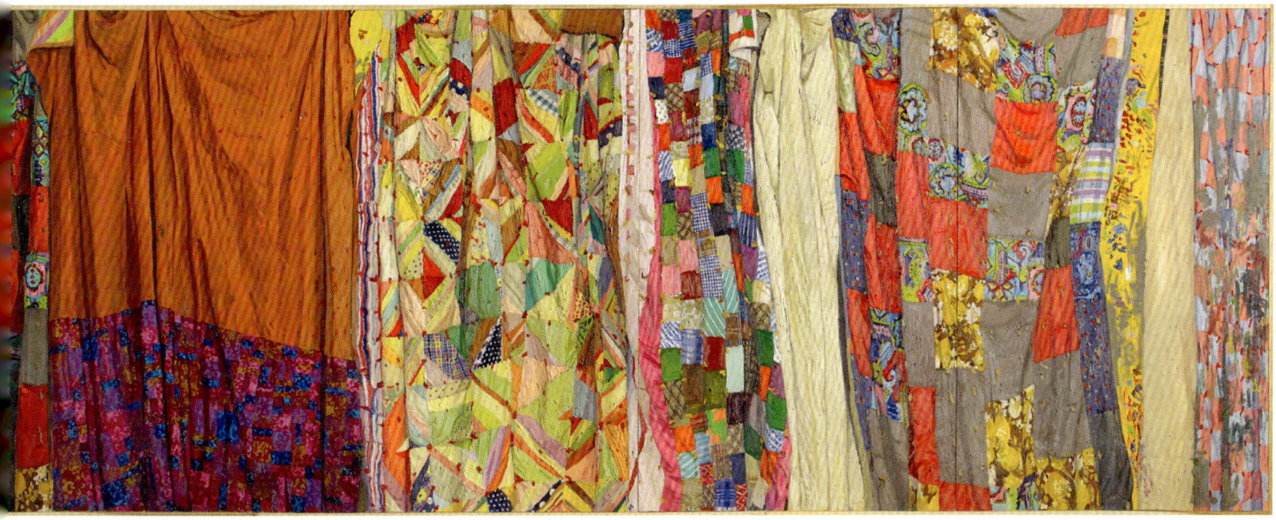

A Love Supreme: Summer, Sedrick Huckaby, 2001–09

LOVIE OLIVIA

Houston artist Lovie Olivia's work draws on her lifelong fascination with quilts. She considers them among her earliest encounters with "architecture for the body." She sees them not only as protectors or objects of comfort, but also as sculptural forms imbued with memory, culture, and care. "Much like food," she notes, quilts are "cultural signifiers," repositories of warmth and tradition passed down like heirloom recipes.[29]

Comforter started as a quilt that Olivia made by hand, then photographed. The final work takes shape as a 400-square-foot fresco painting, rendered through Olivia's signature technique that blends figuration (representation of real-world objects) with excavation (carving or removing layers to reveal what is beneath the surface). As a painter rooted in Southern traditions, she layers texture, color, and history into her work, mining the South through both action and metaphor. The surface of *Comforter* bursts with rich patterns and a spectrum of hues.

The fresco is also an ode to the Southern Black women quilters whose artistry transformed abstraction. "I found joy," she says, "in creating this allegorical abstraction," naming her deep admiration for the Jubilee Quilters of Houston and the women of Gee's Bend, whose bold geometric quilts have become cornerstones of American art history. Olivia's description beautifully captures how Black women's approach

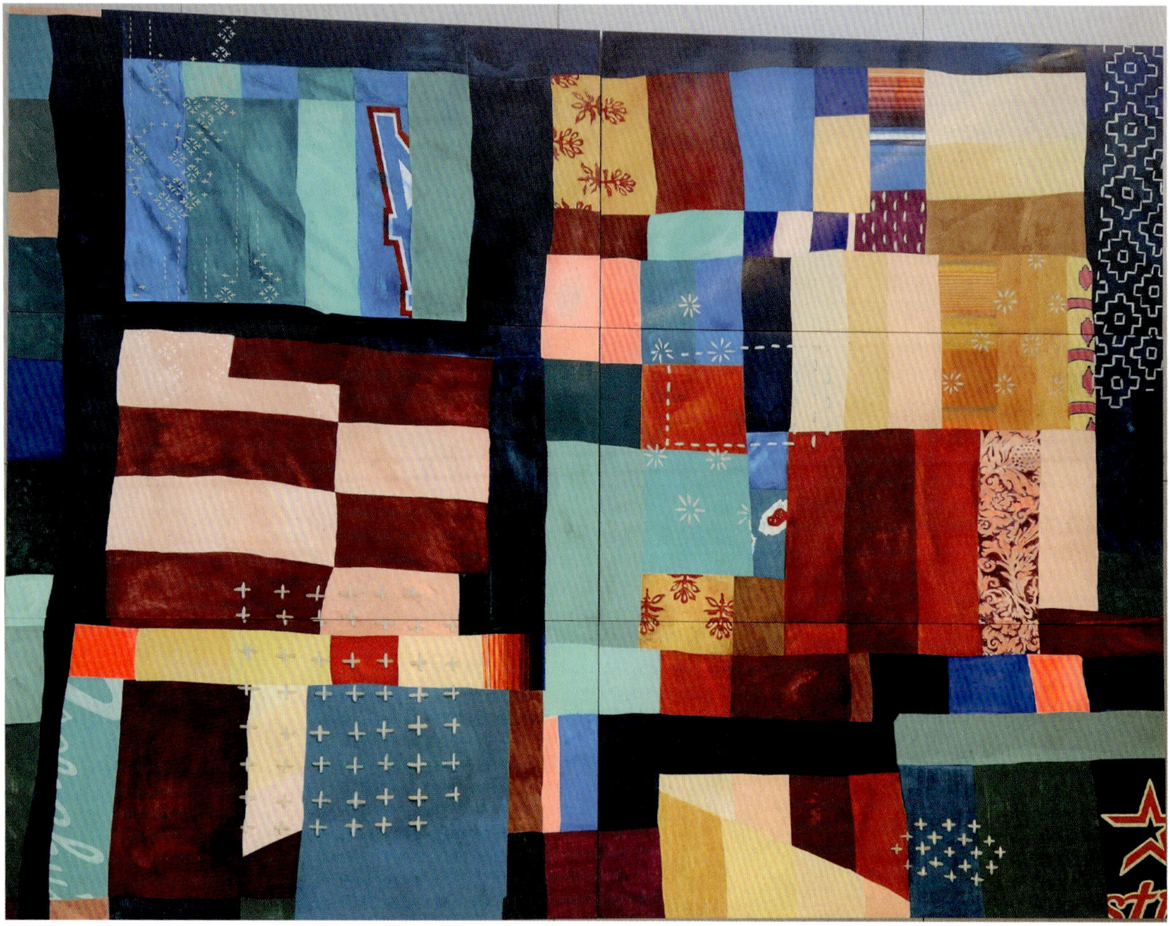

Comforter, Lovie Olivia, 2024

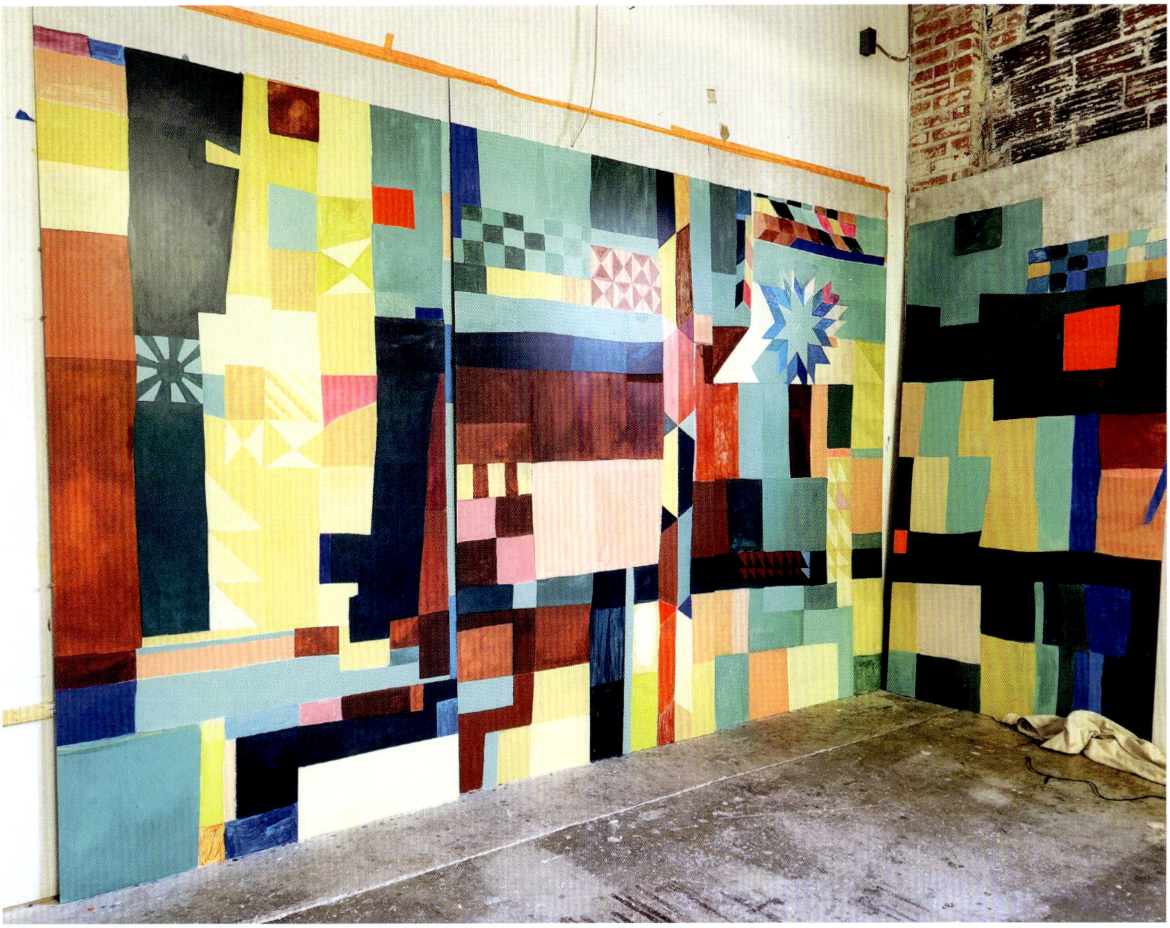

Comforter process (work in progress),
Lovie Olivia, 2024

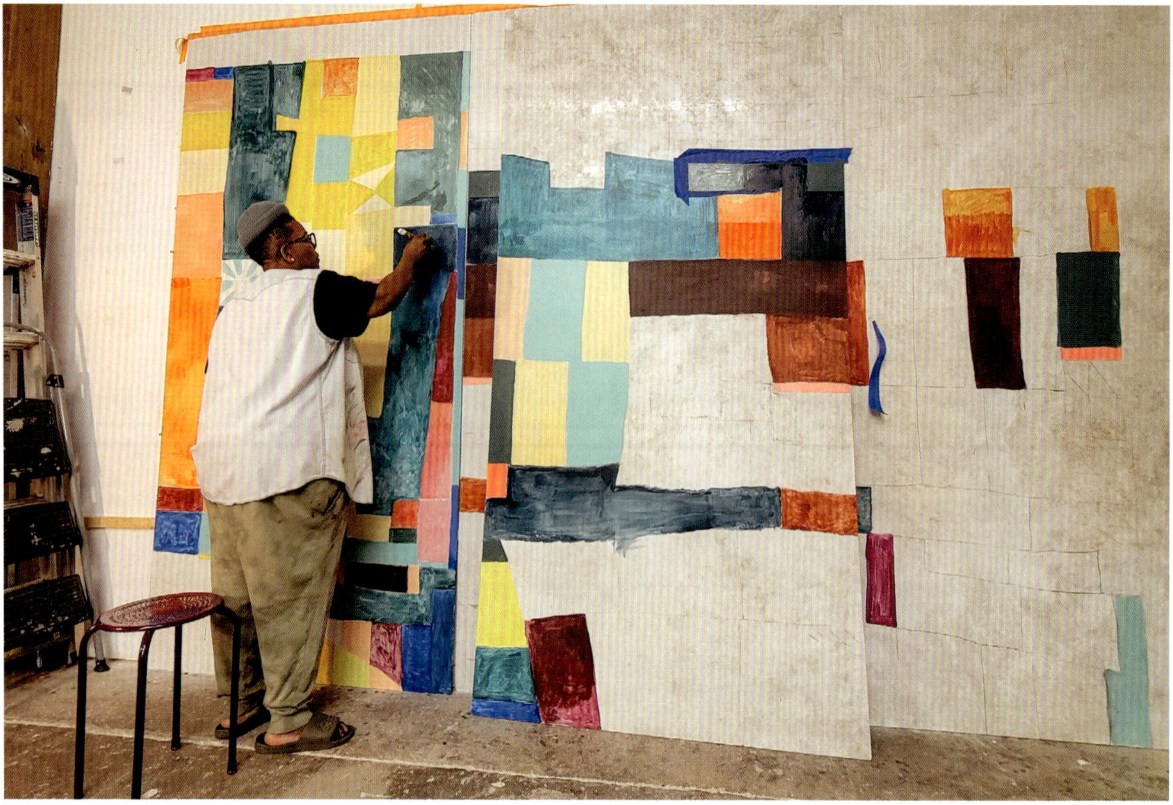

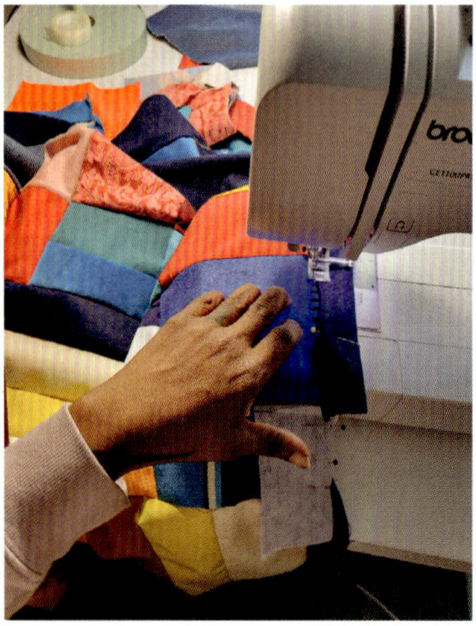

to improvisational quilting has cemented a place within abstraction and should be treated as a pathway that can deepen our understanding of how and why these quilters create. Just as a quilter can use individual patches that connect to moments across their lifetime, Olivia's motifs speak to the diversity and breadth of cultures that represent the city of Houston. Now installed at Houston's George Bush Intercontinental Airport, *Comforter* is a beacon that radiates warmth, welcome, and a deep-rooted sense of belonging. It asks viewers to consider how quilts, and the hands that make them, shape place and identity.

Comforter process (top: Olivia painting in her studio; above: the artist sewing her first quilt), Lovie Olivia, 2024

Quilts and Literature

Black feminist writers have cited quilts as sites of testimony, memory, and self-exploration. They understand how quilts offer windows into the inner worlds of women whose artistry was often anonymized or only recognized by those closest to them. Subtle mentions of quilts can be found throughout Zora Neale Hurston's observations of Black Southern vernacular traditions, as in her book *Their Eyes Were Watching God*. Throughout *Beloved*, Toni Morrison both presents quilts as the nexus of family connections and invokes quilting as a literary device, piecing together fragments of characters' lives to create a tapestry of storytelling that is varied and complex. Similarly, poet Lucille Clifton uses quilting as a vehicle for storytelling and self-reflection in *Quilting: Poems 1987–1990*. The collection focuses on the depths of women's lived experiences through brief poetic fragments, bound with the language and imagery of quiltmaking.

BELL HOOKS

Other writers, such as bell hooks and Alice Walker, have analyzed more intimately the gravity that quilts possess and the significance they hold in the writers' personal lives. In *Belonging: A Culture of Place*, hooks introduces readers to her grandmother, Sarah Hooks Oldham, whom she lovingly refers to as Baba. Baba learned quilting under her mother's tutelage and possessed a certainty about herself and her work. "She was a dedicated quiltmaker," hooks writes, "gifted, skillful, playful in her art, making quilts for more than seventy years, even after her 'hands got tired' and her eyesight was 'quitting.'" She frames Baba's quiltmaking through the lens of a spiritual and meditative practice, one that was restorative and allowed the opportunity to return to oneself. As Baba saw it, quilting involved the art of "calm[ing] the heart" and "eas[ing] the mind." By recalling her grandmother's ritual of showing her quilts and discussing their concepts, hooks gives voice to the intention, process, and precision that have historically been lacking in dialogues around Black quilts. She recognized that earlier generations of quiltmakers were unable to document and share the intricacies of their practice in the way that Baba did. She also knew that the act

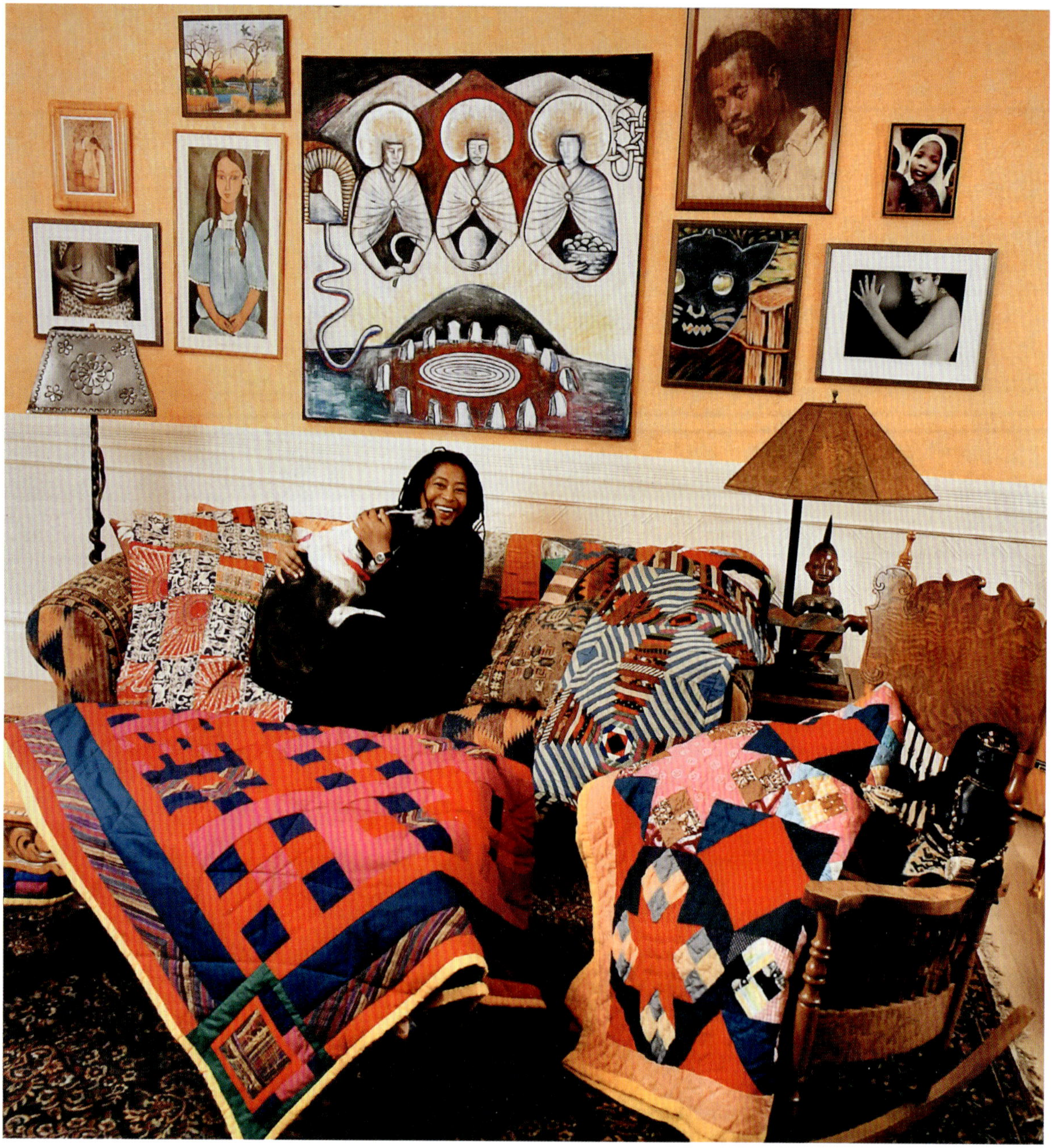

Alice Walker Seated at Her Home, Roland L. Freeman, 1992

of passing down these "aesthetic inheritances" was more than just a hobby; it was the gift of legacy and planted the seeds of creativity to feed one's soul.

ALICE WALKER

Similarly, Alice Walker acknowledged the creative spark of her foremothers and the importance of carrying forward the work of past generations. A daughter and granddaughter of quilters, she knew firsthand the way quilts bind relationships and feed imagination. A lesser-known fact is that quilting was embedded in the development of her Pulitzer-winning novel, *The Color Purple*. As Walker developed the characters for the novel, she felt drawn to create a quilt in tandem with writing. Walker said, "The same voices of my ancestors that dictated the narration in the book also guided me in developing the pattern for the quilt." She chose to use traditional nine-patch blocks, a pattern that is often used to teach aspiring quilters the basics of the process.

Within the book itself, quilting becomes a site of physical mending and emotional repair between the characters Sofia and Celie. Celie's meek disposition is a point of contention for Sofia, whose candor and strength often leave her enraged with Celie. As they grow closer, Sofia begins to empathize with Celie, and Celie learns from Sofia's boldness. The two go on to create a quilt from worn curtains and develop a sisterhood that both are in dire need of. The kinship Walker portrays in *The Color Purple* is but one example of the gift that quilting has offered Black women who seek care and community from one another.

Walker's widely acclaimed short story "Everyday Use" gives us another glimpse into the complexities of quilts within Black life. She specifically draws attention to the tension between portraying quilts as an elevated art form and using them in our everyday lives. The story also highlights how rural Black life possesses a cultural richness that can often go unappreciated by those who are living it. The three main characters, Mama and her two daughters Maggie and Dee (Wangero), are at a crossroads of judgment, entitlement, and appreciation. Wangero is eager to leave home and renounce the rural life that she is ashamed of. She opts to change her name in college and returns home with a newfound attachment to her African heritage. Her mother and her sister

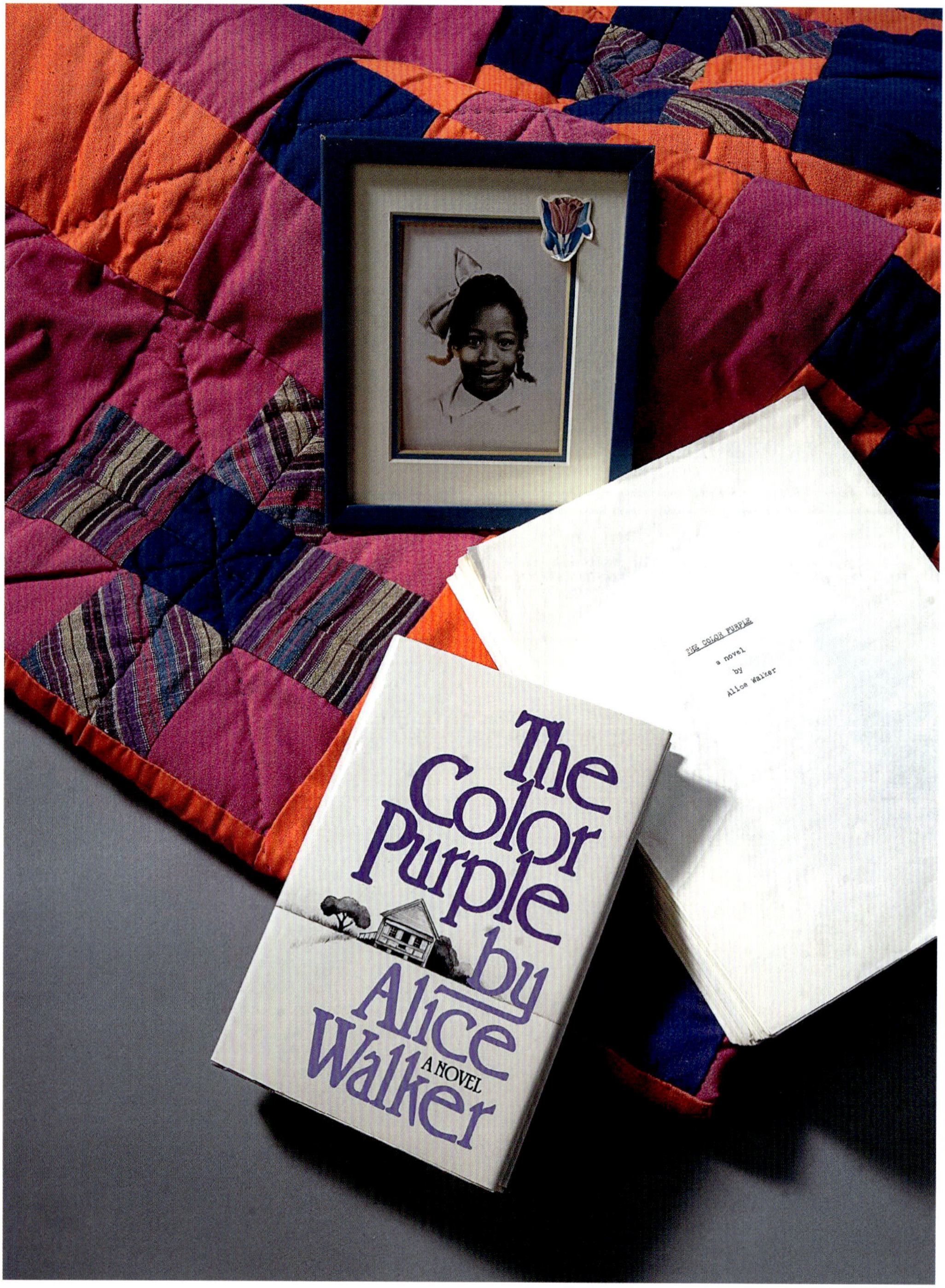

The manuscript of *The Color Purple*, a printed copy of the book, and a childhood photo of Walker atop a quilt made by the author have remained in the small town and continued life as they knew it. Upon her return, Wangero is fascinated by the home and relics she left behind, seeing them through the lens of her perceived enlightenment and success.

As she scans Mama's house for artifacts she'd like to take back to New York, she specifically requests a pair of old quilts from her childhood. Mama rejects her request, stating that they belong to Maggie as a wedding gift. Wangero objects that the quilts will probably be used in a utilitarian way. Mama sees nothing wrong with them having a practical purpose, and she tries to impress onto Wangero the importance of the quilts' familial significance. She notes the hand stitching that she did herself, and the incorporation of fabric from her own mother's dresses. Wangero insists that her mother doesn't understand her heritage and that the quilts should be hung and displayed, but ultimately Mama is set in her decision to pass down the quilts to Maggie as she enters the next stage of her life and her new place within the family.

Walker's story demonstrates that heritage isn't just taught; it's embodied. "Everyday Use" also begs the question: To whom do quilts belong, and how should they be appreciated? For several Black Southern quilters, the interest in their work, without appreciation for the context in which it was made, has often led to one-sided interpretations of the quilts' meaning and purpose. Even when well intended, a desire to possess quilts by Black makers that isn't rooted in humility and care for their stories is an affront to the traditions that brought them into being.

A League of Their Own

The history of Black quilt scholarship is a story of absence, complicated discourse, and self-determination. Throughout history Black people have fought for equitable treatment and recognition of their lived experiences and work across multiple sectors. Historically, when people outside the culture have attempted to define or represent Black quilts, the results have led to misinterpretation or exploitation—especially when power dynamics and profit were involved. For too long Black quilters were either omitted from dominant narratives or presented through a distorted lens that stripped their work of context and meaning. Individuals like Roland L. Freeman, Cuesta Benberry, and Dr. Carolyn Mazloomi have changed that. Their advocacy and research centers community knowledge and affirms quiltmaking as a complex art form and a record of Black life.

For many nineteenth-century quilts stitched by Black makers, little historical information is known because of their creators' position within society. Quilts made during the time of enslavement, although appreciated now, were seen as unworthy of preservation or full consideration until nearly a century after emancipation. Often constructed using old clothing and remnants, quilts made by enslaved women often did not fit within the confines of what was seen by white quilters as traditional quiltmaking. "Acceptable" quilts were often defined by precision, fabric use, and cohesive patterning.

As time progressed and social movements were birthed, interest in Black quilting ebbed and flowed, leading to conflicting approaches to how the cultural practice was described and written about. In the early to mid-twentieth century, most scholarship didn't feature Black quiltmaking as a distinct practice, if they mentioned it at all. By highlighting the servitude of Black women, scholars supported an elite view of quilting and reinforced the social status of white homemakers and the genius of white designers and quilters. At best, Black quilters were alluded to as supporting hands used to execute a project led by the mistress of the household.

The counterculture and civil rights movements of the 1960s and '70s shifted how "women's work," like quilting, was perceived. The feminist movement in particular led to a deepened investment in women's studies and histories, thrusting the quilt into the limelight as a site of personal exploration for several artists. Patchwork quilting also connected to a growing interest in more ecological ways of living that focused on thrift, reduced consumption, and a more harmonious relationship with the earth and others. Exhibitions such as the Whitney Museum's 1971 show *Abstract Design in American Quilts* raised debate about quilts' journey from bedcovers to works of art on walls. Simultaneously, the Black arts and civil rights movements developed an interest in culturally specific practices as a form of resistance and celebration. This led to artists, writers, and researchers developing work and writings that offered a new way of seeing traditional practices. Through these decades there was a shift from traditional quiltmaking to the art quilt movement, which upended how quilts could be defined.

At the same time, a deepening interest in other cultures led to new research on historical objects and traditions. Black quilting became associated with an Africanist aesthetic. Scrappy, patchwork, or improvisational quilts (that is, quilts that don't follow a specific form or pattern), particularly those made by Black women from the rural South, were said to have evolved from African traditions. From fabric and color choice to irregularities in stitches, researchers sought to create a bridge between Black makers in America and West African artisans, with quilts placed at the center. These theories caught on quickly and became accepted as fact thanks to the publication of several works in the 1980s, but these generalizations created tensions within the Black community, as well as the larger quilt community, for a few reasons. First, the patterns and motifs mentioned by early researchers were not always exclusive to Black quiltmakers. Additionally, several of these Africanist theories were developed without the input or voice of the quilters themselves. This exclusion left several Black quiltmakers, especially art quilters, feeling pigeonholed and erased from mainstream quilt discourse. Cuesta Benberry saw that scholars focused on asymmetrical strip quilts that reinforced the theories they wanted to believe. In a 1993 article, art quilter and educator Sandra German captured the frustration of the time, saying:

In a curious twist of fate, we now see that those rare blacks who do achieve visibility within the quilt community often do so en absentia *[*sic*]. In recent history, African American quilts have been subjected to academic, cultural, and artistic exploration by non-blacks who seem to have completed their studies without involving African American quiltmakers in their findings. Our faces and voices have been excluded from the fray. We are left to wonder how it is that the work of so-called experts can be acclaimed in the midst of evidence that they have completely side-stepped our input.*[30]

There were, however, researchers, quilters, and cultural workers who used their disagreement with prevailing theories as fuel to tell a more accurate and comprehensive history. Cuesta Benberry, Roland L. Freeman, and Dr. Carolyn Mazloomi played a pivotal role in shaping spaces and resources where Black quilters could be affirmed while demonstrating the variety found within Black quilt techniques.

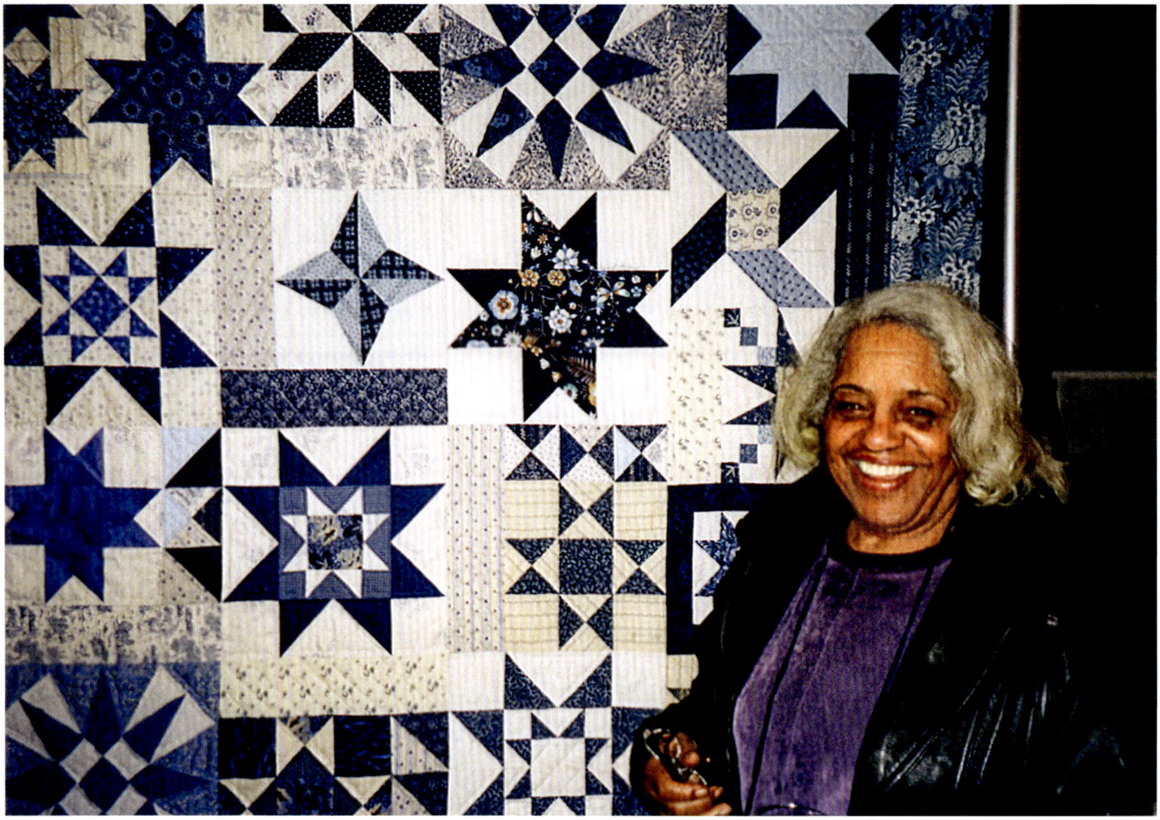

Cuesta Benberry with *Cuesta's Stars* quilt, a gift created for her by the Point Bonita, California, quilt retreat

CUESTA BENBERRY

Cuesta Benberry (1923–2007) was a leading scholar who pioneered the development of Black quilt history. Trained as an educator and librarian, she spent nearly fifty years leading research on pattern history and quilters (particularly Black makers). It was through marrying into a family of quiltmakers in the 1950s that Benberry became interested in the art form. As she learned more about the history of quilts in her husband's family in Kentucky, she set out on a path to better understand quilt patterns. She joined pattern exchange groups, known as round robins, which allowed her to build relationships with other quilters, collectors, and researchers. Benberry became known for writing letters to peers and colleagues in the field that captured her curiosities and findings as she continued her research. As a result, she began the magazine

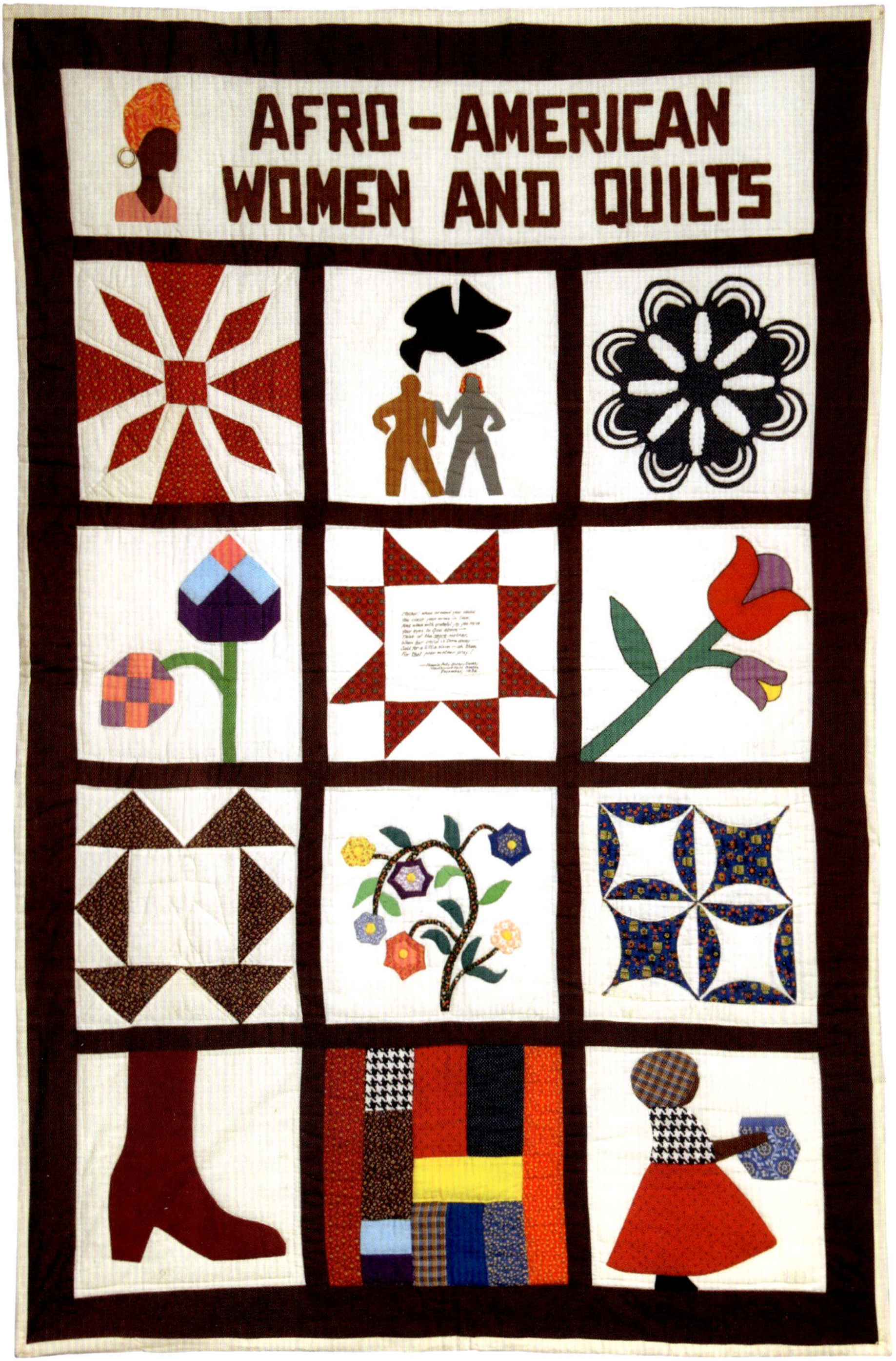

Afro-American Women and Quilts, Cuesta Benberry, Annette Ammen, Lois Mueller, and the Kinloch Community Center Ladies, St. Louis, Missouri, 1979

Nimble Needle Treasures, followed by *Quilter's Newsletter Magazine* and *Quilters' Journal*.

During the 1970s, Benberry was inspired by the writings about ethnic groups that emerged during the US bicentennial. Writings about multiculturalism and pride in cultural heritage gave her a new perspective on quilts. In a 2002 interview with *Quilt Treasures*, she shared, "I ought to study about African American quilts as such." She would quickly find the task to be more challenging than she had originally expected, writing that at the time, "there was nothing in the literature."[31] Soon thereafter, she put out a call in *Quilter's Newsletter Magazine* asking for resources related to quilts made by African Americans. As she amassed her findings, she bridged her love of research and her love of patterns and created her first and only quilt, commemorating the history of Black women and quilting.

In her research, Benberry discovered a range of skills and techniques that could not be solely attributed to an African influence. In 1980, she wrote an essay and presentation—"Afro-American Women and Quilts"—for the first gathering of the American Quilt Study Group and its flagship publication, *Uncoverings*. In the essay she mentions that most of the literature she had encountered was written by researchers in academic settings rather than quilt historians.

For Benberry, it was important that the story of Black women and quilts reflect a more comprehensive view of their existence throughout American history. Rather than focusing on improvisational quilting only, researchers needed to widen their investigation. For example, they could consider quilts from slavery as the earliest form of Black women's creativity and devote attention to traditional quilts that reflected Black quilters' assimilation into Euro-American culture.[32] In addition to becoming a founding member of the American Quilt Study Group, Benberry was also an active member of the Women of Color Quilters Network (WCQN), founded in 1985 by Dr. Carolyn Mazloomi. She often contributed to the WCQN newsletter and was actively involved in research and supporting the network's growth. In a 2004 tribute recognizing Benberry for the donation of her research to the American Folk Art Museum, Dr. Mazloomi wrote,

There is nobody in the United States who has celebrated our success like Cuesta Benberry. As a historian she was the first to write about the wide range of quilting styles in the African American quilt community. I recall the phone calls we've had after looking at quilts from network members . . . the joyful shouts, the awe and shared appreciation of quilts from the African American community. Generosity of spirit, exemplified by her gift to the American Folk Art Museum, typifies Cuesta and I feel privileged to call her friend.[33]

Benberry's research on Black quilt history led to her consulting with museums and organizations on the history and stewardship of Black quilts. In the early 1990s she was invited by the Kentucky Quilt Project to curate an exhibit and publish an accompanying book that presented the results of decades of research. *Always There: The African-American*

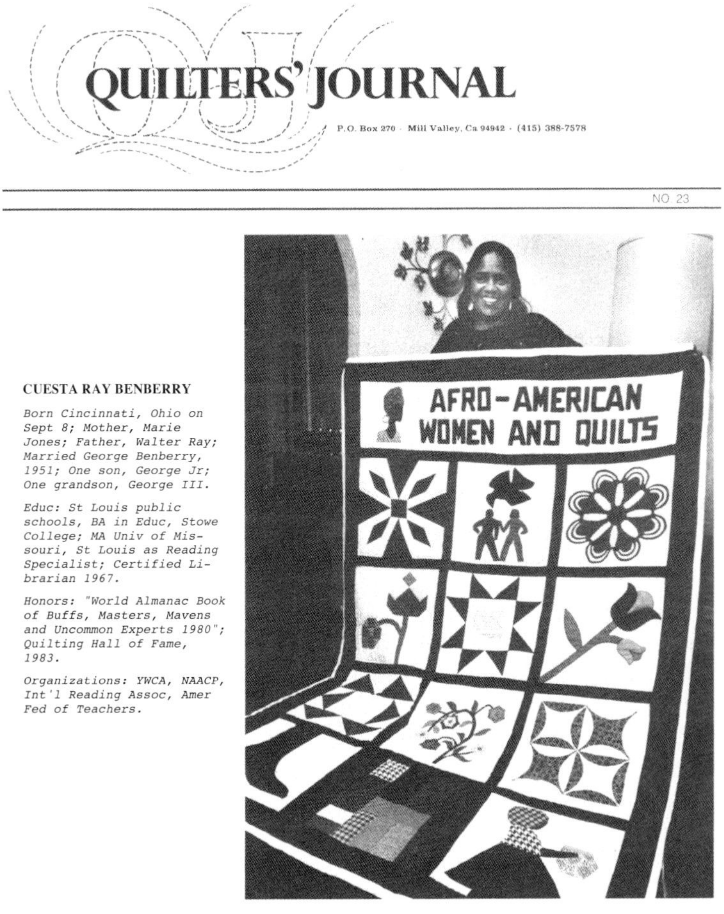
QUILTERS' JOURNAL

P.O. Box 270 · Mill Valley, Ca 94942 · (415) 388-7578

NO. 23

CUESTA RAY BENBERRY

Born Cincinnati, Ohio on Sept 8; Mother, Marie Jones; Father, Walter Ray; Married George Benberry, 1951; One son, George Jr; One grandson, George III.

Educ: St Louis public schools, BA in Educ, Stowe College; MA Univ of Missouri, St Louis as Reading Specialist; Certified Librarian 1967.

Honors: "World Almanac Book of Buffs, Masters, Mavens and Uncommon Experts 1980"; Quilting Hall of Fame, 1983.

Organizations: YWCA, NAACP, Int'l Reading Assoc, Amer Fed of Teachers.

Quilters' Journal, vol. 6, no. 1, featuring Cuesta Benberry, 1984

Presence in American Quilts was a visual response and counterargument to prevailing accounts of Black quilting, and a call to action. Benberry discussed the need for quilters to tell their own stories, saying, "It is important to listen to what African-American quiltmakers say about their work and to give them credence, whether or not their comments coincide with researchers' theories and interpretations."[34] In 2000, she curated and wrote an essay for another show, *A Piece of My Soul: Quilts by Black Arkansans*. The exhibition shone a light on lesser-known Black quilts in the Old State House Museum collection in Little Rock. Benberry's contributions led to her induction into the Quilters Hall of Fame in 1983. She donated her research collection to the American Folk Art Museum in the early 2000s, and it was later acquired by the Michigan State University Museum in 2009.

ROLAND L. FREEMAN

Roland L. Freeman (1936–2023) was a photographer and documentarian committed to the preservation of Black folk tradition and cultures. Although raised in Baltimore, Maryland, Freeman developed his political consciousness after spending time in Paris while serving in the US Air Force in the late 1950s. He came to understand the Black struggle in a global way, learning about Pan-Africanism, Negritude, and the African diaspora through thinkers and artists living abroad. As his awareness of shared struggles grew, he felt compelled to return home to support the burgeoning civil rights movement. After experiencing the March on Washington in 1963, he was inspired to learn photography. He wanted to be engaged and responsive to the political climate, proclaiming, "This is how I can say something about the times we're living in."[35]

Freeman set out to photograph the Black community to counteract the portrayal of Black people in the popular media. To refine his craft, he began studying the work of Gordon Parks and Roy Decarava, two Black photographers whose images captured the depth and beauty of twentieth-century Black life. Following the murder of Martin Luther King Jr. in 1968, Freeman started following the crowds and social unrest in the streets of Washington, DC. Prior to King's assassination, King had been developing the Poor People's Campaign, which would bring together thousands of poor people to descend upon the nation's capital to demand economic equality. The campaign still took place, with a

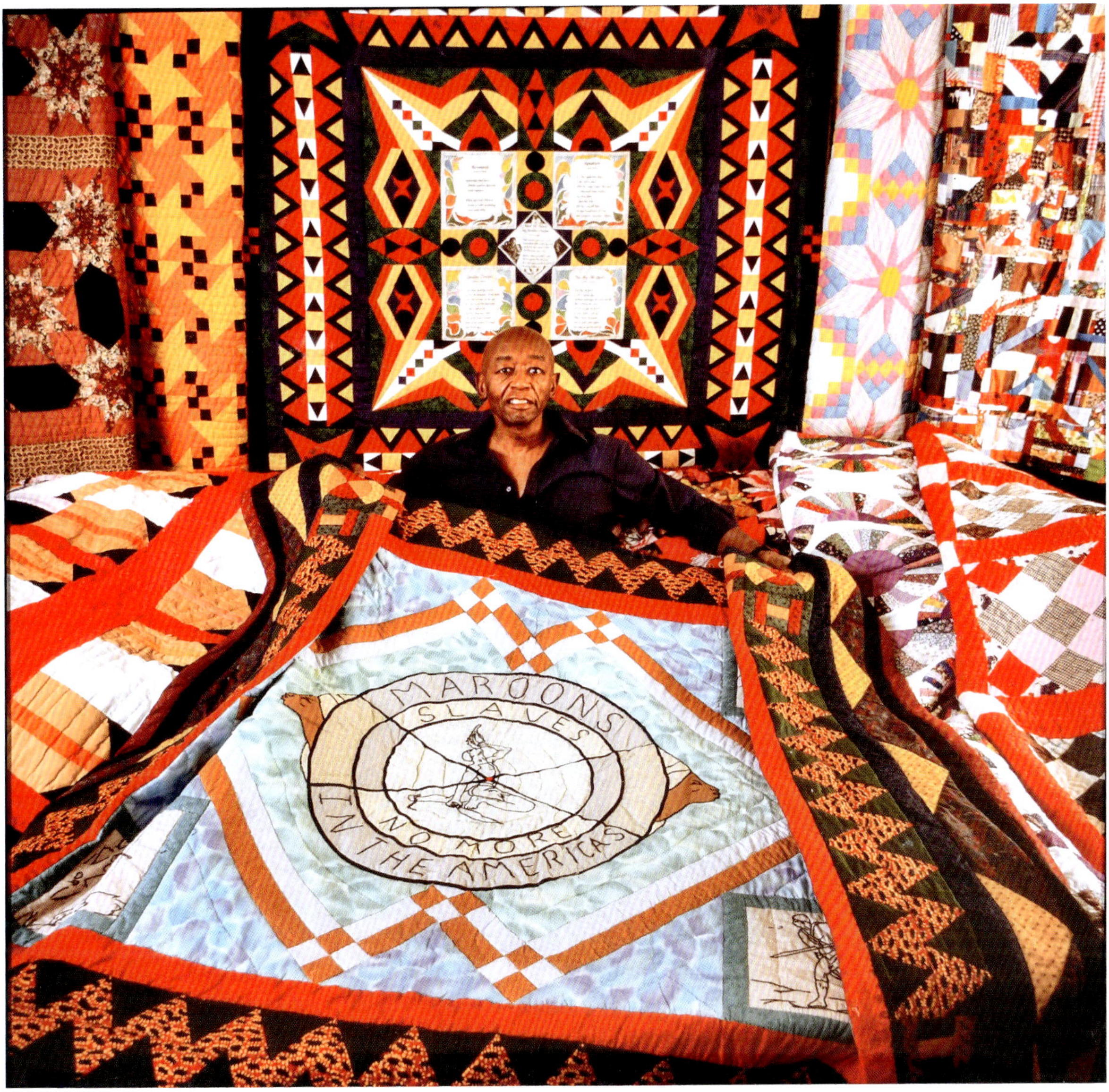

Roland L. Freeman with Nine of the Quilts in His Collection, Roland L. Freeman, 1994

mule train leaving Marks, Mississippi, for a monthlong journey to Washington. Freeman accompanied the participants, learning about the plight of poor, rural Black Southerners in the process.

As his work continued into the 1960s and '70s, he became connected to the Smithsonian's Office of Folklife Programs (now the Center for Folklife and Cultural Heritage). In 1974, the Folklife Festival invited the state of Mississippi to participate and sent Freeman, along with folklorist Worth Long, on assignment to document culture bearers. As he learned about the cultural richness of the state, Freeman felt a "moral obligation" to preserve the folk culture.[36] He feared that when elders died, their traditions would be lost with them.

Freeman went on to codirect the Mississippi Folklife Project, which deepened his understanding of craft traditions and revived his preexisting interest in quiltmaking. For over two decades he documented quilt traditions in Mississippi and across the United States. Freeman also noted the developing interest in improvisational strip quilts in the late 1970s and early '80s. In 1978, having already collected quilts from Black makers during his travels, he developed an exhibit at the Mississippi State Historical Museum called *Something to Keep You Warm: The Roland Freeman Collection of Black American Quilts from the Mississippi Heartland*. One of the first exhibitions of Black quilts, *Something to Keep You Warm* continued to gain national attention, and it was presented at Howard University and featured in the November 1978 issue of *Essence* magazine. During this period he also began communicating with Cuesta Benberry about her explorations into Black quilt scholarship.[37]

By the mid-1980s Freeman knew his project had to grow beyond the borders of Mississippi and the surrounding area. Quilters that he had documented and other folklorists started connecting him to individuals in other areas, imploring him to include them in the continuation of his field research. Concurrently, Dr. Mazloomi's efforts to organize the Women of Color Quilters Network began to take shape, and she later aided Freeman with identifying quilters nationally. A loss of funding meant he had to think creatively about how to chronicle across state lines, and he often combined his surveys of quilters with other photography assignments.

In the early 1990s Freeman was diagnosed with cancer, but after getting treatment and regaining his strength, Freeman had a newfound perspective on his documentation of Black quilters. Up until that point,

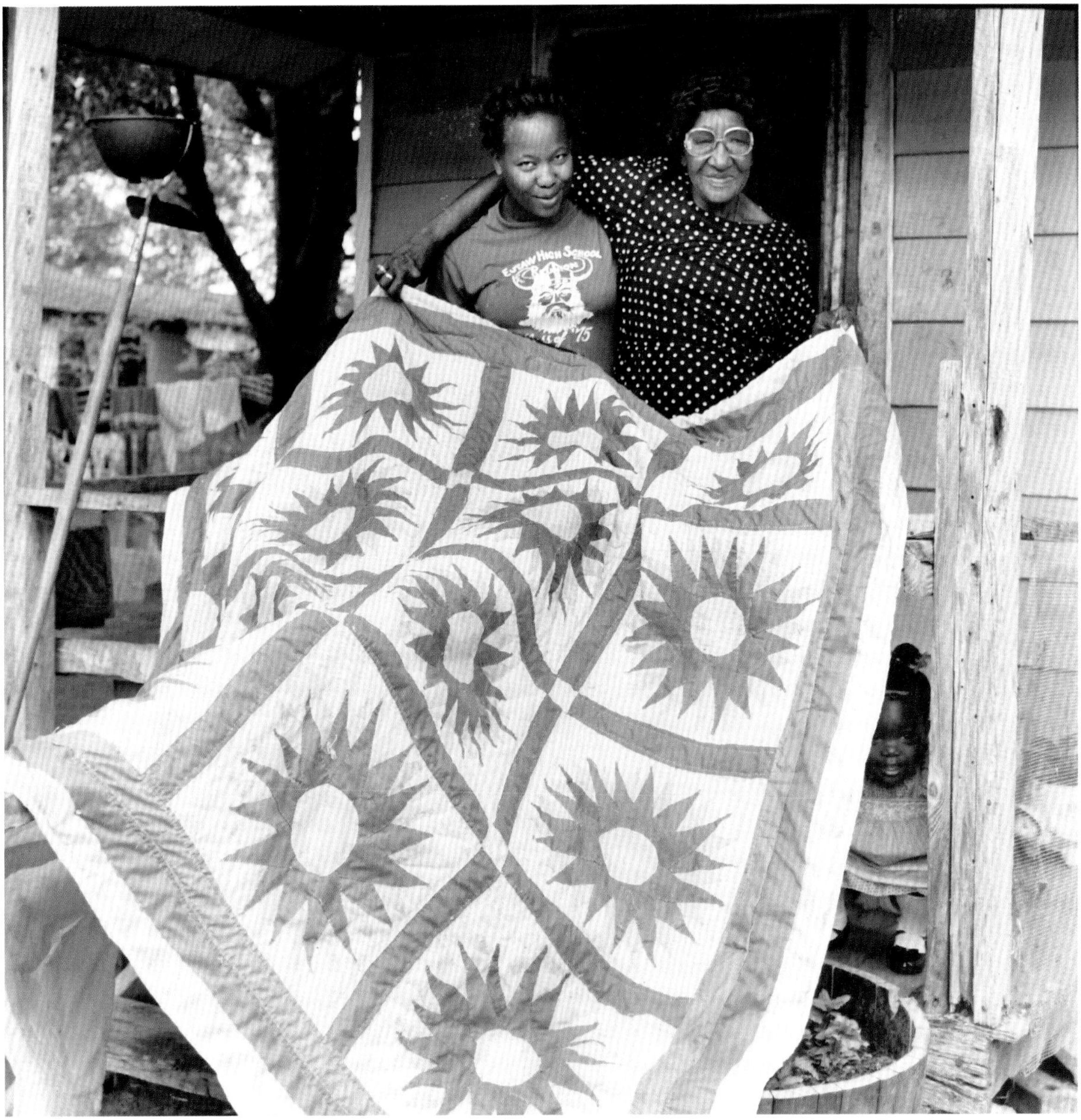

Three Generations of Quilters, Roland L. Freeman, 1986. Left to right: Delois Ann Smith, her mother, Mary K. Williams, and her daughter, LaChandria Smith

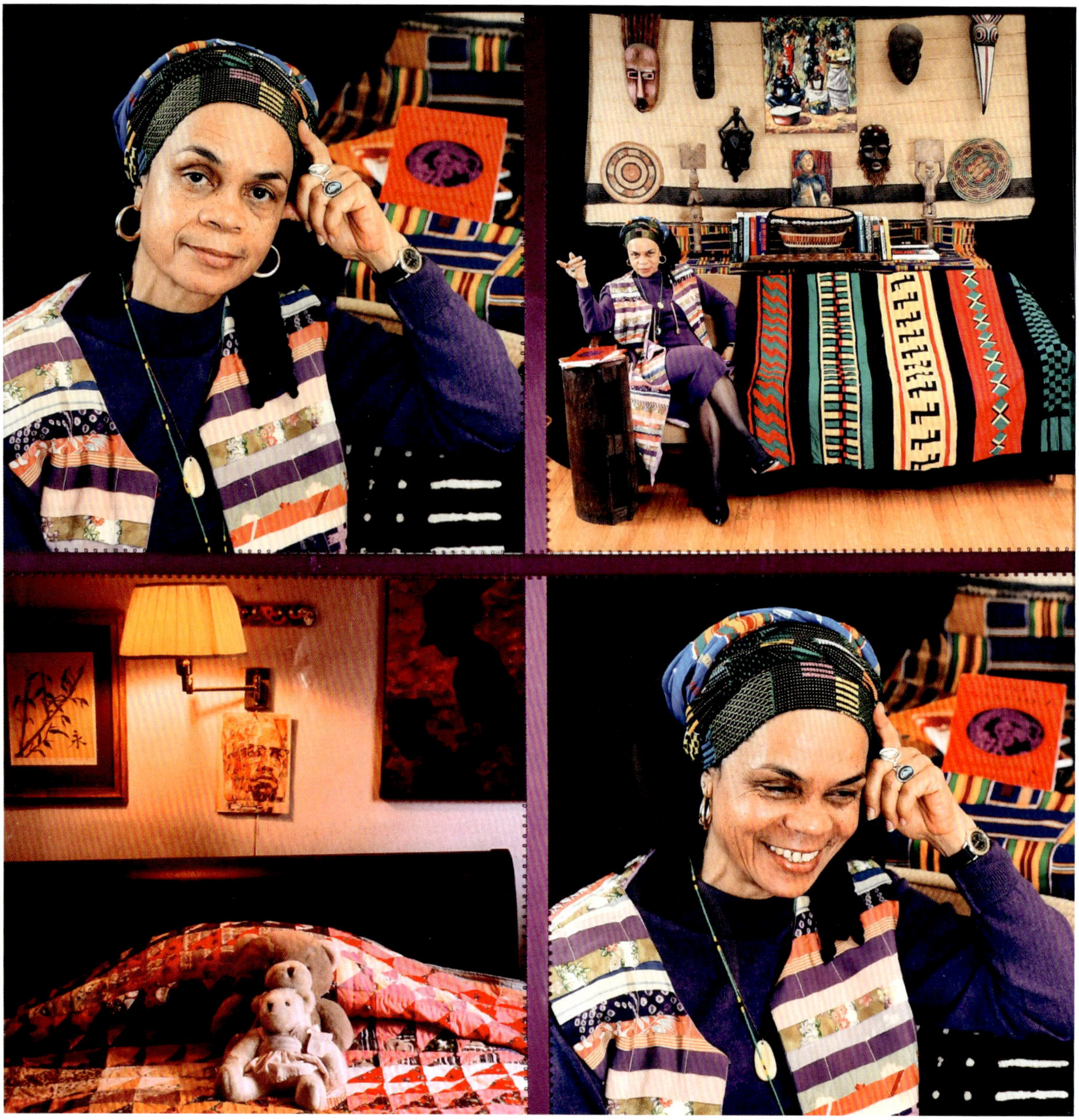

Poet Sonia Sanchez photographed with her quilt collection, Roland L. Freeman, 1992

he had felt that he had "not seen any work based on a full consideration of their remarkable extent and diversity."[38] He hoped that if he could complete a national survey that highlighted the importance of Black quiltmaking, then serious consideration would be extended to the lived experiences of Black quilters and how those experiences shaped their work. In 1996 Freeman published this survey, *A Communion of the Spirits: African-American Quilters, Preservers, and Their Stories*. It was a landmark publication, presenting a compendium of Black quilt stories and practices across thirty-eight states, offering a more complete picture of what had been overlooked for centuries.

In *A Communion of the Spirits*, Freeman also wrote about the controversies around African American quilts being defined strictly as strip quilts. He cited Cuesta Benberry's work, which emphasized how Black quilting encompasses multiple patterns and techniques. He was also critical of how the predominantly white museum field excluded Black scholars who were stewards of their own folk cultures. Nearly forty years later, *A Communion of the Spirits* remains one of the most significant texts to archive Black quilting traditions.

In 1991, Freeman started the Group for Cultural Documentation as a way to continue the preservation and documentation of cultural traditions. In 2007, he was awarded the Bess Lomax Hawes Award by the National Endowment for the Arts. And in 2009, in partnership with the Women of Color Quilters Network, Freeman presented *Quilts for Obama: An Exhibit Celebrating the Inauguration of Our 44th President*, which featured over sixty quilts celebrating the inauguration of President Barack Obama.

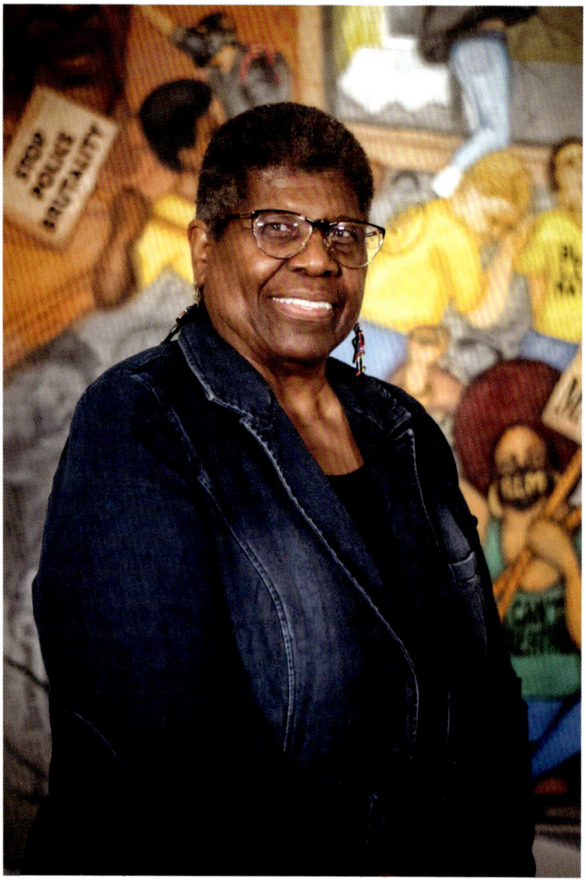

Dr. Carolyn Mazloomi, 2021

DR. CAROLYN MAZLOOMI

Dr. Carolyn Mazloomi continues to be one of the most celebrated and impactful figures in preserving, presenting, and advocating for Black quilters and Black quilt history. Her work as a quiltmaker, historian, author, curator, and mentor—and leader of the Women of Color Quilters Network— has shaped a remarkable legacy and shifted perceptions of Black quiltmaking for over forty years. She originally studied aerospace engineering and took up quilting as a hobby and retreat from her rigorous profession. While living and working in Los Angeles, she taught herself to quilt and joined several groups to improve her artistry. However, many of the groups and spaces she encountered were homogenous and left her feeling isolated as the singular Black member. After teaching a quilting class at the California African American Museum, she was approached by a group of women about organizing a quilting group. This led to the formation of the African-American Quilt Guild of Los Angeles (later renamed the African American Quilters of Los Angeles) in 1981. As the group continued to work together, they wondered where other Black quilters were. Their questioning led Dr. Mazloomi to place an ad in the 1985 issue of *Quilter's Newsletter Magazine* Ten women responded and eventually became the founding members of the Women of Color Quilters Network (WCQN): Claire E. Carter, Arma Carter, Melodye Boyd, Barbara Pietila, Peggie Hartwell, Marie Wilson, Rosalyn Bond, Della Collins, Dorothy Nelle Sanders, and Judy Wellington.

News of the network spread quickly, with other quilters expressing excitement and gratitude after searching for others like them. The WCQN was built upon the unconditional acceptance and validation of all Black quilters. Many of the members had experienced rejection in mainstream quilt spaces because they did not limit their quilting to patchwork or improvisation. Others had even been told that they did not create "African American" quilts because their aesthetic did not match the then-popular African-influenced improvisation. These feelings were compounded by the Los Angeles group's experience at Eli Leon's *Who'd a*

Thought It? exhibition, which was gaining traction as a leading source of Black quilt research. Leon asserted bold claims about improvisation and its origin within the lexicon of Black quilting, positioning it as a defining feature.

In contrast, Dr. Mazloomi was inspired by Cuesta Benberry's position on an all-encompassing spectrum of Black quilting techniques. Mazloomi stated,

We want to celebrate creative freedom, and we frequently break the rules of traditional quiltmaking. Consequently, much of what we do is not always well received by those who don't understand or who are incapable of tolerating different-ness without passing judgement. At the same time, many of our members are masters of traditional quilt forms. They do exquisite needlework. Their work shows exceptional research and attention to detail.[39]

The WCQN set eight primary goals to guide its work:

To foster and preserve the art of quiltmaking among women of color.
To research quilt history and document quilts.
To offer expertise in quiltmaking techniques in order to enhance our skills.
To offer authentic handmade African American quilts and fiber arts to museums and galleries for shows.
To help with writing grant proposals for those persons who may have such needs.
To aid quilters who wish to sell their work obtain the best price possible.
To give quilting workshops.
To facilitate knowledgeable services in quilt restoration and repair.[40]

Cover of the Women of Color Quilters Network newsletter, no. 1

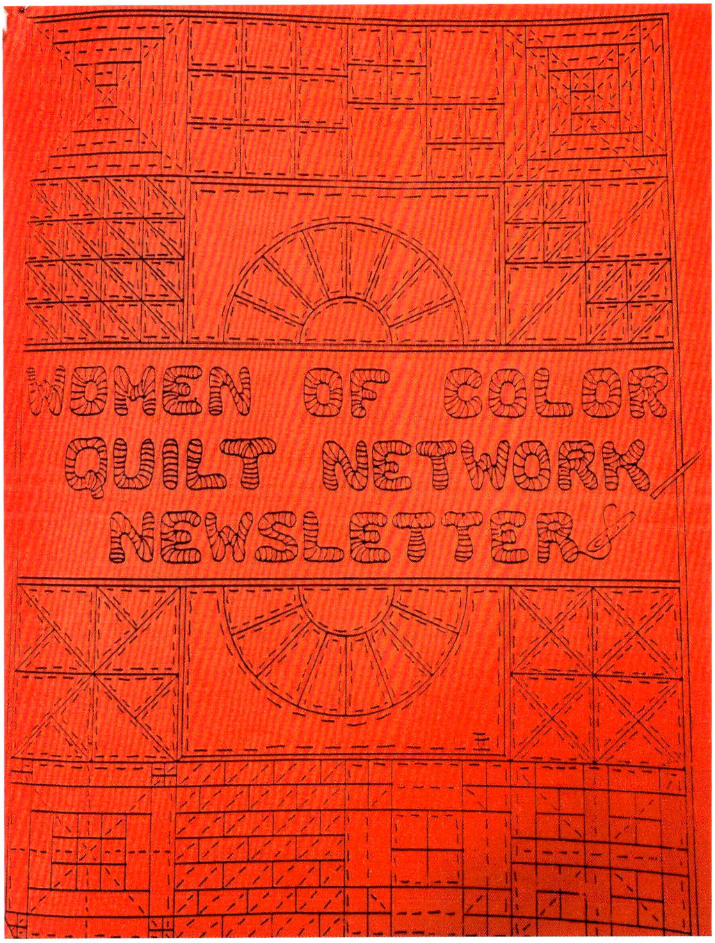

The group released its first newsletter in 1988, which allowed its members to access resources to advance their work and the WCQN's mission. As described by member and quilter Sandra German in 1993, the newsletter "has offered everything from quiltmaking tips to scholarship and grant application forms, humor, and obituaries, hard-hitting original essays and recommended reading lists; letters from members and calls for submissions."[41] In 1989 the group had its first exhibition at the Houston International Quilt Festival, curated by member Della Collins.

Since its inception the WCQN has grown to include over 1,700 members at its peak, with chapters across thirteen cities. With Dr. Mazloomi at the helm, WCQN became known for its critically acclaimed work and advocacy for Black quiltmakers. In 1998 she published the book *Spirits of the Cloth: Contemporary African American Quilts* to celebrate Black quilters through a contemporary lens. *Spirits of the Cloth* was also sponsored by the American Craft Museum as a traveling exhibition, exposing audiences across the United States to the diversity of Black quilters. Through Dr. Mazloomi's curatorial and scholarly leadership, the WCQN has remained steadfast in its use of quilts as a way to preserve Black histories and engage in activism around social issues locally and globally. Among her numerous exhibitions, some of the most revered include *Quilting African American Women's History: Our Challenges, Creativity, and Champions* (2008), *And Still We Rise: Race, Culture and Visual Conversations* (2015), and *We Who Believe in Freedom* (2019). Through publishing texts and sharing others' work, Dr. Mazloomi aimed to help Black quilters give meaning to their own work rather than allowing scholars to project ideas onto them.

Following the murder of George Floyd in 2020, Dr. Mazloomi was deeply impacted as both a Black woman and a mother. The pain of witnessing another victim of police brutality led her to put out a call for quilts that spoke to the issues of racism and police violence. The overwhelming response birthed a collaboration between the WCQN and the Textile Center in Minneapolis called *We Are the Story*. Two exhibitions—*Gone but Never Forgotten: Remembering Those Lost to Police Brutality* and *Racism: In the Face of Hate We Resist*—brought together quilters from across the United States. They gave voice to the ongoing struggles of Black people and made a collective call for change that resonated throughout the nation.

The WCQN never had a formal structure or staff. In lieu of accepting payment for her efforts, Dr. Mazloomi funneled earnings from projects and even personal awards back into the network. While reflecting on this practice in a 2002 oral history interview, she shared, "I don't need it, but our folks need it. The culture needs it. They need this organization. There are certain pioneers within this African-American quilt community . . . like Cuesta Benberry and Roland Freeman that we need to sustain . . . us with their presence and their writings, and I feel like if I didn't do what I set out to do in the network I'm sort of letting them down too."[42] Her commitment to honoring those before her continues into the present. Led by Dr. Mazloomi's advocacy, the WCQN sponsored a replacement headstone for Black quilt ancestor Harriet Powers after hers was broken and removed in 2009.

Dr. Mazloomi has remained true to her initial goals, spending countless years advocating for equitable payment for and archiving of quilts, both by network members and by folk artists in the field. Her efforts and artistry have been commemorated through several awards, including the Bess Lomax Hawes NEA National Heritage Fellowship, United States Artists Fellowship, American Textile Society Fellowship, Ohio Heritage Fellowship, and American Craft Council Honorary Fellowship.

Harriet Powers's headstone, sponsored by the Women of Color Quilters Network, Azuree Holloway, 2023

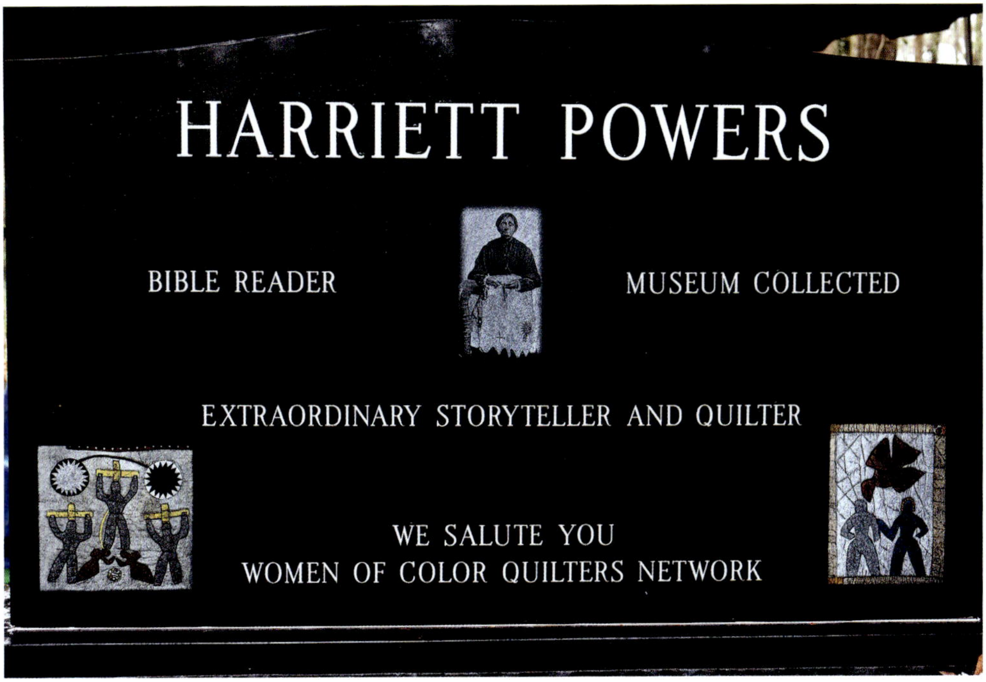

PART II

METHOD

Here I investigate the reasons Black quilters create and what inspires them.

These chapters carry us into the *how* and *why* of Black quilting, the use of quilts for political messaging, and the role that women and maternal figures play in quilting wisdom and assurance into future generations. I feel compelled to present work that is both visually robust and varied in an attempt to resist defining Black quiltmaking through a single lens. The quilts in the following three chapters are as varied and complex as the quilters who created them.

"Handled with Care," is a meditation on intergenerational instruction and the encouragement experienced through relationships with mothers, grandmothers, and other matriarchs. It spotlights artistic collaborations that were formed at sewing tables and through invisible nudges from those who have passed away. From the family legacy of Phoeba Johnson and her daughters to the collaborative genius of Faith Ringgold and Madame Willi Posey, we witness how skill is passed on as a rite of passage and artistic inheritance. These stories honor the careful instruction and knowledge that have been poured into people and quilts.

"Personal and Political" is a presentation of quilts that are anchored in resistance and boldness. The quilts in this chapter refuse to be silent. Using their methods as a vehicle for justice, these quilters create to make sense of violence and imagine freedom when language isn't available. Examples include the fierce iconography of L'Merchie Frazier, the unapologetic typography of Chawne Kimber, and the historical citation of Dindga McCannon and Betty Leacraft. Their work reminds us that revelation can be found at the sewing machine.

The final chapter in this section is a celebration of difference. Rather than attempting to reduce Black quiltmaking to a singular method or aesthetic, this chapter finds beauty in variety. Inspired by the phrase meaning "everybody talking at once," "Gumbo Ya Ya" asserts that cathedral window quilts, strip quilts, and political portraiture all have a place within Black quilt history. Legacy quilters Anna Williams and Michael Cummings are discussed along with younger voices like Kewon Hunter to demonstrate how quilting evolves and returns across generations.

Handled with Care

Although quilting is not an exclusively woman-led practice, most seasoned quilters will tell you that their earliest memories of the craft are connected to the women in their lives. Mothers, grandmothers, and other loved ones often passed down the art of quilting to those seated at their feet. Through observation and direct instruction, quilting became a familial practice among many women. From the hum of the sewing machine to sorting through fabric and thread, these memories cultivated creativity that was shaped by culture and love. Earlier generations of Black women were able to present quilts as heirlooms to let future generations know that they were loved and to remember how far their families had come. As a result of these teachings, we have been able to experience some of the most impressive artists (and quilts) of the twentieth and twenty-first centuries that carry their loved ones' legacies forward.

To speak of quilting in a Black cultural context is to speak of the maternal beyond biological mothering. Mothering has existed as a way of being in the world for Black women, regardless of whether or not they birthed children of their own. Quilting is an extension of care work that encourages others and allows them a place to feel seen and heard. Black women have constructed homeplaces where, as bell hooks writes, "we could restore to ourselves the dignity denied us on the outside in the public world."[43] Quilts were often sewn in these very places, which acted as spaces of radical love where Black women could teach, affirm, and protect. Through fabric scraps and inherited gestures, generations of women have modeled how to build something beautiful with whatever you have. Their teachings have guided generations of children, both kin and chosen, toward their own creativity.

Quilting as Lineage

Matriarch Phoeba Johnson (1883–1984) and her daughters Annie Dennis (1904–97) and Emma Russell (1909–2004) are shining examples of the beauty that can carry through generations. According to their family history, quilting in their family stretched back nearly five generations, beginning with Johnson's namesake, Phoeba Mae (b. 1814), a skilled dressmaker and quilter who made quilts with and for white people. Phoeba Mae was originally enslaved in Maryland and was later moved to Virginia. She gave birth to Johnson's grandmother, Thomsy (b. 1830), who was sold down to Mississippi at the age of fourteen, becoming the plantation's seamstress after learning the skill from her mother. She would later give birth to Johnson's father, Isaac, who took on his mother's textile-based sensibilities, even though he was a man, by learning to craft garments and quilts. Phoeba, the third of seven children, had fond memories of her father also being present with her and her mother, Virginia, at the quilting frame.[44] Phoeba reflected fondly on her quilting journey, saying, "I started piecing quilts when I was seven or eight years old. First thing I pieced was a little nine-patch, and Papa made the biggest fuss over it you ever saw. My grandmama quilted, my mother quilted and two of my three daughters, Annie and Emma, quilt. Course they do that fancy piecing and quilting. I don't do any more quilting. My hands won't take it, but I can still piece up one of the prettiest spreads around."[45]

In Roland L. Freeman's *A Communion of the Spirits*, Phoeba Johnson shared that the pattern for her quilt *Slave Chain* was adapted from a family heirloom of similar style that was given to Thomsy by Phoeba

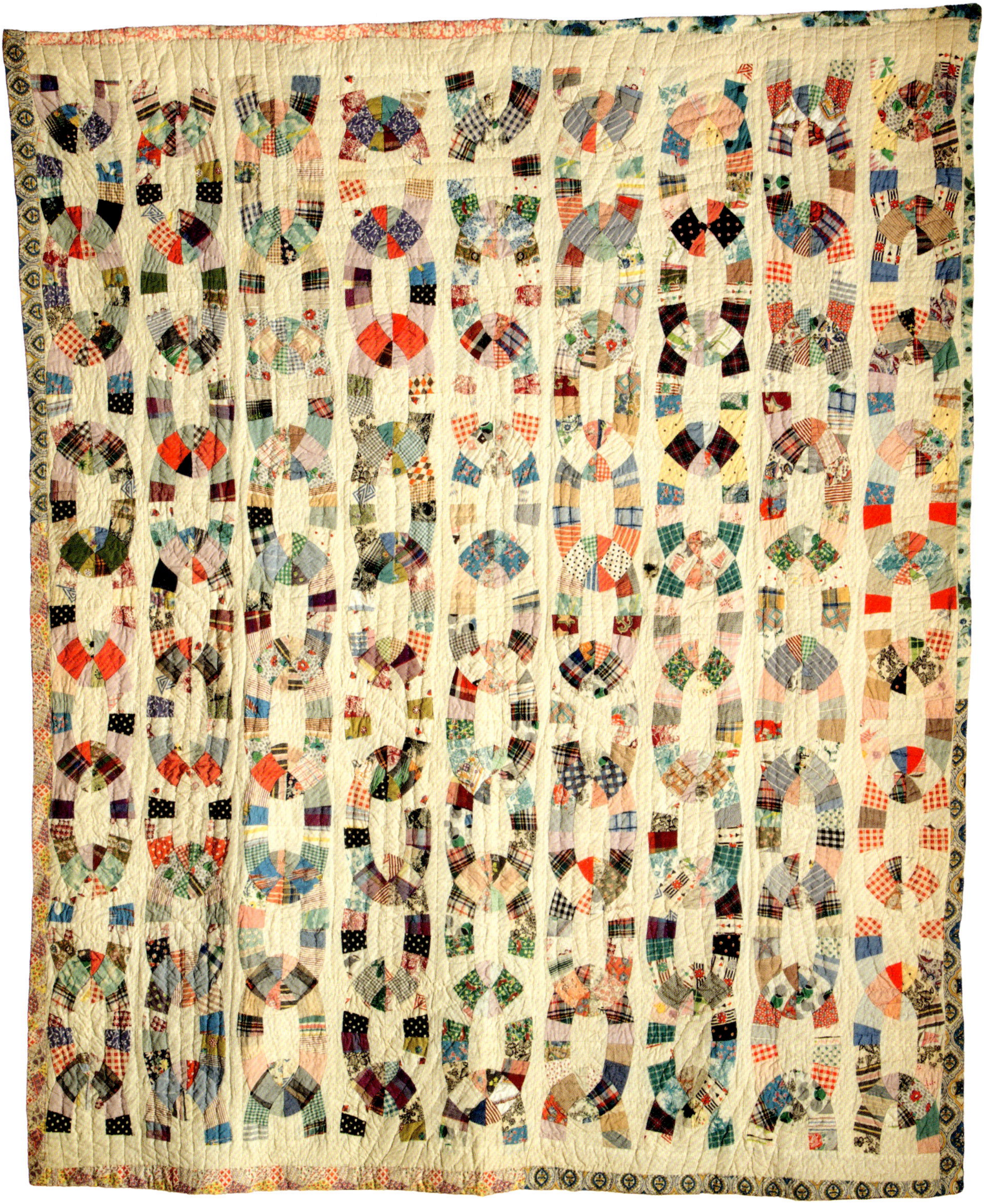

Slave Chain, Phoeba Johnson, 1969

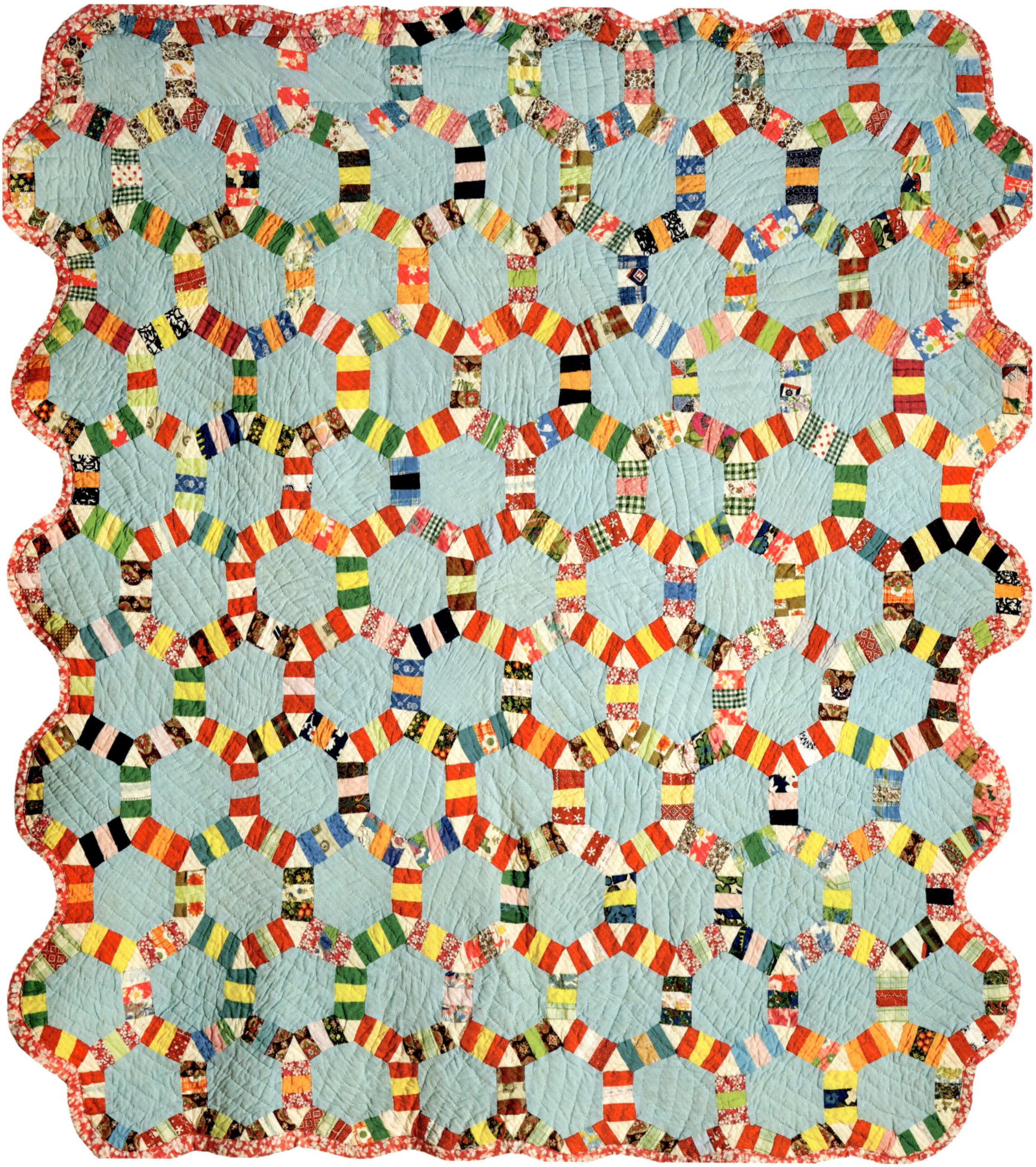

Honeycomb Quilt, Annie Dennis and Phoeba Johnson, 1976

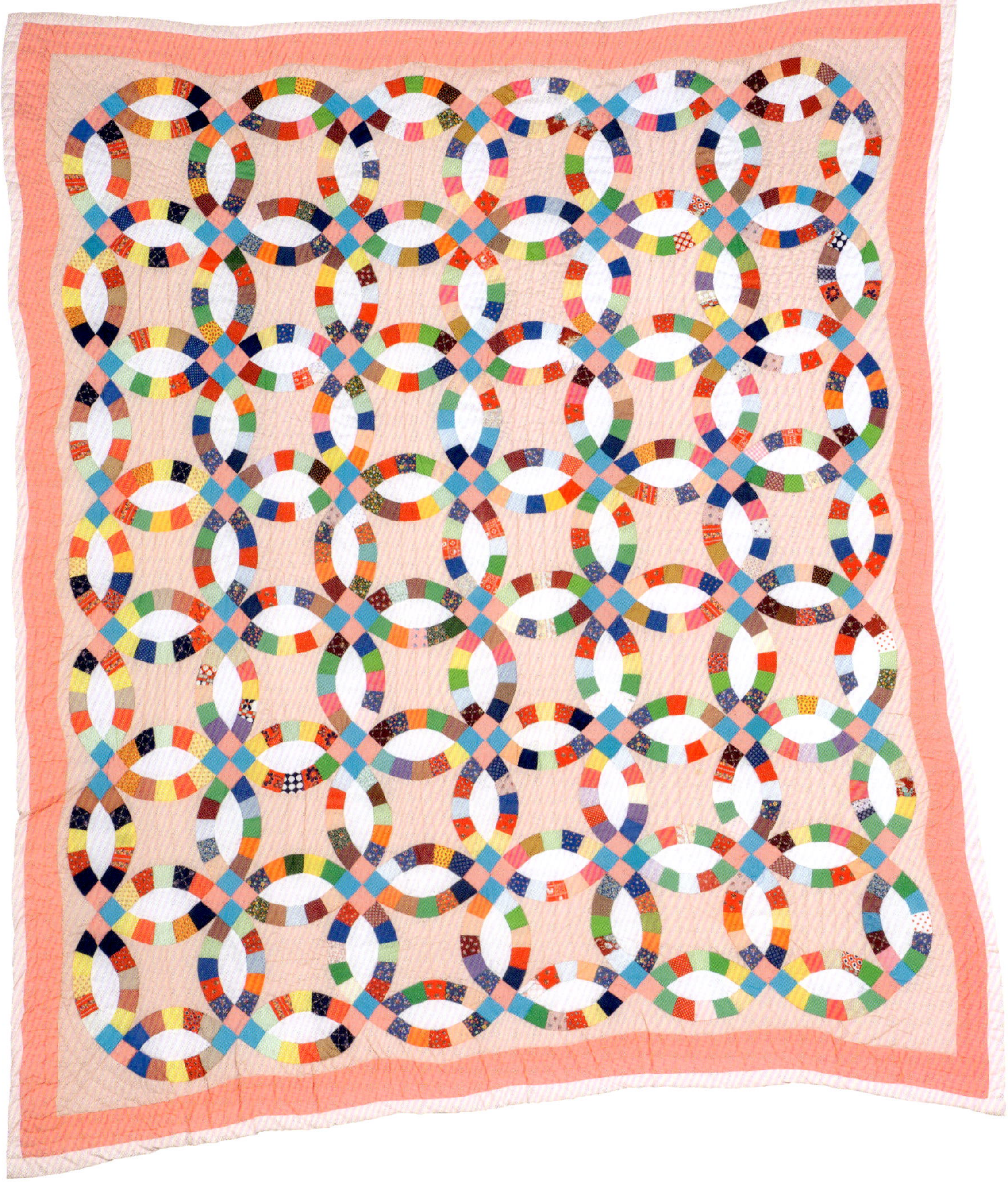

Double Wedding Ring Quilt, Annie Dennis, 1986

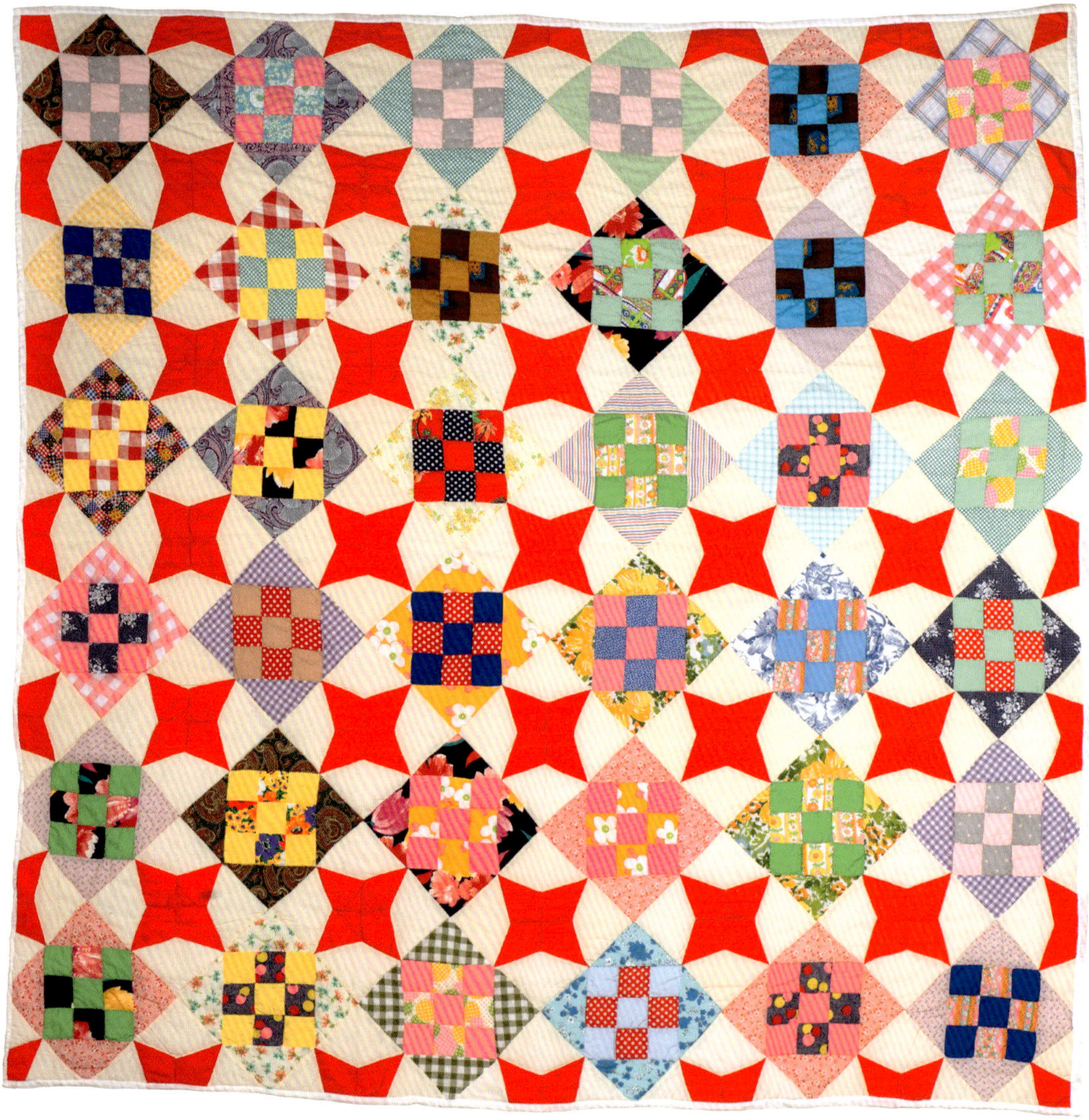

Circle of Stars Quilt, Emma Russell, 1986–90

Mae when she was sold. The original, which was no longer usable, featured links of brown and black over a white background. Johnson would go on to make future versions in lighter fabrics, such as her 1930s replica, to bring some light to a dark history.

Of her three daughters, two—Emma Russell and Annie Dennis—would follow in the family tradition. Despite Russell relocating to Louisiana as an adult, the three continued to collaborate. Russell and Dennis worked on projects together, and in some instances Dennis worked with her mother on projects like *Honeycomb Quilt* to complete the quilting when Phoeba's arthritis wouldn't allow her to do so. Both Dennis and Russell adopted an expert ability to piece and use color in striking ways, similar to that of their mother.

From their mother's instruction, both Russell and Dennis were able to inspire others through quilts and the art of stitching. Dennis was known for making quilts for members of her community who were sick, and she also introduced quilting to friends who would later become known for their expertise, such as Mississippi quilter Cleola McFarland.[46] Both Dennis's *Double Wedding Ring Quilt* and Russell's *Circle of Stars Quilt* were made roughly a decade after the creation of their mother's *Honeycomb Quilt*, all of them subtly connected through colors that are mirrored across the three quilts.

In addition to piecing traditional patterns, Emma would often appliqué narrative quilts that depicted biblical scriptures and her memories of growing up in Mississippi. Possessing an entrepreneurial spirit, she even introduced her friend and neighbor, Effie Bates Cooper, to quilting, with the two later becoming business partners.[47]

Care Through Community

Renowned quilter and National Heritage Fellow Hystercine Rankin was not only known for her storytelling through quilting, but she was also a beloved teacher to generations of quilters in Mississippi. She was a loving instructor to many, sowing seeds of creativity in aspiring and seasoned quilters alike. Born in 1929 in southwest Mississippi, she learned quilting at the age of twelve from her grandmother. Whether seated in front of the fireplace on a rainy day or by a lamp in the darkness, the two maintained this practice throughout Rankin's childhood.

Decades of refining her craft would prove helpful in 1981, when she was invited to be an artist in residence by Mississippi Cultural Crossroads, an arts agency based in Port Gibson, Mississippi. Her gift for instruction quickly became evident, leading to her getting additional support from the Mississippi Arts Commission to teach six local apprentices and work with middle school students.[48] She became recognized in the region for her mastery of quilting, later joining Cultural Crossroads as a teacher and cofounding the Crossroads Quilters, a cooperative of quiltmakers who sold their work through Cultural Crossroads. She even worked with the state to help start two quilting clubs in housing projects in Hattiesburg that were later supported by the city's recreation department. Many women benefitted from studying under Rankin, describing her as a kind but particular teacher who encouraged the correction of mistakes and a dedication to precision.[49] Most notably, Rankin possessed an ability to help others see the possibilities for themselves and develop their own approach to quilting.[50]

Hystercine Rankin and teacher's aide Gwen Aikerson Brooks with a group of local students, Patricia Crosby, date unknown

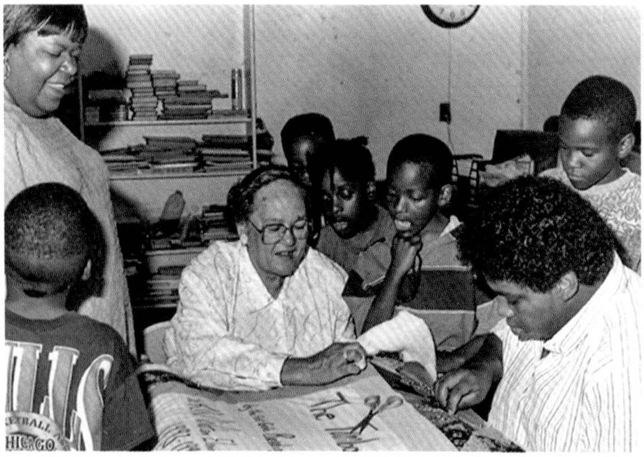

In a 2007 interview with *Craft in America*, Rankin reflected on her time teaching in schools, sharing that she could often take the most challenging students and shift their behavior. She recognized when students were hurting or troubled, and she believed care was the antidote. When asked by other teachers why she was able to help them, she simply stated, "'Cause I love them."[51] Her passion for quilting also translated into her love for her own children and her investment in their well-being. As the recognition of her quilts grew, collectors became more interested in purchasing them. As a result, Rankin was able to fund a college education for her seven children, all of whom graduated from Alcorn State University.

Stitched Collaborations

FAITH RINGGOLD AND MADAME WILLI POSEY

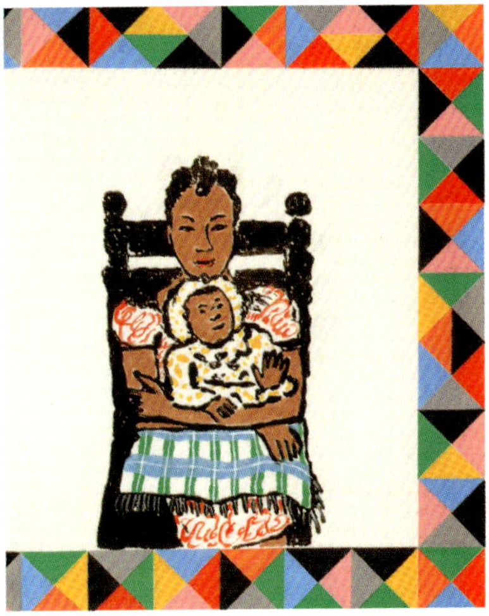

Willi Posey Jones and Faith Ringgold, Faith Ringgold, 1998

Faith Ringgold (1930–2024) is one of the most celebrated and accomplished Black quiltmakers in US history. As an artist, activist, and movement builder, Ringgold used story quilts to chronicle Black history, her inner world, and the everyday experiences that shaped her community and culture. Originally trained as a painter, she spent the early years of her practice creating politically charged work that spoke to the struggles of the civil rights, Black Power, and women's movements of the 1960s and '70s. She dared to be a full-time artist and mother at a time when that felt unattainable for many Black women. In addition to her own perseverance, she credits her mother, Madame Willi Posey (1903–81), with modeling persistence and dedication, which left a lasting impact on her life. In her autobiography *We Flew over the Bridge*, she reflected lovingly on her mother, who inspired her as both a parent and an artist:

> *My mother was a treasure. We adored her. Not only did she raise me carefully and lovingly, but she was also my best friend. She was intelligent, forceful, and physically and mentally agile. She could do a split, headstand, and even learned to swim at 70. Later when she became a collaborator, she inspired my new medium: the quilt. We made our first and only quilt together in 1980. Since then, with the wealth of knowledge and skills she imparted to me, I made 85 or more quilts. There was nothing Willi Posey Jones could not do once she set her mind to it.*[52]

Madame Willi Posey was a fashion designer who began sewing and quilting as a young girl under the guidance of her mother, Ida Posey, and grandmother, Betsey Bingham. When Ringgold was a child, Posey made clothing for her and her siblings, in addition to being sought out to mend and tailor for community members and family friends. She was later able to enroll at the Fashion Institute of Technology, where she learned to cut patterns. As a result, she secured a position at the famed Eisenhower Jacket Factory and later took on her own entrepreneurial endeavors. Ringgold remained in awe of her mother's self-determination throughout her life, and she was encouraged by Posey to explore her own creativity. Remembering her childhood, Ringgold recalled the freedom she had to try her hand at assembling works at the family sewing machine. "Mother would give me scraps of fabric or pieces of patterns she had discarded," Ringgold said, "and I would

Faith Ringgold with her mother, Willi Posey Jones, photographer unknown, date unknown

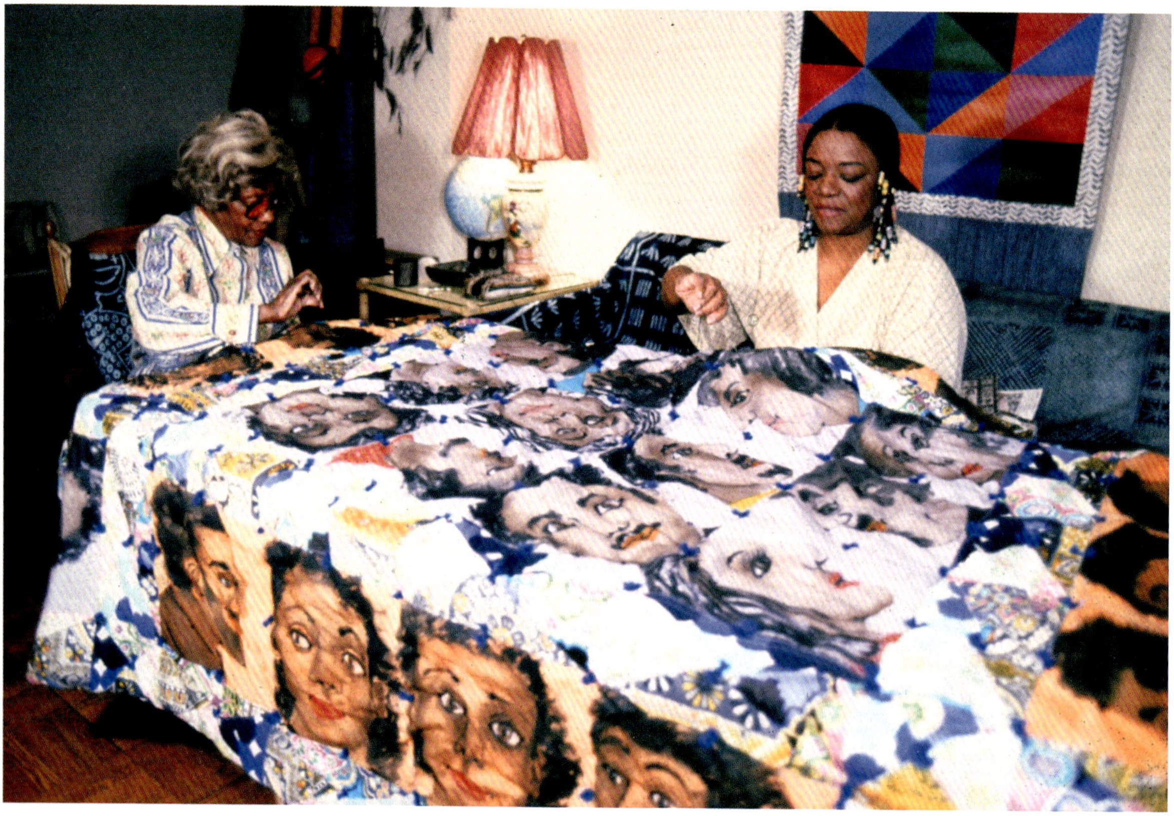

sew them together in an attempt to make outlandish-looking shoes and pocket-books—once I even try to make a brassiere. I never thought I was making art, and though I love the process, I never liked the results because they always looked so homemade."[53]

In 1972 Ringgold reached a crossroads in her artistic career. She encountered intense discrimination in the New York art scene, which impacted her ability to show her paintings and publish her writing. On an international trip she was inspired by Tibetan thangkas—Buddhist paintings depicting sacred images—at a museum. This led to Ringgold pivoting to painting on and assembling textiles. Her mother became a collaborator on those early works, offering input on what Ringgold called "design problems." With Posey's support and guidance, she was able to create her own interpretation of thangkas that combined elements of the Tibetan aesthetic with African influences.

Ringgold's inspiration deepened as she learned about the roles that her enslaved ancestors played in creating quilts and needlework on plantations. The combination of her feminist values and renewed engagement with fabric opened the door for her to fully embrace quilts as a medium. In 1980 Ringgold created her first quilt, *Echoes of Harlem*. This moment would also mark her last collaboration with her mother, who passed away the following year. *Echoes of Harlem* combines fabric, painted canvas, and handwritten text to display thirty faces that represent the voices and stories found throughout Harlem. By passing on her family legacy, Posey lit a fire in Ringgold that led to the creation of many narrative works that tell a rich and expansive story of Black life in the United States.[54]

JOYCE J. SCOTT AND ELIZABETH T. SCOTT

Elizabeth T. Scott (1916–2011) and Joyce J. Scott are another example of a dynamic mother-daughter duo brought together through the bond of quilting. Award-winning MacArthur Fellow Joyce has been internationally recognized for her bold, dynamic sculptures and beadwork. Her work—spanning quilting, performance art, and installations—draws from African American history, folklore, and personal narratives while also integrating influences from Native American, African, and global artistic traditions. Her mother, Elizabeth, was her earliest teacher and her bridge to making art, teaching Joyce beadwork at the age of five.[55]

Elizabeth's artistic journey and knowledge of quilting began in Chester, South Carolina, where she was raised alongside thirteen siblings. Her motto, "Take what you have. Make what you want," was undoubtedly shaped by the women in her life who handed down quilting as a ritual of necessity.[56] After relocating to Baltimore, Maryland, in the 1940s, she put aside quilting until Joyce left for school in 1970. It was at that moment that she pivoted into an exploration of quilts beyond utility and everyday use, creating complex quilted pieces that were embedded with rocks, buttons, and any other materials that spoke to her. When comparing their works, it's easy to see how Elizabeth's maximalist, layered method of quilting influenced Joyce's own expressiveness and otherworldly imagery.

For nearly six decades, Joyce and Elizabeth shared a home and collaborated on numerous projects like the *Three Generation Quilt* before Elizabeth developed dementia. *Three Generation* is, in some ways, a visual manifestation of the maternal legacy and familial tradition of quilting. The middle block on the top row, according to Joyce, illustrates her situated in a garden of innocence as a child. The center block of the quilt is an "initiation rite," with Elizabeth handing over the knowledge of quilting represented by a threaded needle. Surrounding them are their ancestors, the Caldwells and Scotts, watching lovingly as the metaphorical torch is passed to their grandchild. The bottom of the quilt is anchored by Joyce being held and supported by her mother and father. Between them is the "heart of the family," which consists of a yellow thread that runs through each person sewn into the quilt,

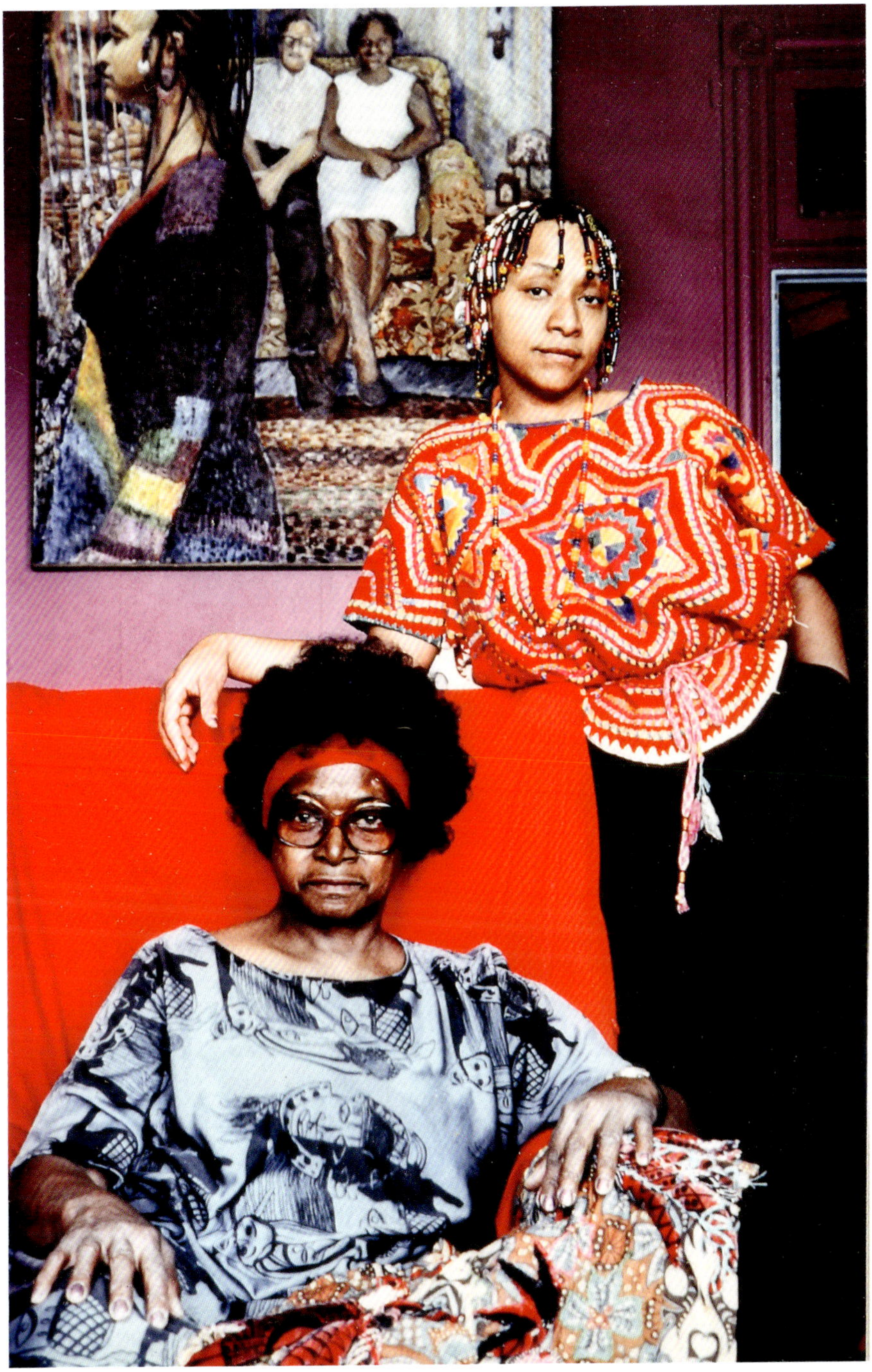

Elizabeth T. Scott and Joyce J. Scott, Roland L. Freeman, 1982

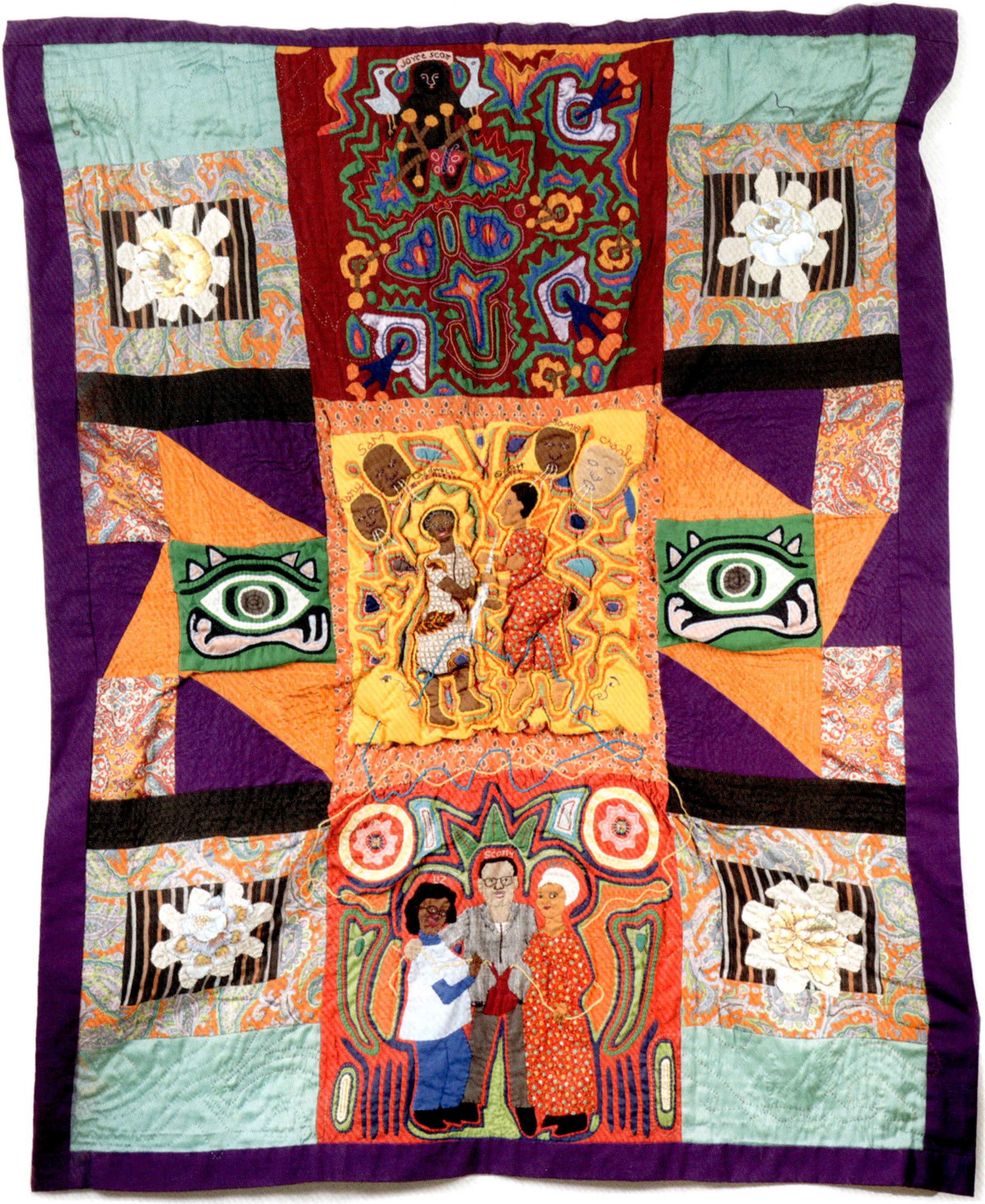

Three Generation Quilt I, Elizabeth T. Scott in collaboration with Joyce J. Scott, 1983

representing the interconnectedness of Joyce's sewing with what she calls the "family thread."[57]

Joyce credits her mother with sharing a gift that allowed her to advance her life in unimaginable ways. She says, "My mom gave me a passport. It was needle and thread and I added on the beads. And that passport . . . that artistic endeavor, has taken me around the world."[58]

Contemporary Perspectives

BASIL KINCAID

Quilting is a tradition spanning multiple generations in Basil Kincaid's family. As a contemporary quilter, he is celebrated for his ability to honor traditional quilting while also remixing patterns in innovative and unexpected ways. Kincaid's quilts are crafted from repurposed materials, including donated clothing and fabrics with personal significance. He also uses traditional Ghanaian textiles, such as kente cloth, symbolizing a fusion of African and African American cultural practices. This approach not only emphasizes sustainability but also weaves personal narratives into each piece, as the materials carry the energies and histories of their previous owners. He likens this process to musical sampling, as he creates new stories through the combination of diverse fabrics.[59]

Kincaid is profoundly inspired by the women in his life, especially his mother and grandmother. He has often spoken about a dream involving his grandmother—also a skilled quilter—that led him to quiltmaking. In the dream, she stood in front of a house wrapped in a quilt and glowing with golden light. This vision wasn't just symbolic. It was a turning point that propelled him toward working with cloth. He began quilting during a 2014 residency in Accra, Ghana, inspired by the closeness he felt to his family heritage.[60]

Kincaid also credits his mother with encouraging his creativity from a young age and informing an evolution in his adult practice.

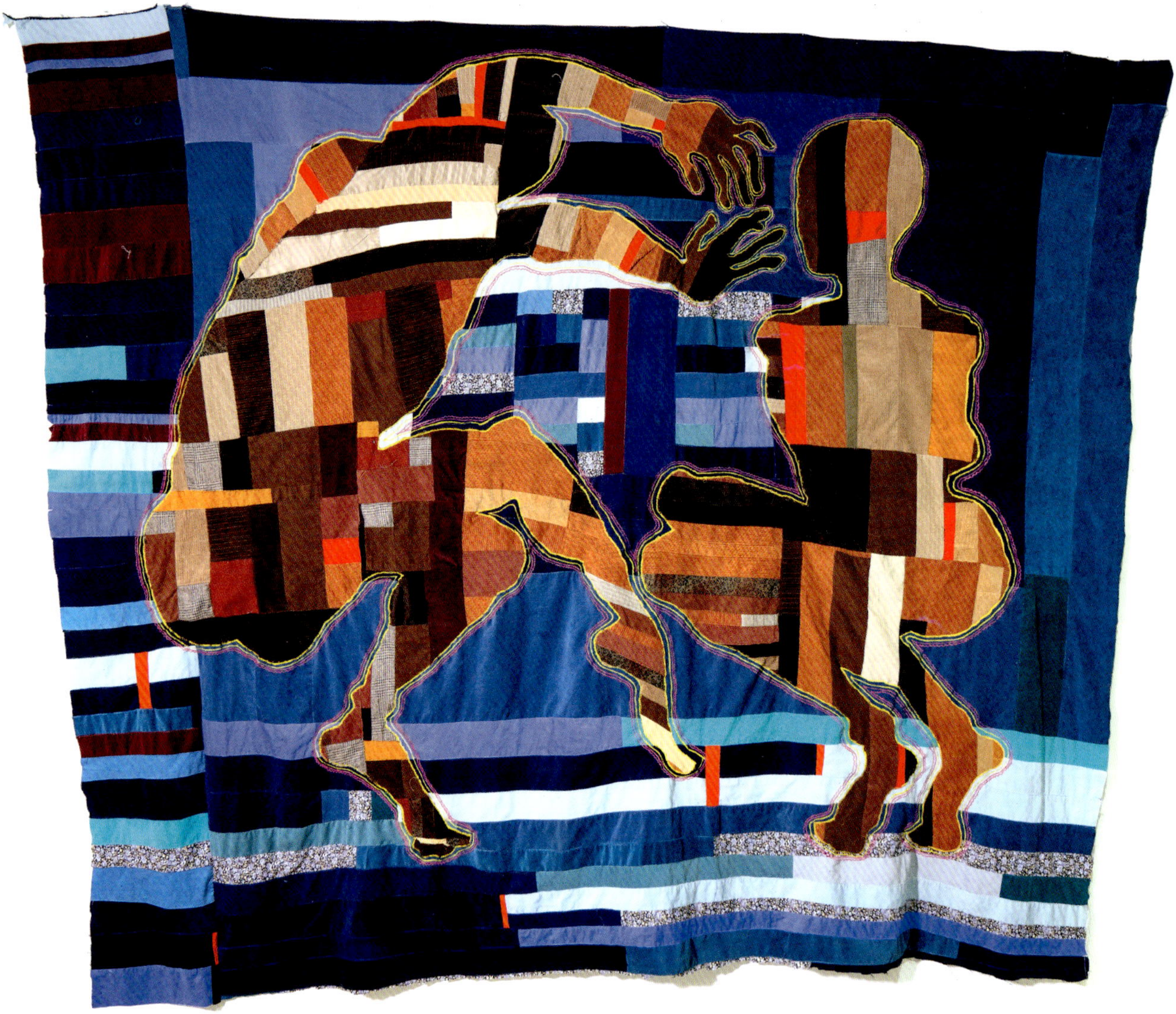

My Momma's Prayers Work, Basil Kincaid, 2019-20

"Most of the time I haven't taken [her ideas for my art] but this time she asked why I wasn't integrating drawing and collage into my quilting, and I could see it in my mind," he recalls. "It just made sense. So I decided to test it out and see where the experiment leads."[61] What emerged was the inclusion of figures that combined his more traditional quilts with expansive forms and playful compositions. He created *My Momma's Prayers Work* in honor of his mother, citing her love, prayers, and other practices as actions that have "cloaked" him throughout his life. He also continues to heed the messages and encouragement from his grandmother and mother by pushing the boundaries of quilting, and he acknowledges the artistry of his foremothers, who were often unrecognized as artists. He sees himself as ushering their legacy forward, saying, "I am carrying on the tradition to keep it alive and to honor those women who didn't get the recognition they deserved for their amazing works of art."[62]

ALIYAH BONNETTE

Aliyah Bonnette approaches quilting with tenderness, connecting to her maternal lineage as she gives voice to the Black female experience. Her entry into quiltmaking was less a deliberate choice than a moment of ancestral calling. While studying African American history she began reflecting on material culture as a vessel for storytelling and survival. When she shared her interest in quilting with her grandfather, he reminded her that her late grandmother, Sarah, had once been an avid quilter who was taught by her own mother.[63] This revelation sparked her to return to her roots, and Bonnette and her mother traveled to Georgia. There they recovered barrels of Sarah's unfinished quilts, neatly folded and waiting. When discussing her homecoming, Bonnette says, "I was stunned. It was a sign that my grandmothers were alive within me, guiding me all along."[64]

Rather than seeking out formal instruction, Bonnette taught herself improvisational quilting. Her grandmother's fabrics became her actual and metaphorical foundation. She began a visual conversation with her grandmother, blending her background in figurative painting with her newfound outlet. Referring to her ancestral guides as her "kindred," she invokes them through a shared practice. Quiltmaking allows her to

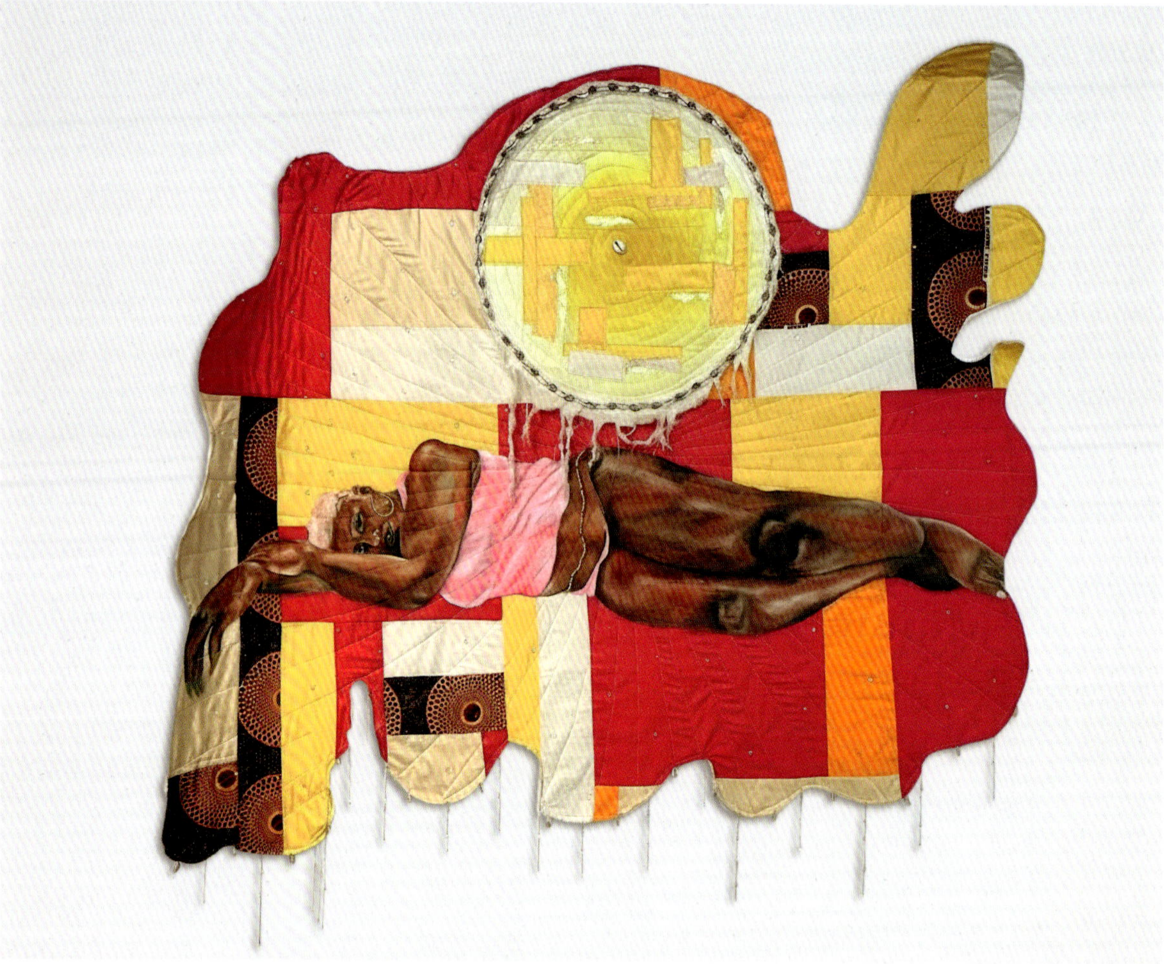

She Realized You Weren't the Sun, Aliyah Bonnette, 2023

create a through line across time between herself and the women whose lives shaped hers.[65]

Bonnette's use of inherited fabric, intuitive approach to composition, and spiritual alignment with her foremothers all point to quilting as a method of remembering. Through this vessel, she centers the interiority of Black women and encourages them to take up space. Figures appear in silhouette, resting or stretching. These portrayals resist spectacle, offering instead a vision of Black femininity that is self-defined. The women are meant not to be consumed but to be witnessed and revered.

Personal and Political

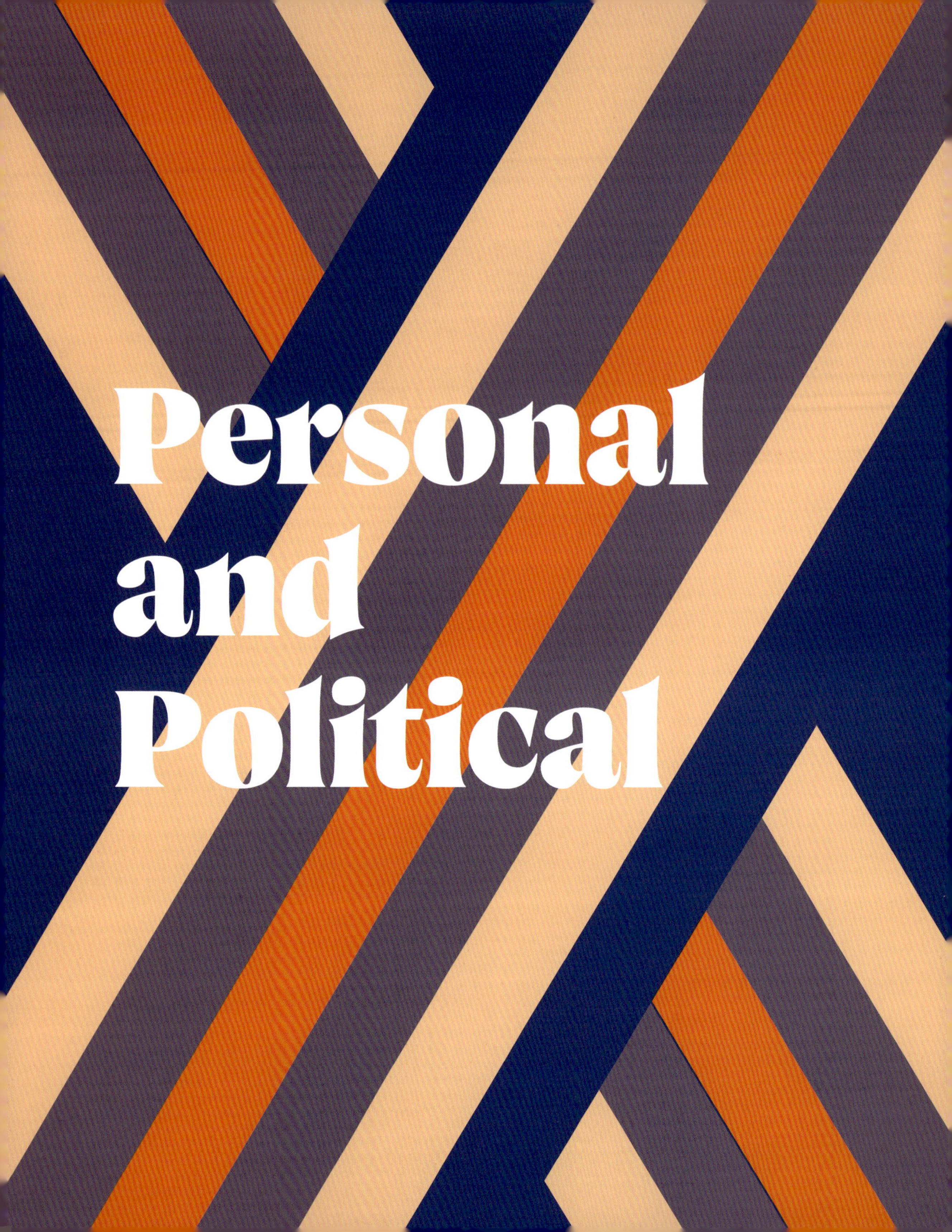

Quilts have historically been used as a form of protest and resistance against racial and cultural injustice. They have been used as tools for campaigning, to reflect women's feelings about social issues, and to build awareness of sociopolitical causes.[66] Abolitionists during the Civil War era used quilts and needlework to rally resources for the antislavery movement. During the civil rights movements, groups like the Freedom Quilting Bee raised funds and support for freedom riders. Contemporary quilters have leveraged quilts for mutual aid, to support community causes, and as backdrops to protests.

The year 2020 unearthed a rawness of emotion that needed a home that could hold both ancestral history and present urgency. In the wake of COVID-19 and racial uprisings across the nation, Black quilters once again turned to cloth and thread as vessels for truth telling. Black makers chronicled their feelings about state violence, memorialized those lost, and reasserted Black power. Quilts became banners to reflect mourning and a defiant love of the creators' communities. The pandemic intensified calls for justice while also isolating communities. Yet quilting circles—virtual and otherwise—offered continuity, care, and space to grieve and mobilize. In choosing to create during crisis, Black quilters

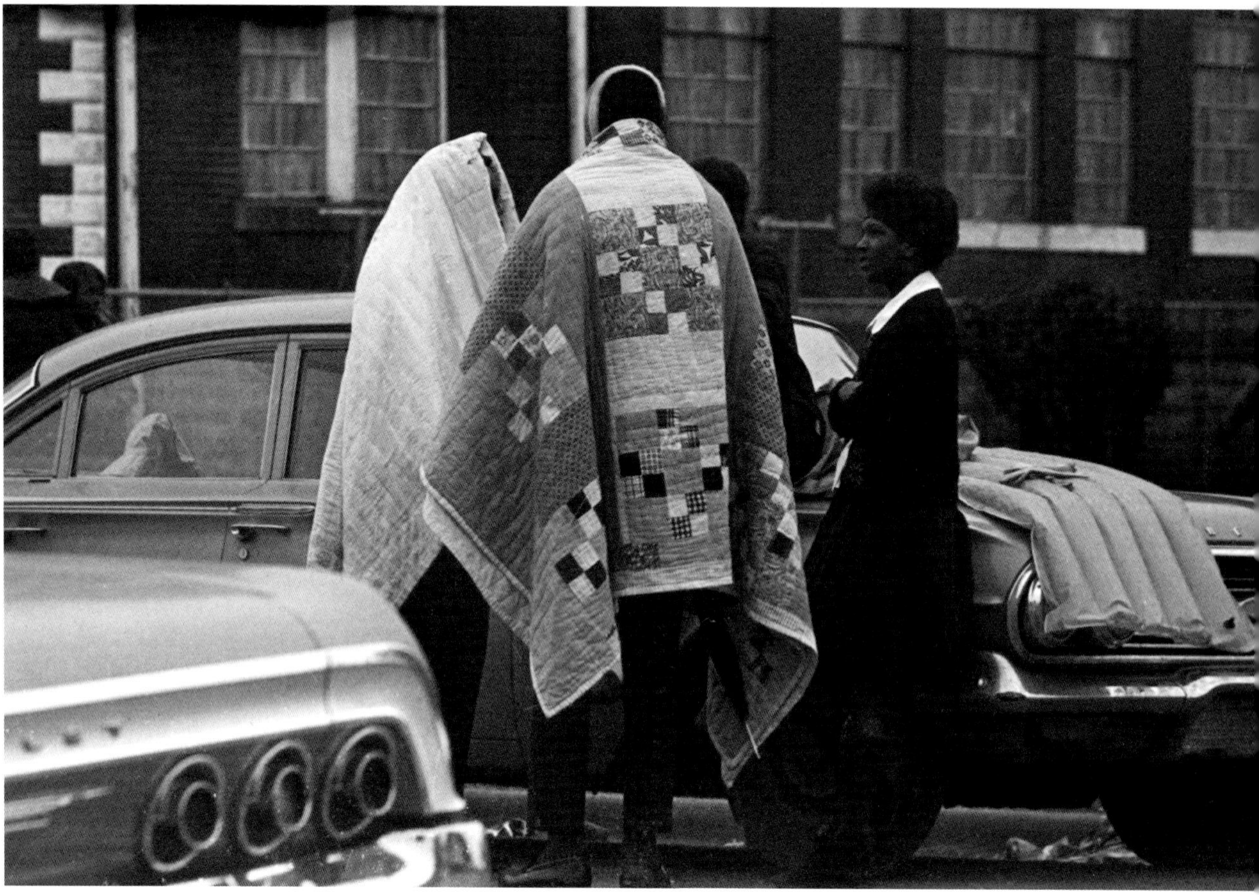

Civil Rights Demonstrators Wrapped in Quilts Outside of Brown Chapel AME Church in Selma, Alabama, during the "Berlin Wall" Demonstrations, Haywood Paravicini, 1965

carry forward the work of their foremothers, finding ways to extend hope, comfort, and support in the most unimaginable circumstances.

Projects like *Racism: In the Face of Hate We Resist*, a traveling exhibition organized by the Women of Color Quilters Network and the Textile Center of Minnesota, offered a platform for quilters to engage in unfettered dissent. The quilts confronted white supremacy with sharp visual narratives that included portraits of victims such as George Floyd, Breonna Taylor, and Elijah McClain. For many Black quilters, the choice to engage with these themes through traditional and improvisational techniques is also a rebuttal to widely recognized aesthetic norms (for example, the use of traditional shapes, clearly defined layers, and apolitical themes) imposed by mainstream art and quilt spaces. Such works affirm that beauty and protest are not mutually exclusive and can, in fact, make for a more compelling narrative when combined.

For Black quilters, choosing to create outside of social expectations has always been inherently political. Choosing to be unapologetic about one's self-expression while existing in a world that expects assimilation has been essential for generations of artists. This form of creative resistance has been deepened through quilts that portray political messages, criticize unjust systems, generate empowering images, celebrate the beauty of Black life, and demand it be valued accordingly. The following quilts offer a glimpse at how quilters are using their talents to communicate their beliefs and values in visually compelling ways.

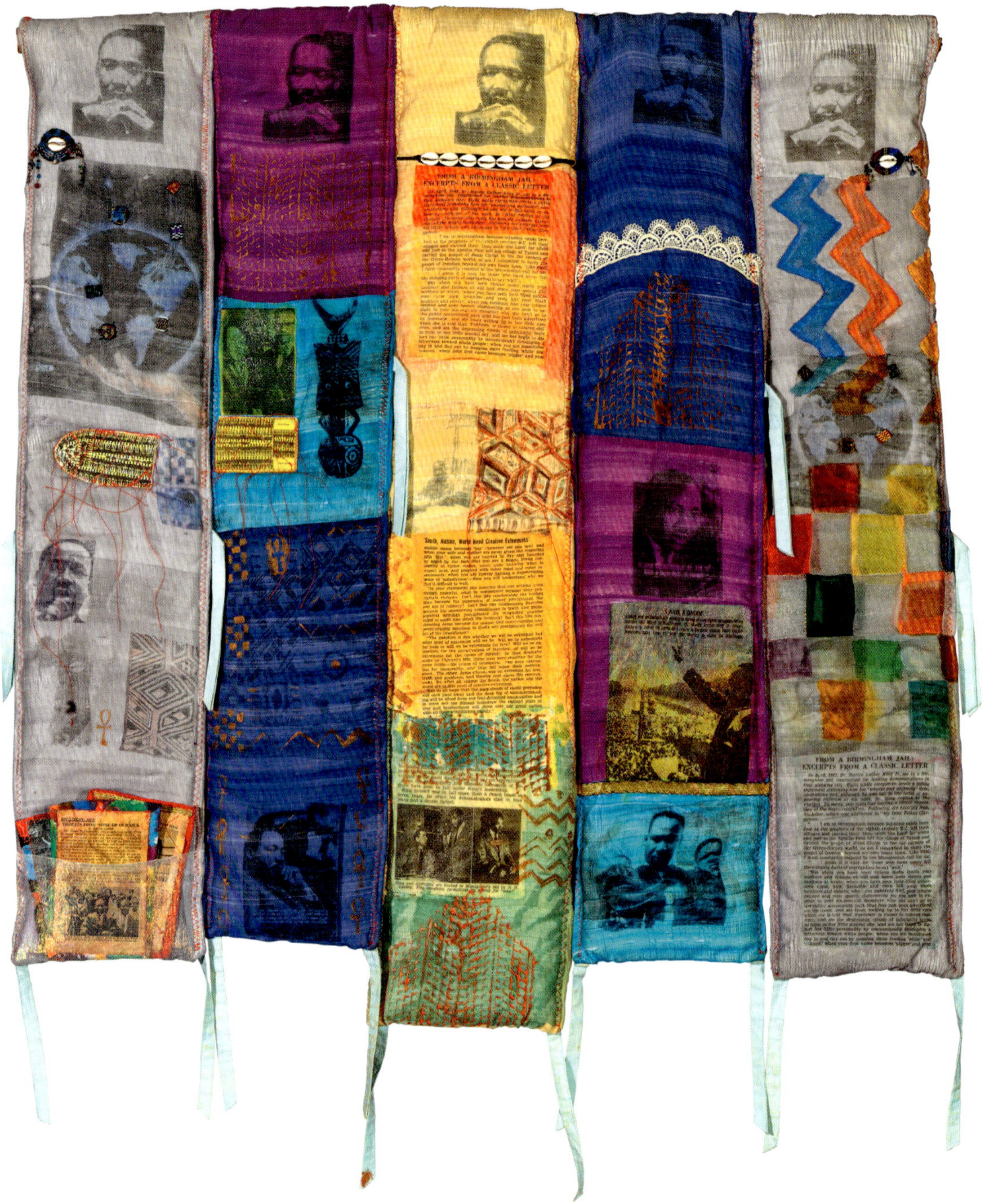

From a Birmingham Jail: MLK,
L'Merchie Frazier, 1996

L'MERCHIE FRAZIER

L'Merchie Frazier's *From a Birmingham Jail: MLK* (1996) bridges her work as a visual activist and public historian by honoring the efforts of Dr. Martin Luther King Jr. According to Frazier, "The quilt deifies the life and work of Dr. Martin Luther King. In his response to the clergy embodied in a letter he wrote in 1957, while jailed for his stance on Civil Rights in Birmingham, Alabama, Dr. King extolled the need for more of what his accusers, the clergy, termed 'Creative Extremists.'"[67] Embedded in the quilt are images and excerpts of speeches and events from King's life. Frazier chose to emulate an African strip quilt, invoking that pattern's original purpose of calling for the "protection of the community via the presence of the ancestors."[68] Throughout the quilt are references to Central and West African iconography, such as masks, cowrie shells, and ankh symbols, to reinforce themes of protection and ancestral connection. In the bottom left corner a pocket houses three freestanding panels that feature scanned images of pages from an issue of *Jet* magazine that memorialized King's life. The panels chronicle King winning the Nobel Peace Prize as well as his assassination, and they invite viewers to interact with the quilt and add their own stories, continuing the dialogue that the quilt began. Through this piece Frazier not only honors King's legacy but also asks viewers to engage with the ongoing struggle for racial equality and social justice and further her artistic call to action—"I Remember, Reclaim, Restore, Reimagine."

JESSIE BELL WILLIAMS TELFAIR

Jessie Telfair's *Freedom Quilt* speaks to the tension within the civil rights movement. Telfair, who resided in Parrot, Georgia, during the height of the movement, was inspired by the work of the Student Nonviolent Coordinating Committee (SNCC), which played a significant role in facilitating voter registration efforts across the South, including in southwest Georgia. Telfair decided to register to vote as part of the wave of Black citizens taking social action, but when her employer found out, she was fired from her job as a cafeteria worker at an elementary school. As the pain from that experience persisted, she was encouraged to put her feelings into a quilt. With the colors of the American flag, Telfair used a simple one-word declaration to state her belief in her personal liberation and desire for freedom for all.[69]

Freedom Quilt, Jessie Telfair, 1975

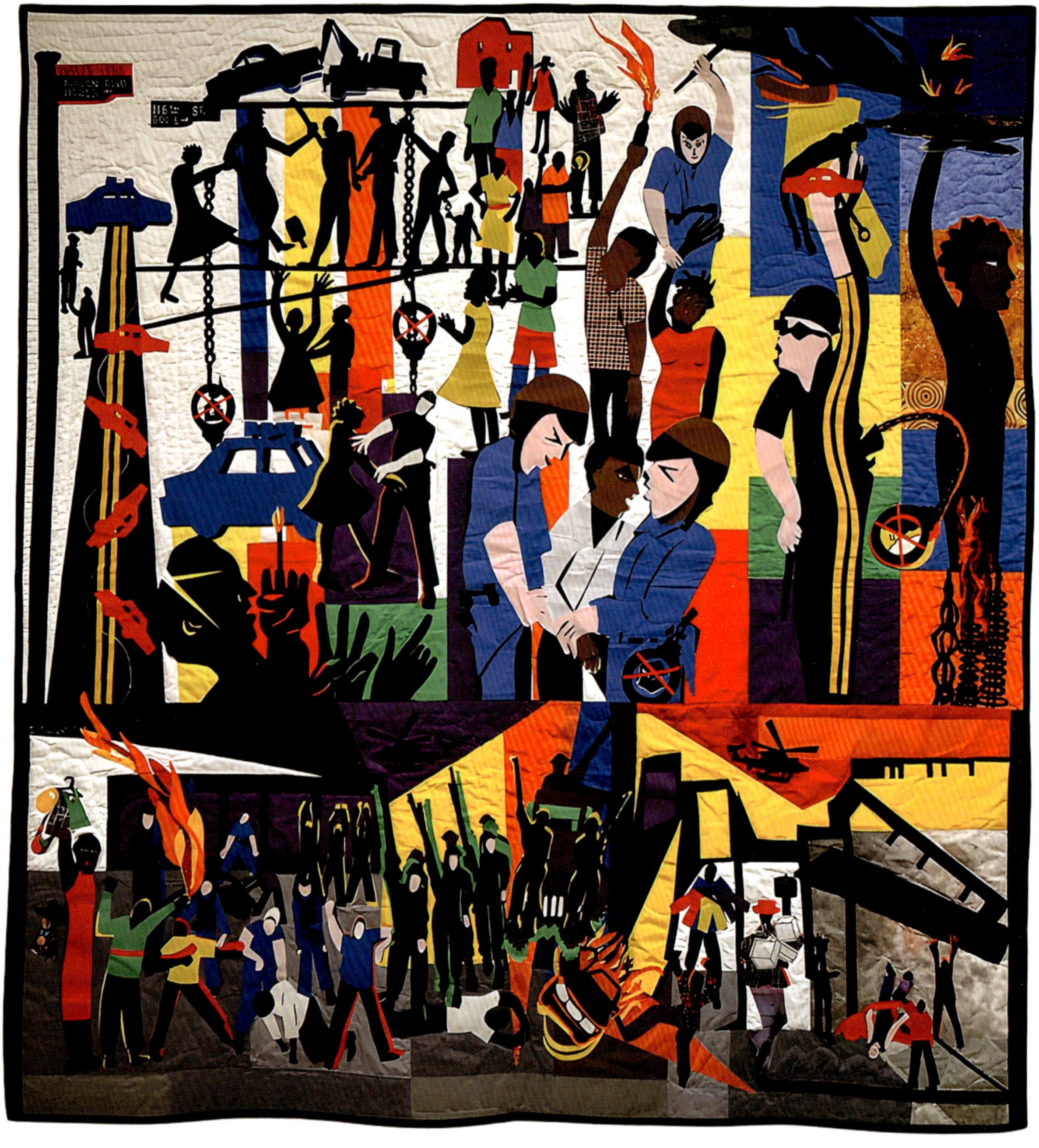

Watts Riot, Viola Burley Leak, 2021

VIOLA BURLEY LEAK

Other Black quilters have used their medium to capture historic protests and raise awareness about current activism. *Watts Riot* by Viola Burley Leak portrays riots that occurred in 1965 and the challenges that preceded them. From August 11 to August 17, 1965, the predominantly Black neighborhood of Watts in Los Angeles, California, was the location of the largest rebellion of the civil rights era. The unrest began after a routine traffic stop of a Black motorist, Marquette Frye, who was arrested by Lee Minikus, a white member of the California Highway Patrol, under suspicion of driving under the influence. Onlookers gathered at Frye's arrest, and tensions boiled over due to long-standing racial injustices, including ongoing police brutality, economic disparity, and inadequate living conditions.[70]

Over the next six days, widespread rioting, looting, and clashes with law enforcement ensued. Approximately thirty-four people were killed, over one thousand injured, and more than four thousand arrested. The National Guard was deployed to restore order, and property damage exceeded $40 million. The riots underscored deep racial tensions in Los Angeles and the broader United States. In response, the McCone Commission was established to investigate the causes of the riots, ultimately attributing the violence to systemic racial discrimination and economic inequality. However, there remained a lack of substantial reform, and the Watts riots foreshadowed future urban uprisings in American cities.[71]

Leak captures the essence of the nearly weeklong riots in five parts, starting with the intersection where the arrest took place. Throughout the connecting panels, she captures the spirit of the rioters' chant, "Burn, baby! Burn!" by featuring silhouettes and profiles of protesters carrying torches and igniting fires throughout the neighborhood as they clashed with police and military forces.

SHARON RAY

Sharon Ray uses *Hamtramck, My Home* to illustrate a story of protest and displacement in her hometown of Hamtramck, Michigan. The 1968 case of *Sarah Sims Garrett et al. v. City of Hamtramck* is one of the most significant milestones in civil rights litigation in the United States. The city of Hamtramck, outside of Detroit, saw an influx of immigrants from Eastern Europe in the early 1900s due to an increase in blue-collar jobs. Hamtramck grew into a largely Polish community, and Black residents were caught in the crossfire of housing discrimination in Detroit and plans for urban development in Hamtramck in the 1950s and '60s. The city's development initiatives focused on areas they felt were "blighted," disproportionately targeting neighborhoods primarily inhabited by African American families. They demolished many homes, displacing a significant portion of Hamtramck's Black population—a pattern that was also rippling throughout the United States in other Black enclaves.[72]

In 1968, Sarah Sims Garrett led a group of fellow residents in filing a class action lawsuit against the city of Hamtramck that would later become one of the longest-running civil rights housing cases. They argued that the city's residential projects were intentionally designed to remove Black citizens, violating their constitutional rights under the Fifth and Fourteenth Amendments along with other statutes.[73] In 1971, US district judge Damon Keith ruled that the city of Hamtramck was guilty of racial discrimination, violating the plaintiffs' rights to equal protection under the law. A decade later the city agreed to a settlement that mandated the construction of two hundred units for the displaced families. Financial constraints and administrative challenges prolonged fulfillment of the settlement, and the final units weren't completed until 2024.

Ray's imagery in *Hamtramck, My Home* simultaneously captures Garrett's bravery and vulnerability. She is shown embroiled in a struggle outside of her Hamtramck home after wrongful eviction, pushing against a bulldozer that is headed to dismantle the house, which has had its contents tossed onto the street. Garrett, her home, and the bulldozer are appliquéd onto a black-and-white map of the city.[74] The quilt is a harsh reminder that for Black people, definitions of home can be complicated. Community is ultimately found in people rather than physical structures.

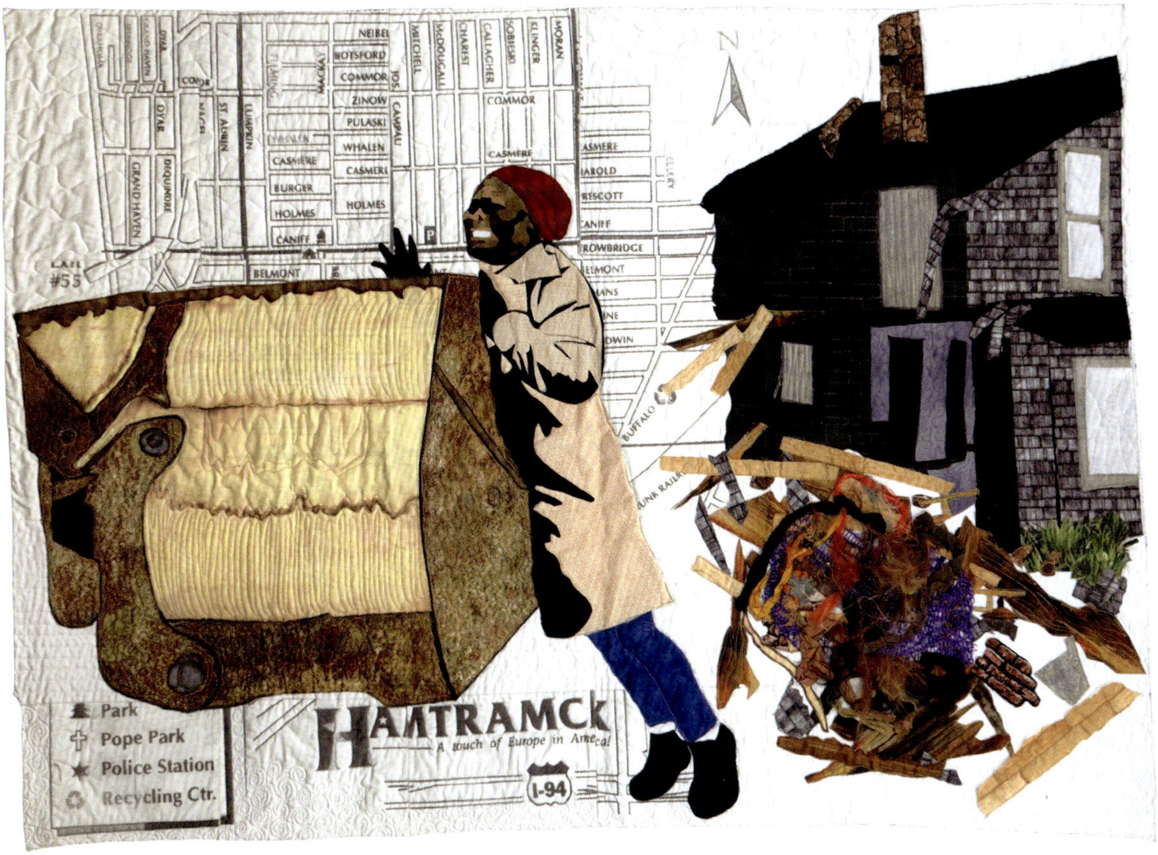

Hamtramck, My Home, Sharon Ray, 2021

BETTY LEACRAFT

The reckonings of 2020 gave way to a collective cry for justice, particularly within Black communities. The murder of George Floyd shook the nation, with his final words, "I can't breathe," igniting a flame in many. Needless to say, Black citizens' distrust in police and the justice system deepened as a result of the unwarranted violence that tragically took Floyd's life. While some took to the streets in protest, many quilters also took to their machines.

Betty Leacraft created *Nation Time 2020: Power and Protection from Racial Terrorism* in response to the ongoing crisis of racial violence in the United States, particularly highlighting the resurgence of lynching and state-sanctioned brutality following the murder of George Floyd. Leacraft intentionally avoided explicit depictions of violence, such as lynched bodies, focusing instead on culturally encoded symbols, colors, and other items to shape her commentary on injustice and the collective memory of trauma. Through *Nation Time* Leacraft also sought to bring awareness to the Emmett Till Antilynching Act, which was finally passed in 2022 after nearly two hundred failed attempts. Prior to passage of the bill, lynching was not formally classified as a hate crime in the United States, but now it is considered a criminal act that is punishable by up to thirty years in prison.[75]

The quilt's color scheme prominently features red, black, and green arranged vertically, representing the Pan-African flag. These colors represent unity and solidarity among people of African descent, particularly in North America. Red signifies the blood shed in the struggle for liberation, black represents the people, and green embodies the richness of the African continent.[76] Central to the composition are the motifs of eyes and fingers, serving as metaphors for past and present victims of lynching. These elements symbolize the act of witnessing and pointing out perpetrators, enablers, and those who remain silent in the face of racial terrorism. The inclusion of these body parts underscores the collective gaze and an accusatory stance toward systemic injustice.

Leacraft also incorporated protective symbols, drawing inspiration from her personal collection of amulets and talismans. The quilt features a stylized hand of Fatimah (also known as a hamsa) and a Black Power fist. Within these symbols are two Ghanaian adinkra motifs. The open hand displays the Eban symbol, which represents a fence that encloses a home, signifying protection and safety from external harm. The raised fist contains the Eban symbol as well, interpreted here as links in a chain, symbolizing unity and collective strength in the pursuit of communal well-being. The quilt's surface is further textured with irregularly stitched "trauma lines" within the red and green quadrants, symbolizing the deep-seated wounds inflicted by racial violence. Additionally, blood-splattered letters emphasize the brutal reality of these atrocities and the urgency for societal acknowledgment and action.[77] Leacraft not only addresses the ongoing legacy of lynching in the United States but also issues a call to action, urging viewers to confront the persistent realities of racial injustice and to participate in the collective movement toward systemic change.

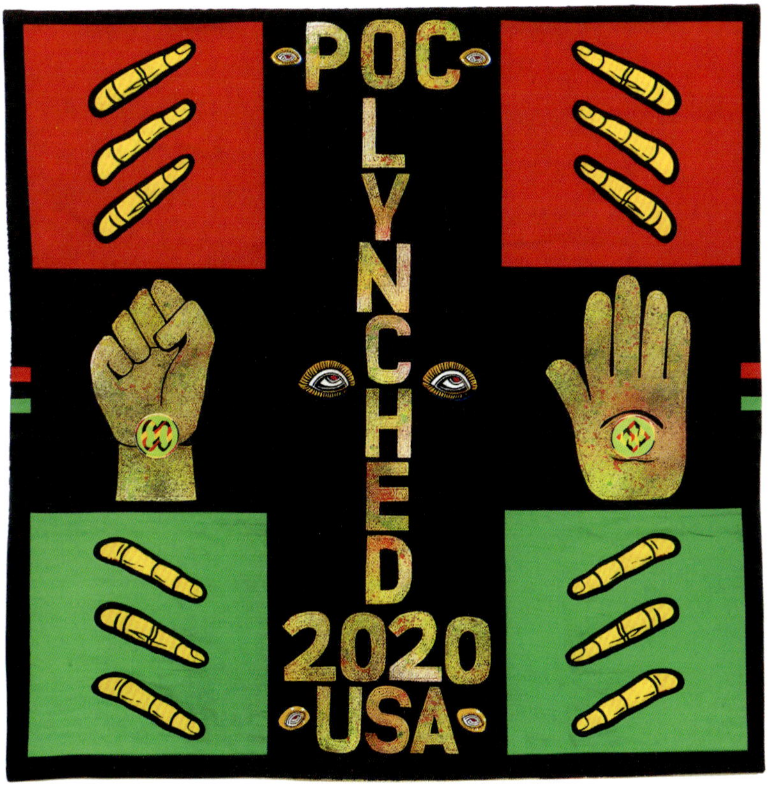

Nation Time 2020: Power and Protection from Racial Terrorism, Betty Leacraft, 2020

CHAWNE KIMBER

Through the pointed use of text, quilter Chawne Kimber makes bold statements that don't leave much room for misinterpretation. Not one to shy away from social critique, she subverts conventional expectations of what quilts should say—or rather, what they are allowed to say. She has often been met with resistance and attempts at censorship, but she hasn't been deterred from using spite as a tool to "entice people to think about an issue a little differently."[78] Using her training as a mathematician, she created a "needlework handwriting" that disrupts how the average person might perceive quilts.[79] And she goes further by using commanding language and often incorporating profanity, protest slogans, and African American vernacular.

In Kimber's hands, quilting pivots from the genteel to the bold and arresting. She often references her family—descendants of enslaved people who labored in cotton fields and quilted for necessity and expression—embedding her work with a layered understanding of how labor, history, and identity converge. Her works challenge national myths, expose racial violence, and count the toll of systemic oppression.

Kimber frames *Get Woke* as her take on a protest poster. She created it in 2017, on the day of Donald Trump's inauguration, to immortalize the resistance that was brewing throughout the nation at the time. She speaks to American nationalism by using red, white, and blue as the quilt's primary colors. "It flows from red to blue to show that there are people from both sides of the aisle who have concerns," she says, "who are resisting."[80] She also likens the red to blood and the blue to breath, imagery that could speak to police brutality and the fragility of Black life.

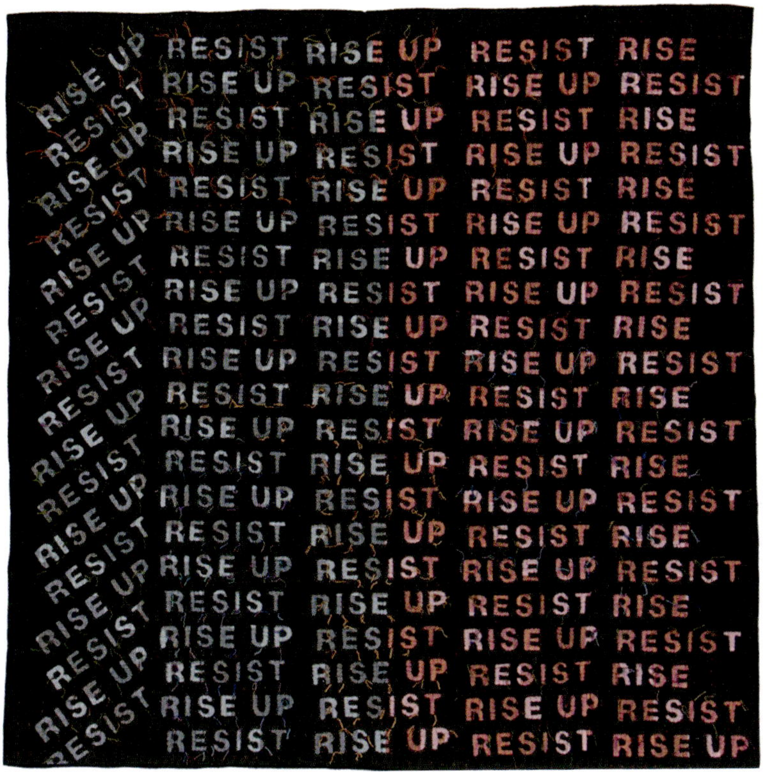

Get Woke, Chawne Kimber, 2017

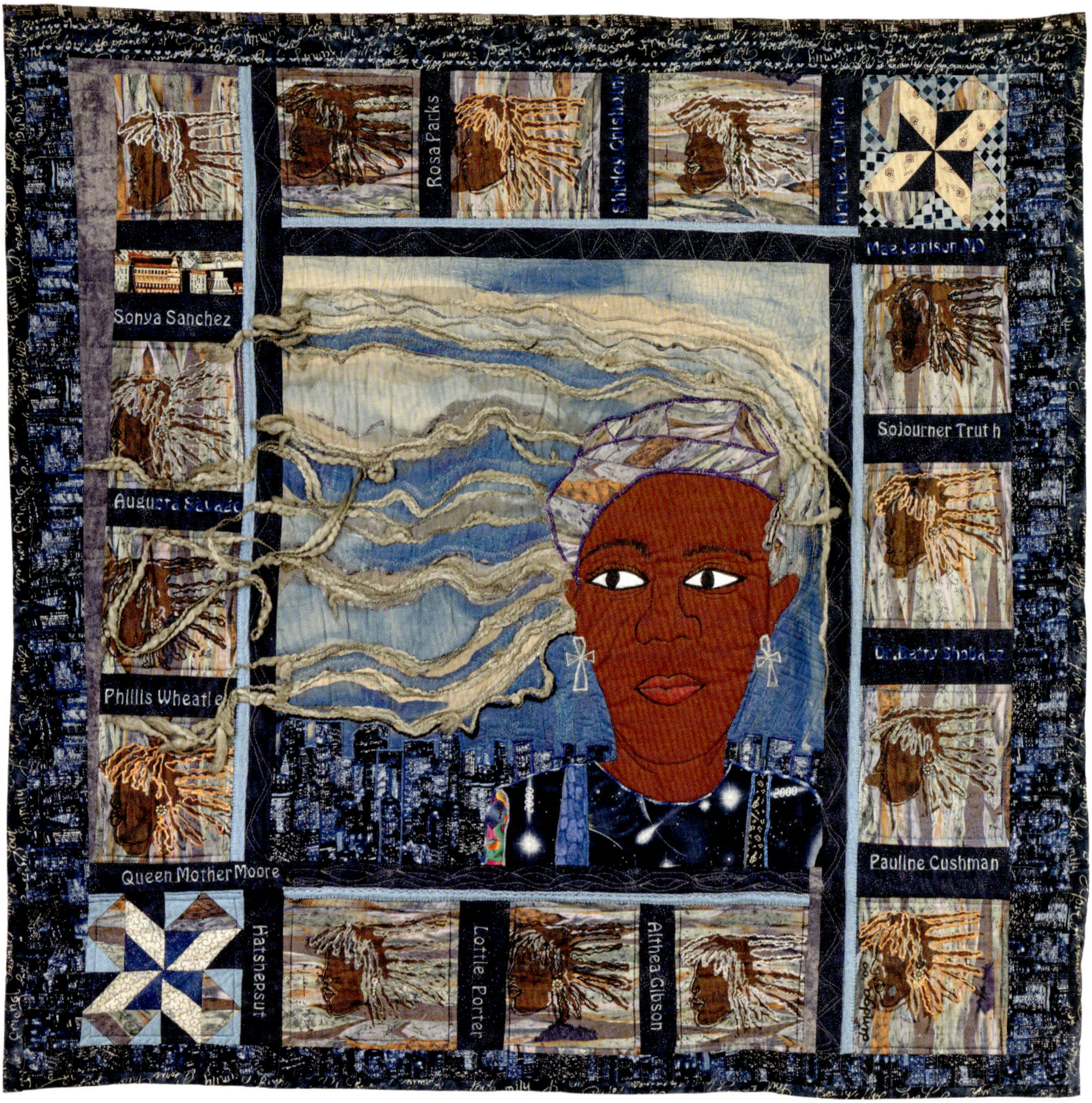

Threads of the Past, Inspiration for the Future, Dindga McCannon, 2000

DINDGA MCCANNON

For some, quilts align with deeply personal politics. In *Threads of the Past, Inspiration for the Future*, Dindga McCannon's self-portrait anchors the center of the quilt. Her image is surrounded by inspirational Black women whose lives are a beacon for McCannon, ranging from Hatshepsut to Sonia Sanchez. In a 2020 interview she shared the following context for the piece:

I created this piece because every once in a while, I get a little bit discouraged. When those moments occur, I think back to what other women have been able to accomplish under the worst circumstances possible. And when I think about that, it allows me to get out of the depression and move forward. The woman in the center is probably myself. At that time, I had a lot of hair. You know, I had locs, which was another issue.[81]

Alluding to the policing of Black women's bodies and other social scrutiny, McCannon uses *Threads of the Past* to remind herself to not lose sight of her personal power.

Throughout her career McCannon encountered her share of disappointments, and she had to navigate the racism and sexism of the 1960s and '70s as a Black woman artist and single mother. To do so, she drew on the power of the collective. She cofounded Where We At Black Women Artists with Faith Ringgold and Kay Brown in 1971 after having difficulty showing her work in white-run museums and galleries in New York. Her interest in the intersection of Black art and women's work led her to explore quilting, as well as other forms of mixed media. Through her practice McCannon has continued to critique the injustices experienced by Black women in America, often highlighting erased histories and the contributions of cultural figures and women in her personal life. After a nearly sixty-year career as an artist, McCannon finally received long overdue recognition with her first major exhibition in 2021. Titled *In Plain Sight*, the show presented a survey of her body of work spanning from 1980 to the present.

ERIN LEANN MITCHELL

Erin LeAnn Mitchell also invokes Black feminist legacies as a source of inspiration in her piece *Extreme Times Call for Extreme Heroines*. Mitchell initially drew inspiration from artist Betye Saar, who is best known for her assemblage art, which uses found objects, Black folk practices, and esoteric symbolism to explore themes of race, history, spirituality, and feminism. Saar's 2017 work of the same name—*Extreme Times Call for Extreme Heroines*—pays homage to the Black domestic workers who toiled tirelessly after the Civil War. Saar's work features a mammy figure in the center of a washboard, with a clock frozen in time to represent a lack of progress. The figure holds a rifle while donning an apron fashioned from an image of a slave ship, referencing both the atrocities of the slave trade and the resistance of abolitionists like Harriet Tubman.[82]

Mitchell's work also speaks to the relationship between time and social progress (or the lack thereof). She developed this quilt in 2023, as the war in Gaza worsened, as an act of solidarity. The figures are crying out for freedom for Black people and all oppressed people of the world and speaking out against the modern atrocities connected to centuries of colonialism. Images of Black feminist writers and activists like Audre Lorde, bell hooks, Angela Davis, Nikki Giovanni, and Fannie Lou Hamer are placed throughout the quilt as a reminder that although injustice persists, so does a school of women who continue to fight for change.

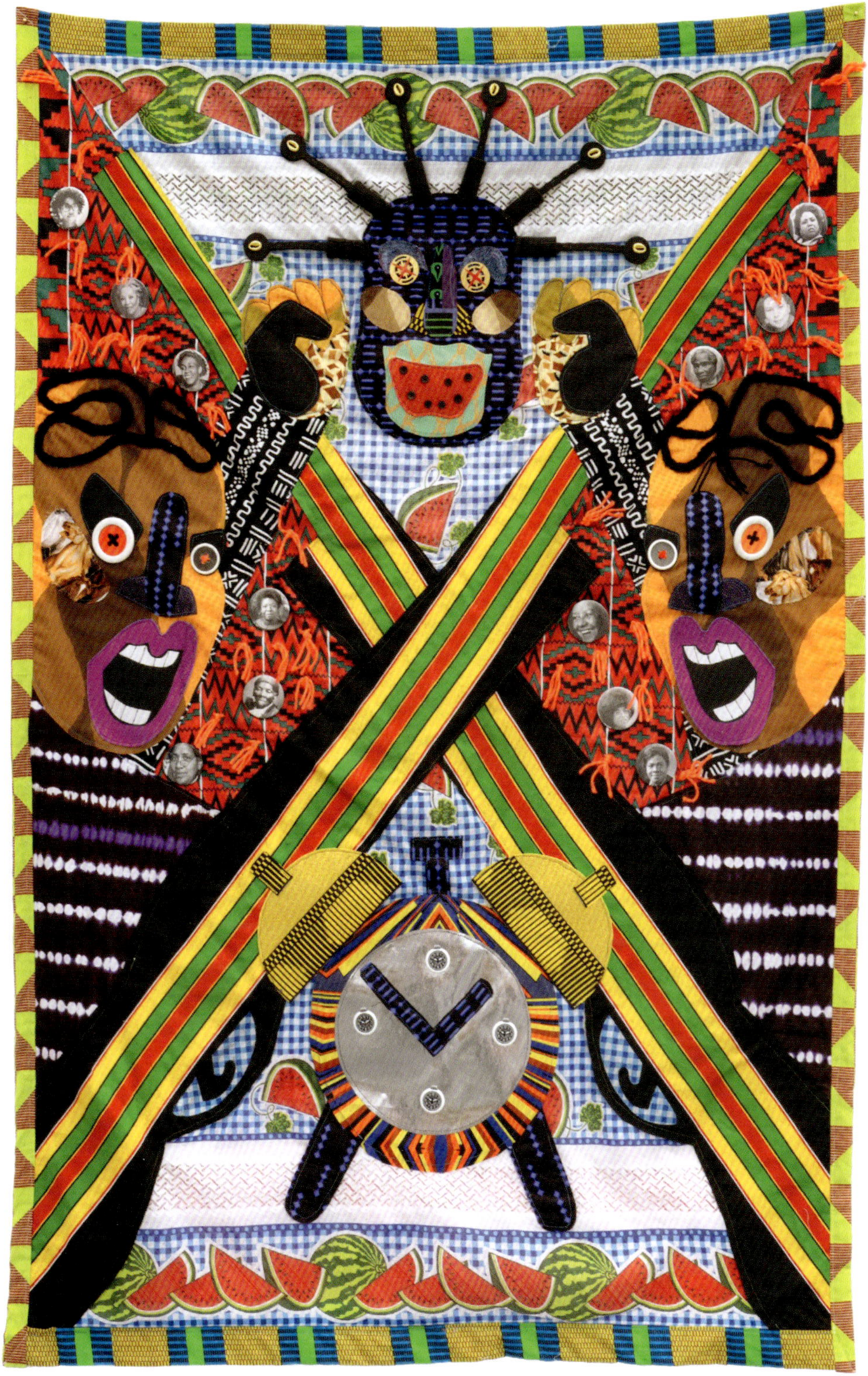

Extreme Times Call for Extreme Heroines,
Erin LeAnn Mitchell, 2023

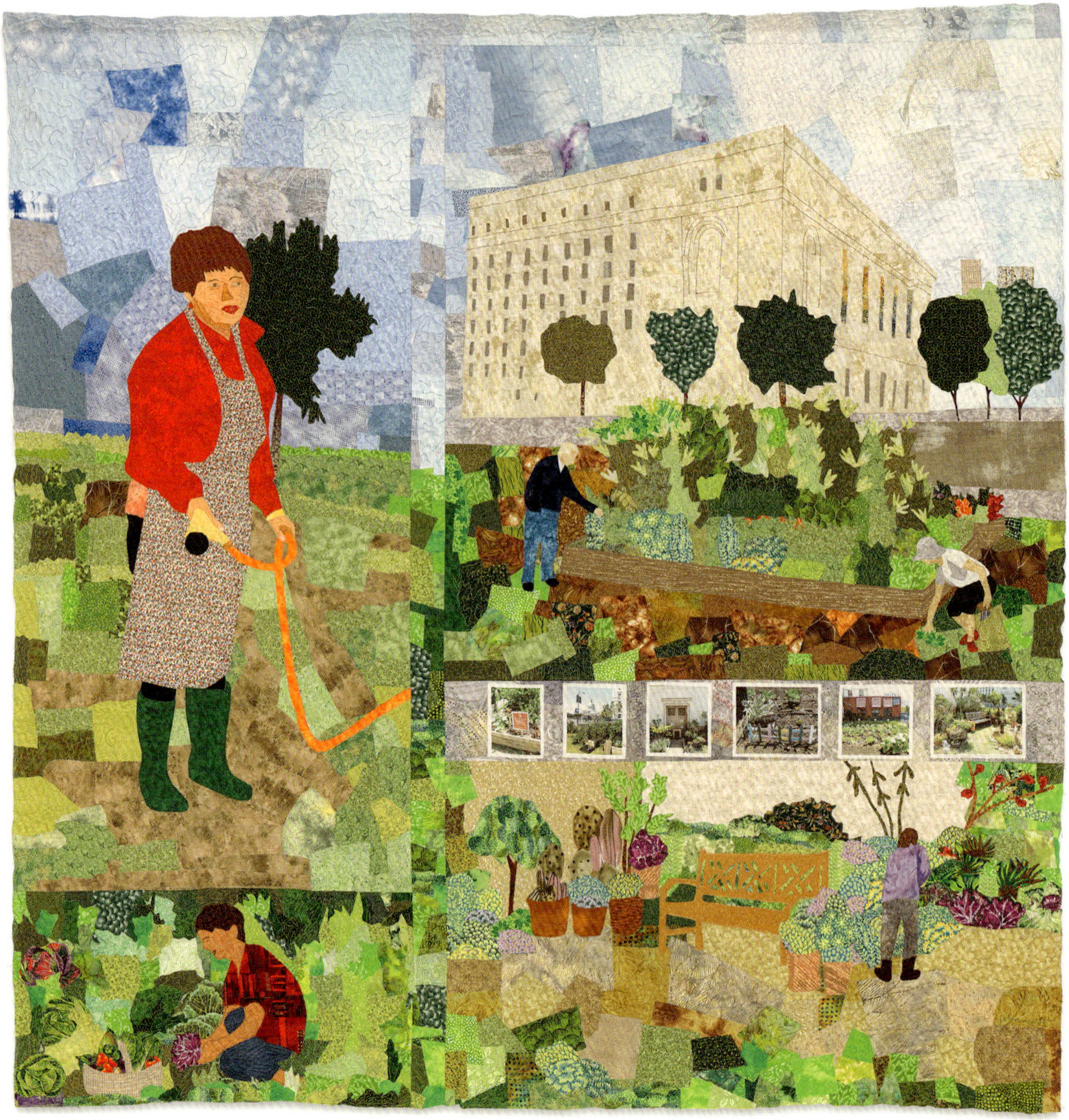

Tender Gardens, Marion Coleman, 2014

MARION COLEMAN

Marion Coleman's 2014 *Tender Gardens* stands as a testament to communal resilience and care as a political act. The piece portrays the evolution of a vacant lot in San Francisco's Tenderloin neighborhood into a thriving urban farm known as the Tenderloin People's Garden. Established in 2010 by local residents and the Tenderloin Neighborhood Development Corporation, this communal space addresses the scarcity of fresh produce in the neighborhood and serves as a hub for community engagement.[83]

The Tenderloin, home to approximately thirty thousand residents, has historically lacked a full-service grocery store, making access to fresh, affordable food a significant challenge. The garden directly addresses this issue by offering free produce weekly, contributing to local food security and fostering a sense of community ownership. Unlike community gardens that have individual plots and long waiting lists, this one embodies openness, welcoming all community members to participate in planting and harvesting every Saturday.[84]

Tender Gardens presents vignettes of individuals tending to the garden, interspersed with photo transfers depicting lush greenery and the backdrop of San Francisco's Civic Center. This juxtaposition highlights the contrast between the urban environment and the cultivated oasis within it, paying homage to the everyday people who maintain this resource for all to enjoy. While the systemic problems in the neighborhood may not be resolved, *Tender Gardens* reminds us that we have the power to create an oasis in the midst of imperfection.

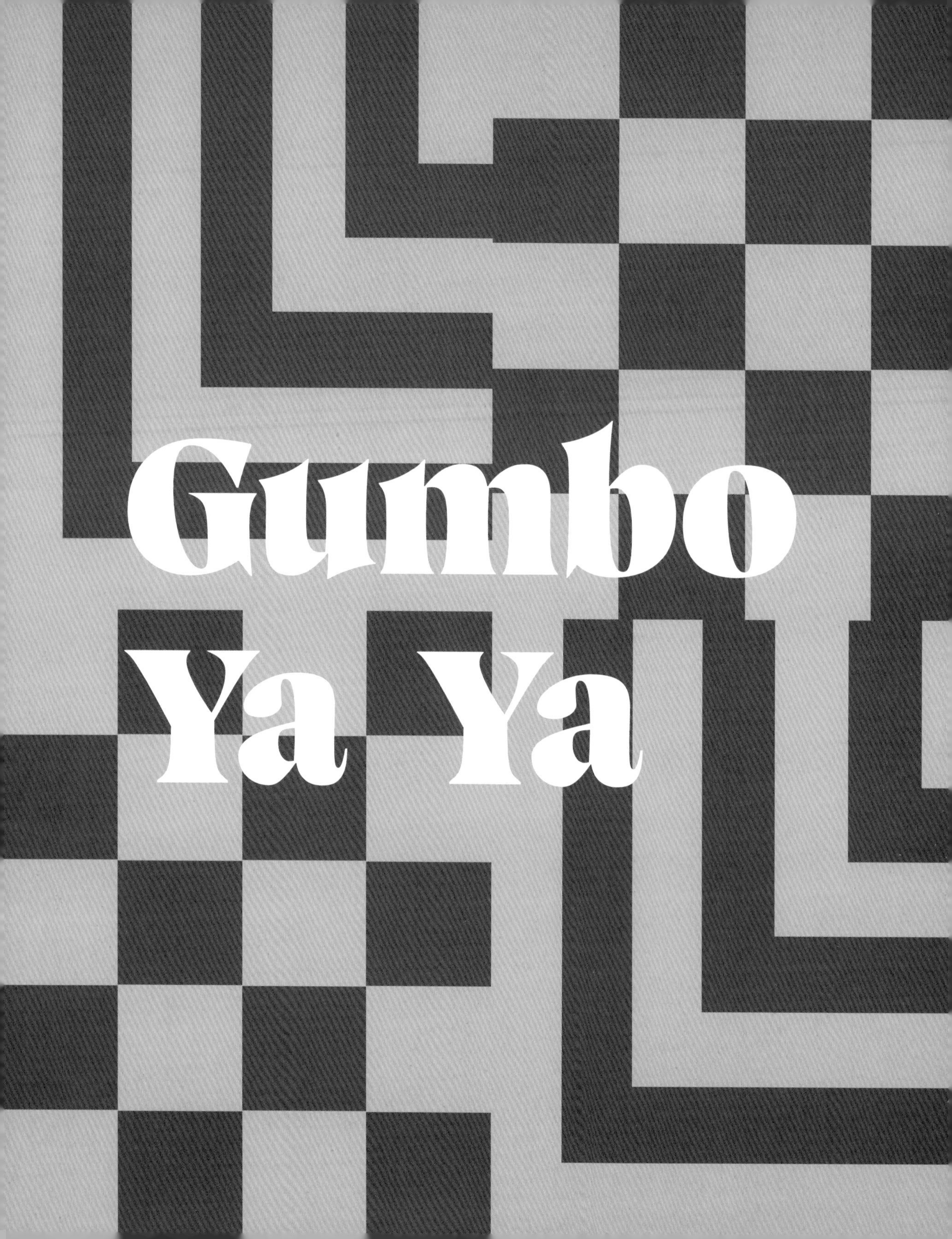

Gumbo Ya Ya

"Gumbo ya ya" is an expression from Louisiana meaning "everyone talks at once." In keeping with that energy, this chapter, inspired by the 1995 book *Gumbo Ya Ya: An Anthology of Contemporary African-American Women Artists*, offers an exciting look at the depth and breadth of patterns and techniques used by Black quilters. Highlighting 150 Black women artists working across a range of mediums and processes, the book was a response and antidote to the erasure endured by Black artists for centuries. In her introduction, art historian Leslie King-Hammond beautifully describes the tug-of-war experienced by Black women who feel compelled to create work about their lived experience in a world that has historically invalidated it. For them, the process of making in spite of erasure and oppression exists as a "continuum of battles against the hegemony of political, social and economic systems vehemently resistant to the inclusion of Black women as vital to the cultural and intellectual fabric of the world."[85]

This experience also extends to Black quilters. Commentary on American quilting has often prioritized Western aesthetics and sidelined the diversity of cultural and historical narratives embedded in Black quilts. These quilts are archives of centuries of life that have gone underrecognized in the dominant art historical canon. As King-Hammond writes, "Undaunted in the will and spirit to survive, these women began to transform traditional mediums to create new visual languages through the medium of fiber. This elevated the quilt to a new level of understanding, critical to the African American experience."[86] Just as Black people are not monolithic, neither are their quilts. Part of righting the representation of Black quilts means celebrating the innumerable ways that quilters of all backgrounds tell their stories, shape their own worldviews and the perspectives of others, and amplify their voices through their artistry.

AOLAR CARSON MOSELY

Aolar Carson Mosely (1912–99) was introduced to quilting by her mother, Elizabeth Pettway Carson, and the other women in her extended community in Gee's Bend, Alabama. Mosely differed from other local quilters in that she began at a machine rather than starting with hand piecing. She was knowledgeable about all steps of quilting, from fabricating a frame to assembly and stitching.

Mosely was also one of the founding members of the Freedom Quilting Bee, working with the group from 1966 until she withdrew in 1981, after which she continued to mentor and guide cooperative members through tasks like co-op management, quilt construction, and machine repair. She was the mother of seventeen children, one of whom was famed Gee's Bend quilter Mary Lee Bendolph.[87]

Her quilt *"Housetop"—"Half-Log Cabin" Variation* fuses the related styles of housetop and log cabin blocks to create a hybrid quilt. Housetop quilts use repeated squares to mimic an aerial view of a shingled rooftop. They are often assembled as a wholetop design, which typically features concentric squares growing larger until they occupy the entire width of the quilt. Log cabins, although similar, are typically a bit more uniform. They feature a square to anchor the center of the block, which is then wrapped with strips that alternate between light and dark colors in a spiral pattern. In Mosely's variation, she takes smaller blocks to create a more organic layout across a spectrum of colors.

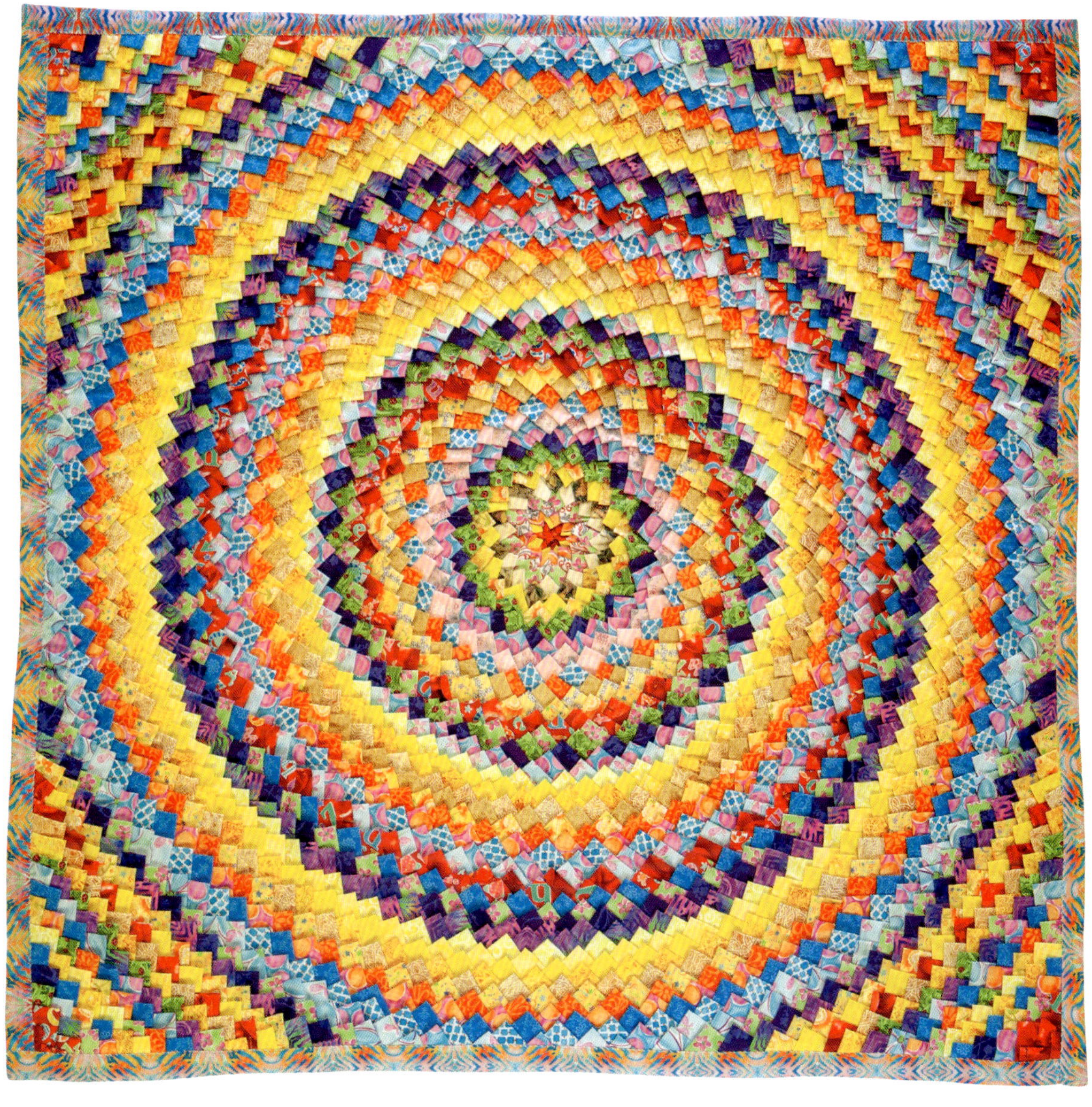

Pinecone Quilt, Betty Ford-Smith, date unknown

BETTY FORD-SMITH

Betty Ford-Smith's journey into pinecone quilting began under the mentorship of Miss Sue (Arlene Dennis) in Sebring, Florida, in 2004. Enamored by the beauty of the ninety-two-year-old's hand-sewn quilts, Ford-Smith began a six-year apprenticeship with Dennis to learn the elaborate process of constructing pinecone quilts.[88] Also known as pine burr quilts, these are distinguished by their conical shapes formed through concentric circles of folded triangles. This technique holds deep significance within the Black community and is often associated with the most technically skilled quilters. Pinecone quilts are revered for both their scale and the time it takes to complete just one full-size quilt, which might be composed of thousands of triangles. Ford-Smith emphasizes the importance of this tradition, saying that she continues to make these quilts to ensure the pattern doesn't disappear.[89] Her dedication extends beyond her personal creations; she also teaches and shares the art of pinecone quilting, hoping to inspire others to appreciate the persistence, time, and patience that go into these detailed works of art. Prior to quilting, Ford-Smith had a rich professional life, including roles as a fashion designer, dance teacher, and educator, teaching subjects from home economics to special education in New York, St. Thomas, South Carolina, and Florida.

NORA EZELL

As a young girl, Nora Ezell (1919–2007) would stand and fan her mother as she quilted, longing to make her own quilts. Although skilled in a variety of traditional techniques, she was best known for her narrative quilts that paid homage to Alabama and civil rights history. Some of her achievements included a solo show at Stillman College in 1986 and other exhibitions at the Birmingham Public Library and the Alabama Artists Gallery in Montgomery. She also became well known at multiple fairs, such as the Kentuck Festival of the Arts in Northport, Alabama. She spent over a decade as a master teacher in the state's Folk Arts Apprenticeship Program and was recognized by the National Endowment for the Arts as a National Heritage Fellow in 1992.[90]

She often wrote in a journal and kept records of her quiltmaking process, which allowed her to track her time spent making the quilts and to price them fairly. She was known to wake up in the middle of the night to work on a piece or jot down an idea, afraid that she wouldn't remember the designs if she waited. These reflections would later come together in a book titled *My Quilts and Me: The Diary of an American Quilter*, published in 1992. As a quilter, Ezell always strived to have a distinct visual language that left a lasting impression. In a 1990 interview with Alabama Folkways, she shared, "I like to put a little bit of me in my quilts. Because I think this is one thing that lives on after us. Maybe you will have forgotten my name but you'll remember that I always used certain colors that went together so well."[91]

Her *Everybody (Sampler) Quilt* is one of a handful created by Ezell showing the breadth of her abilities. She embedded her quilts with signature elements, like a donkey motif, along with more traditional blocks like stars, log cabins, and Dresden plates. When asked about what inspired her, Ezell simply replied, "I grab things off the top of my head and run with 'em. I can't tell you no more. I just do it."[92]

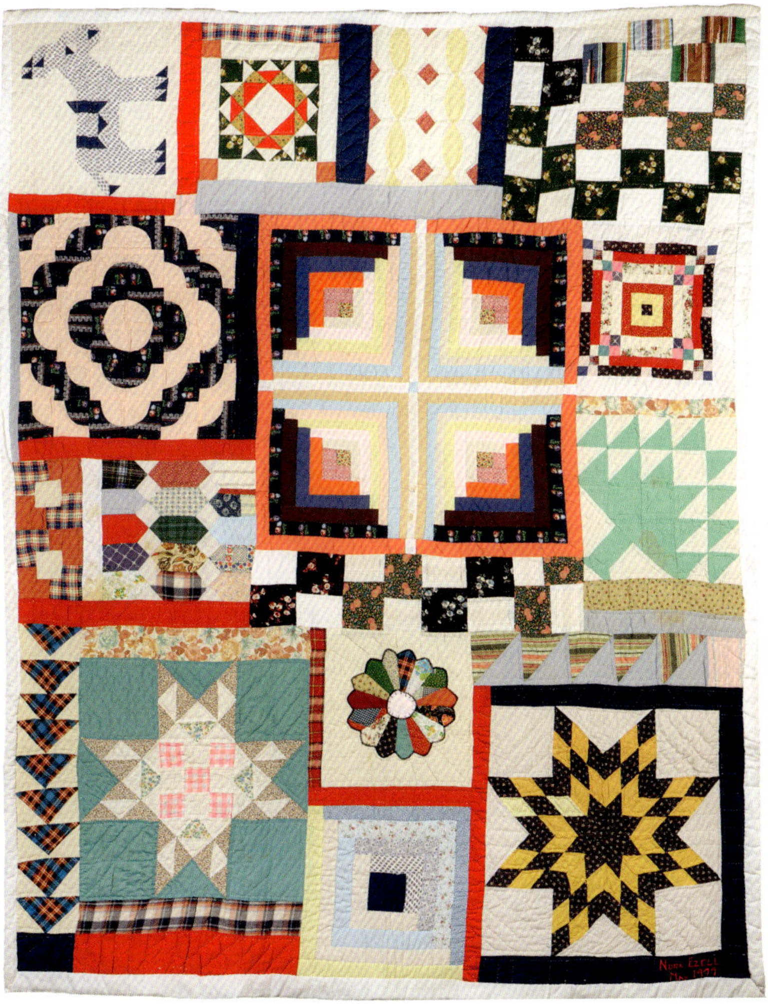

Everybody (Sampler) Quilt, Nora Ezell, 2007

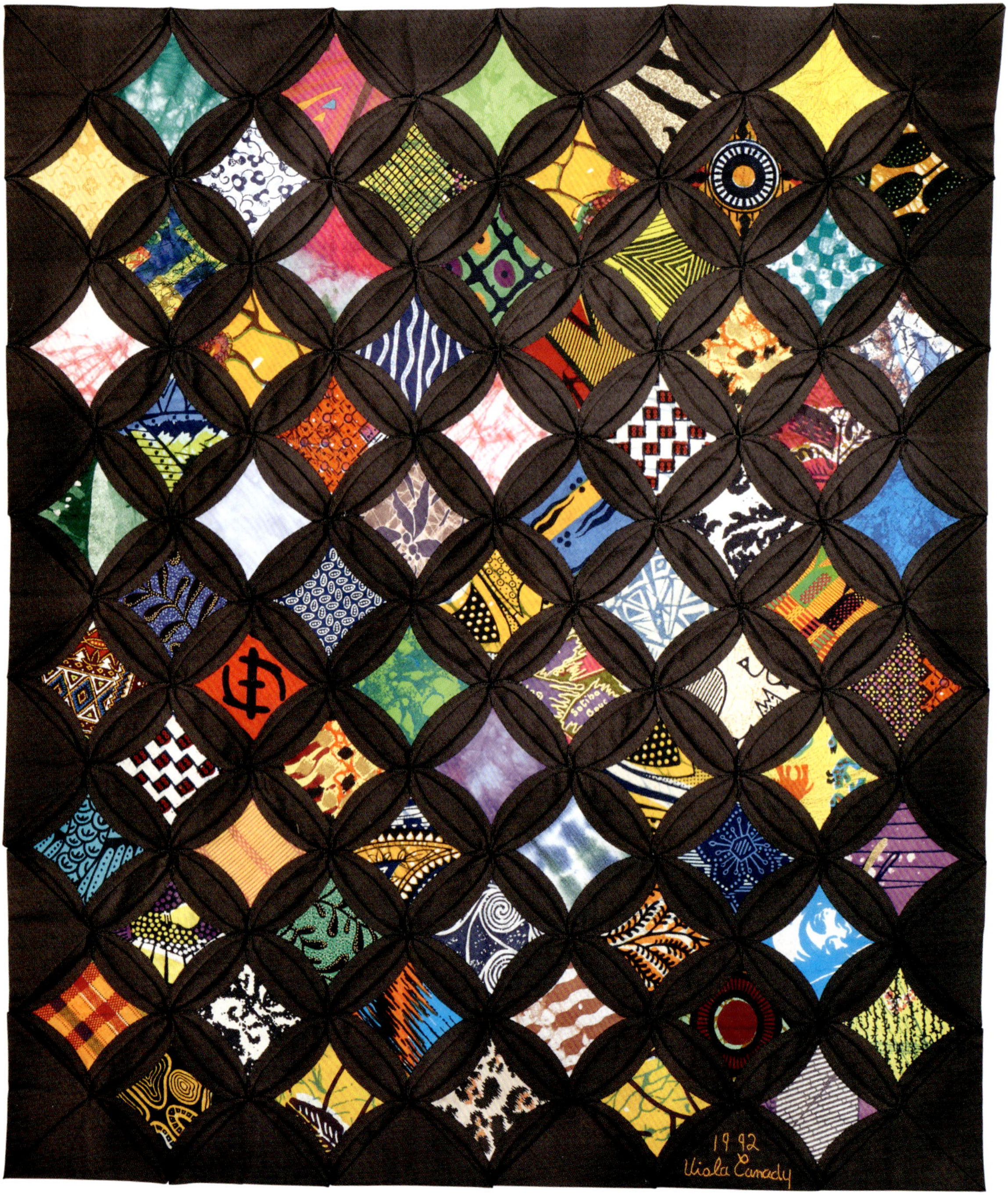

Cathedral Window, Viola Canady, date unknown

VIOLA CANADY

Viola Canady's (1922–2009) *Cathedral Window* is a beautiful take on one of the more intricate and ambitious traditional quilt patterns. Inspired by stained glass, cathedral window quilts require precision and an eye for detail in order to create a curved effect. Whereas many cathedral window quilts feature a light-colored base, Canady leaned into a bolder palette. Squares of African batiks and wax print fabrics are nested into each matrix, creating a stunning contrast while integrating elements of diasporic culture. She became known for her stained glass appliqué technique and her use of colorful fabric bordered with black cloth.[93]

A lifelong seamstress, Canady was often sought after to teach for organizations such as the National Quilters Association, which allowed her to connect with other Black quiltmakers. As a result of those connections, in 1980 she would cofound the Daughters of Dorcas and Sons Quilt Guild in 1980, one of the oldest African American quilt guilds. Named after the biblical character Dorcas, who served as a seamstress for the poor, the Washington, DC–based organization dedicates itself to teaching and sharing knowledge among Black quilters.[94]

WENDY KENDRICK

Wendy Kendrick has always felt a calling to be an artist. In the 1970s she attended Dartmouth College to pursue art. However, a traumatic experience with a studio professor was so discouraging that, after graduation, she vowed never to create art again. She returned to making at the encouragement of colleagues while working as a docent at the Columbus Museum of Art and taking classes at the neighboring Columbus College of Art and Design. Inspired by the work of Romare Bearden, she began making collage work that incorporated fabric. She later shifted to strip quilting, then more dimensional work like her African mask quilts. Kendrick saw her quilting work as a return to traditions instilled by her grandmother, who originally taught her how to sew.[95]

She describes her work as dealing "with the special bond that women enjoy with one another. The joy we share as mothers, daughters, sisters, grandmothers, nieces, neighbors and sister friends. It's

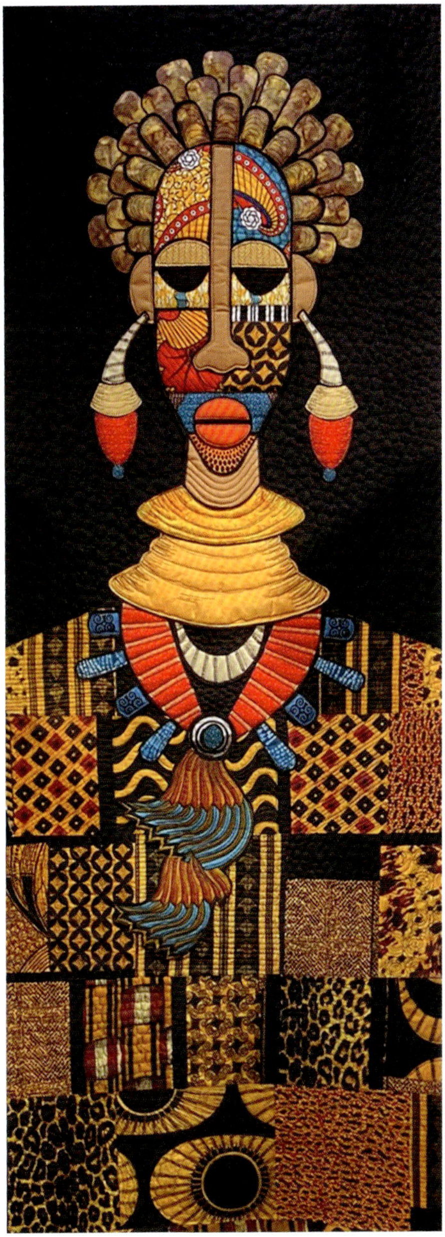

Queen Mother, Wendy Kendrick, 2022

about inner strength, nurturing and sharing our spiritual journey."[96] A women's artist exchange trip to Tanzania in 2010 changed her use of color, pattern, and even layering. This experience led Kendrick to commit to a more African-inspired approach to making and representation. Through the creation of stitched portrait masks, she now highlights and celebrates African diasporic culture and physical features that have historically been misrepresented and othered. Her appliquéd quilt *Queen Mother* pays homage to the late Aminah Brenda Lynn Robinson, a profound artist and storyteller from Columbus. According to Kendrick, the quilt "depicts the strength of all mothers" but pays special tribute to Robinson's role in the Black Ohio artist community as a storyteller and creator.[97]

AMINAH ROBINSON

Aminah Brenda Lynn Robinson (1940–2015) was an artist and griot known for her one-of-a-kind works that captured stories of home, community, and liberation. Her mother and father encouraged her creativity, and she continued her training at the Columbus College of Art and Design. Robinson spent over six decades creating multimedia artwork that chronicled everyday Black life in monumental ways. From hand-bound and illustrated journals that captured her personal journeys to sculptures made of "hogmawg"—her own homemade material—Robinson utilized media that spoke to her to illustrate history in a vivid and imaginative way.[98] Her home, which now hosts artist residencies, was known for its eclecticism, as it was filled with collections of materials, writings, and works in progress.

Many of her stories connect to her early life in Columbus's Poindexter Village, which was one of the earliest federally funded apartment complexes for African Americans in the United States. Later travels to Africa, the Middle East, and the Gullah region would shape work that centered on migration, resilience, and identity, often focusing on historical figures and overlooked stories of Black achievement. In 2004, she was awarded the MacArthur "Genius" Award for her achievements as an artist and visual historian.

Some of her most notable works are her RagGonNons, which combine layers of fabric, buttons, beads, drawings, paint, dolls, and found

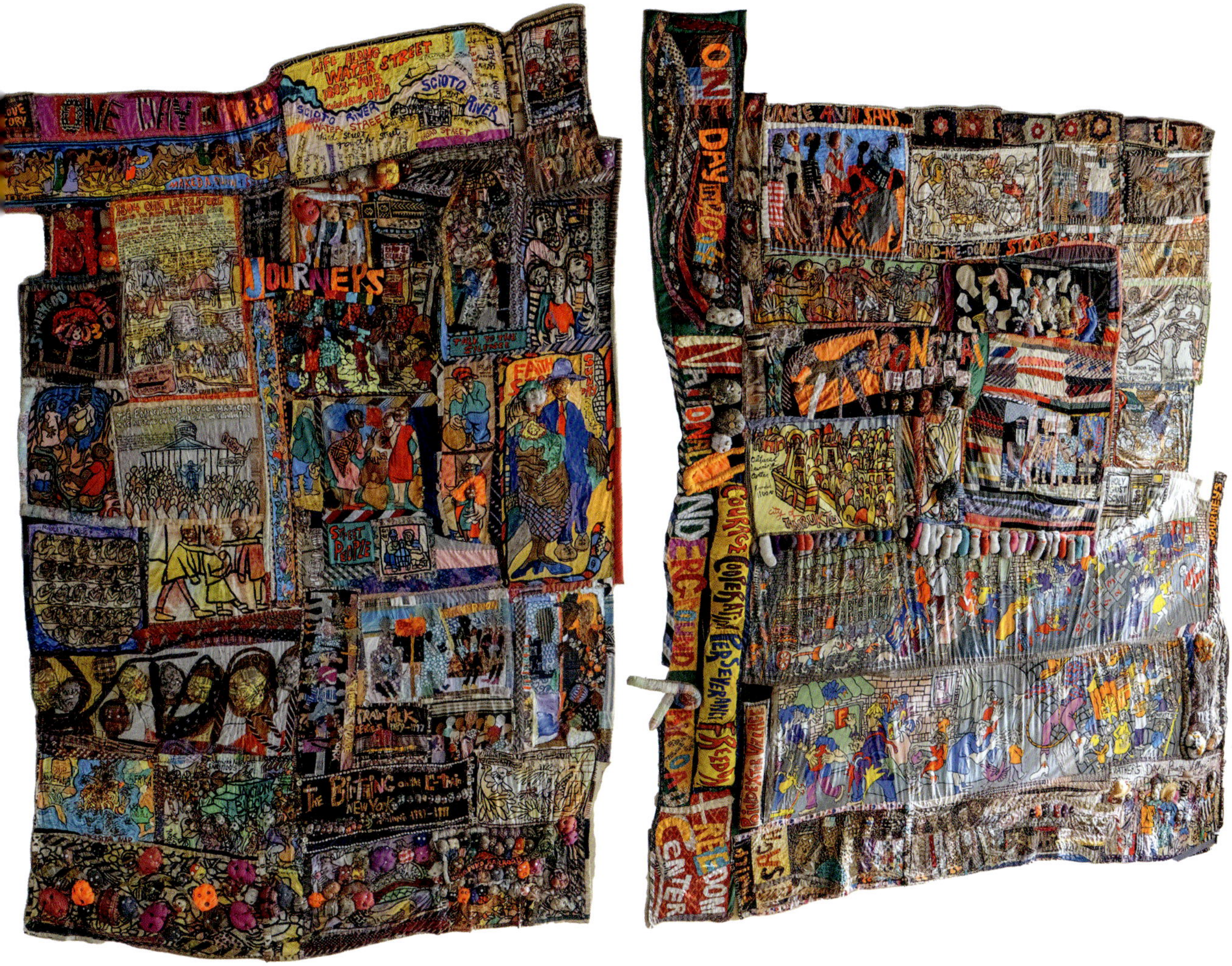

objects to create textured, quilt-inspired tapestries. These massive works hold decades of memories that will, in Robinson's words "rag on and on," thus inspiring the term.[99] Her RagGonNons combine a myriad of materials to bring years of research to life. *Journeys I* and *Journeys II* in particular act as a textile-based diptych that portrays Robinson's ancestral history. Taking several decades to complete, these two pieces take the viewer on a journey through her family's history, from West Africa, through the transatlantic slave trade, to Columbus, Ohio.[100]

Journeys I and *Journeys II*, Aminah Robinson, 1968-ongoing

MOFAD *LEGACY QUILT*

The Museum of Food and Design (MOFAD) Legacy Quilt Project (2022) is a tribute to the Black food and beverage producers and purveyors who have shaped American cuisine since the country's inception.[101] MOFAD has written about the complexity of sourcing centuries of material to create 406 commemorative blocks:

> *The* African/American: Making the Nation's Table *exhibition Advisory Board—28 of the country's most distinguished scholars, writers, chefs, and food and drink producers—was tasked with coming up with names of iconic figures and noteworthy moments in food culture. Those for the contemporary period were easier to add and discover; individuals and items for the 17th, 18th, 19th, and early 20th centuries were more daunting. So, the curatorial team began to research African Americans and food's more profound history and came up with more names and concepts and contributions, and the list grew. The culmination of this research was vetted by Dr. Scott Barton alongside Dr. Jessica B. Harris, the exhibition's lead curator. Writer Osayi Endolyn was tasked with amplifying and verifying the biographies and creating a series of brief synopses that would be used to inform visitors about the quilt's contents.*[102]

Building upon the cultural tradition of quilting and collective work, the museum commissioned Harlem Needle Arts (HNA) to lead the creation of the quilt. Founded in 2005, Harlem Needle Arts has been steadfast in its mission to both preserve and transform the narrative surrounding fiber, textile, design, and needle arts within the African diaspora. The organization is dedicated not only to preserving these vital cultural traditions but also to expanding their relevance and visibility, ensuring that the rich legacy of textile crafts continues to evolve and inspire new generations. Artists Laura Gadson, Sylvia Hernandez, and Ife Felix joined together to construct over four hundred distinct blocks featuring illustrations by designer Adrian Franks, guided by the research and leadership of HNA executive director Michelle Bishop. At nearly 14 feet tall and 30 feet wide, *Legacy Quilt* is composed of fabrics that were carefully selected to correspond with the time period associated with the

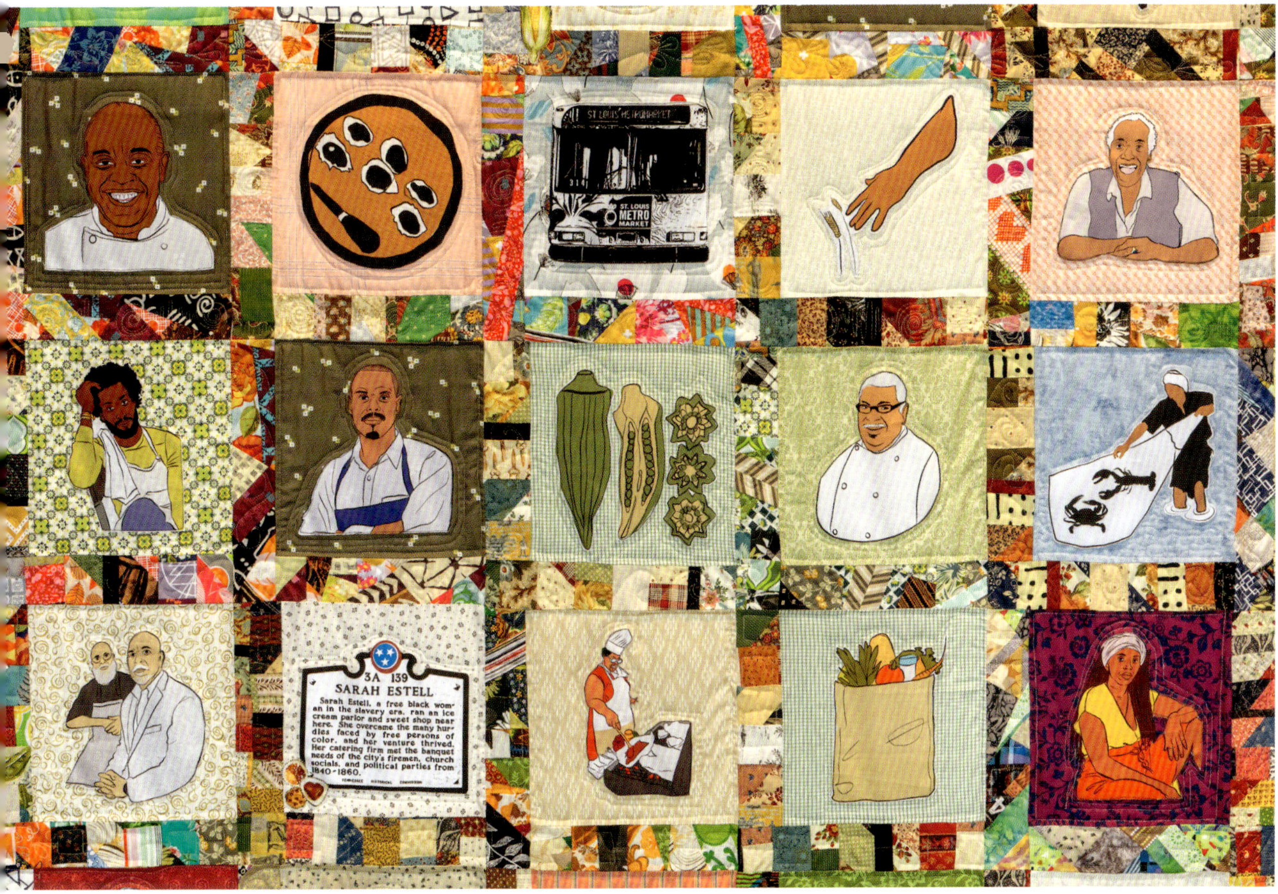

contents of each block. The fabrics used include "cotton, corduroy, flannel, gingham, muslin, chintz, croaker, calico, chambray, wool, brocade, toile, and denim along with batiks, Adire, and Ankara prints."[103] Today the quilt can be explored through MOFAD's website, which allows viewers to engage with individual blocks and the richness of the stories they capture.

Legacy Quilt, (detail) image 412, 2020.

Top row, left to right: Francois Kwaku-Dongo, Emmanuel "Manna" Bernoon, Rafia Zafar, Annie Fisher, Mildred Cotton Council

Middle row, left to right: DeVonn Francis, Preston Clark, okra, Leon West, Sebastian Cane

Bottom row, left to right: Ben and Robert Bynum, Sarah Estell, Bessie Lou Cathey, Solomon Humphries, Kia Damon

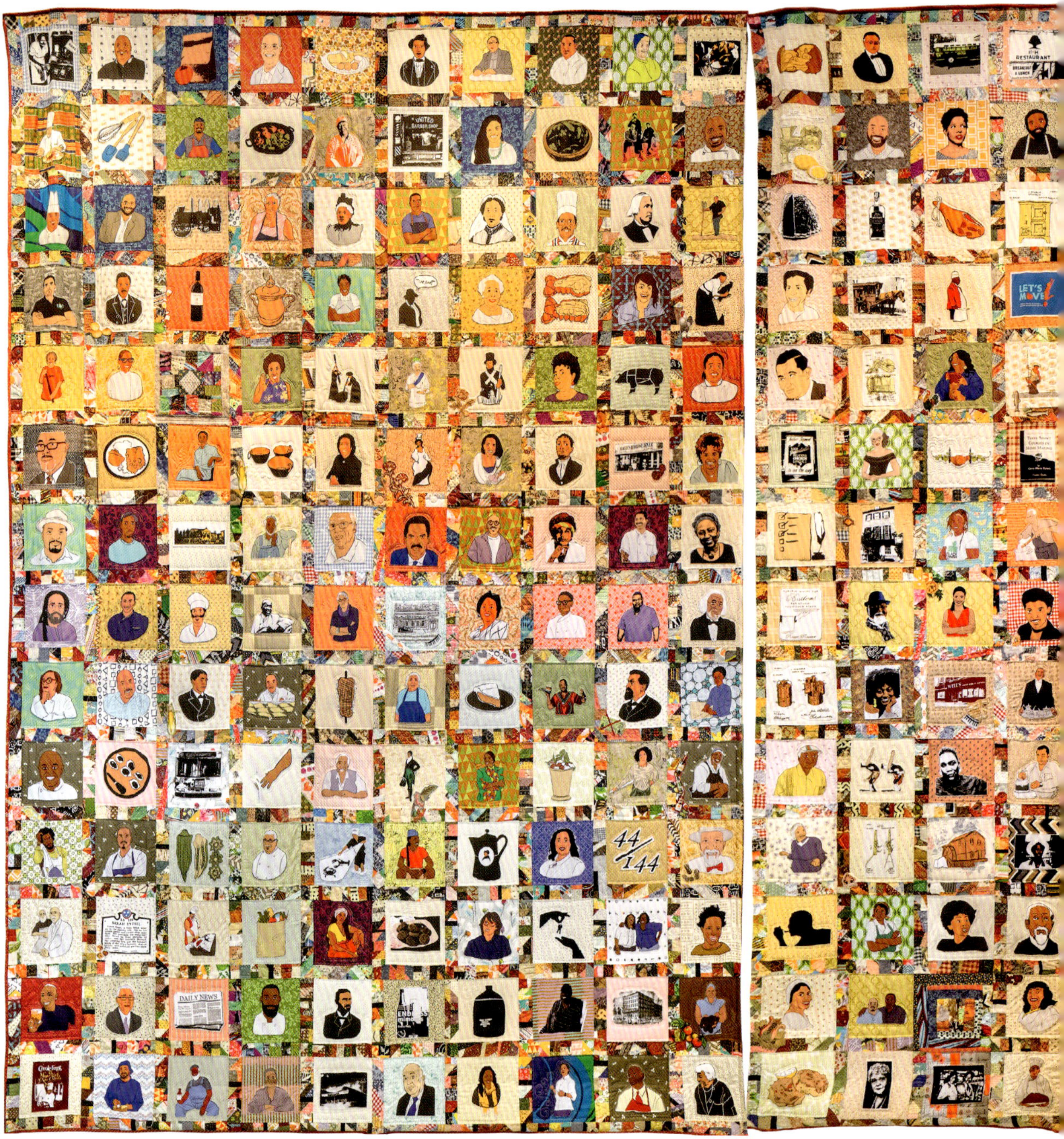
RESTAURANT
LET'S MOVE!
44/144
DAILY NEWS

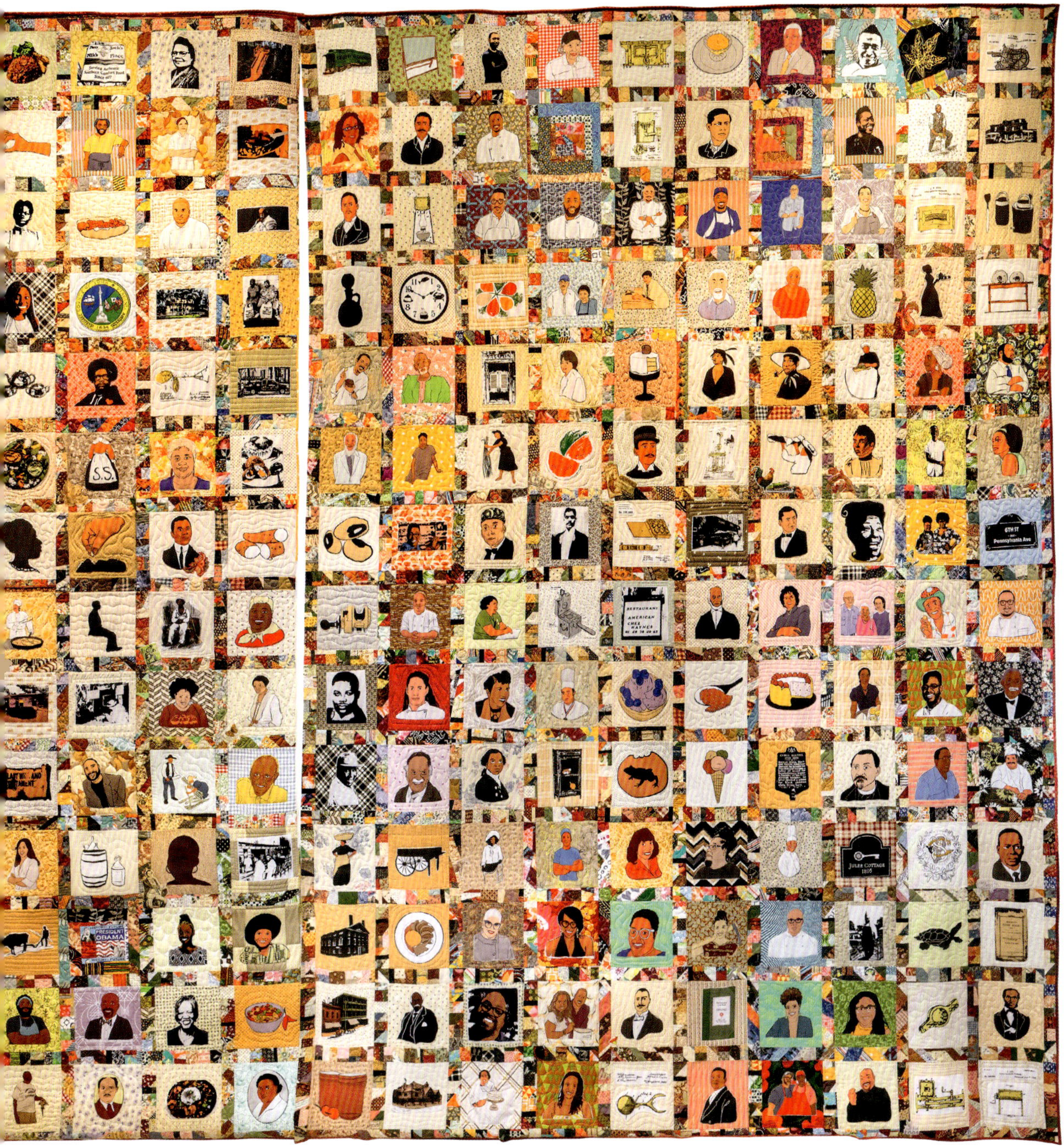

Legacy Quilt, Harlem Needle Arts, executive director Michelle Bishop and quilting artists Laura Gadson, Sylvia Franks (graphic designer) and Osayi Endolyn (writer), 2020

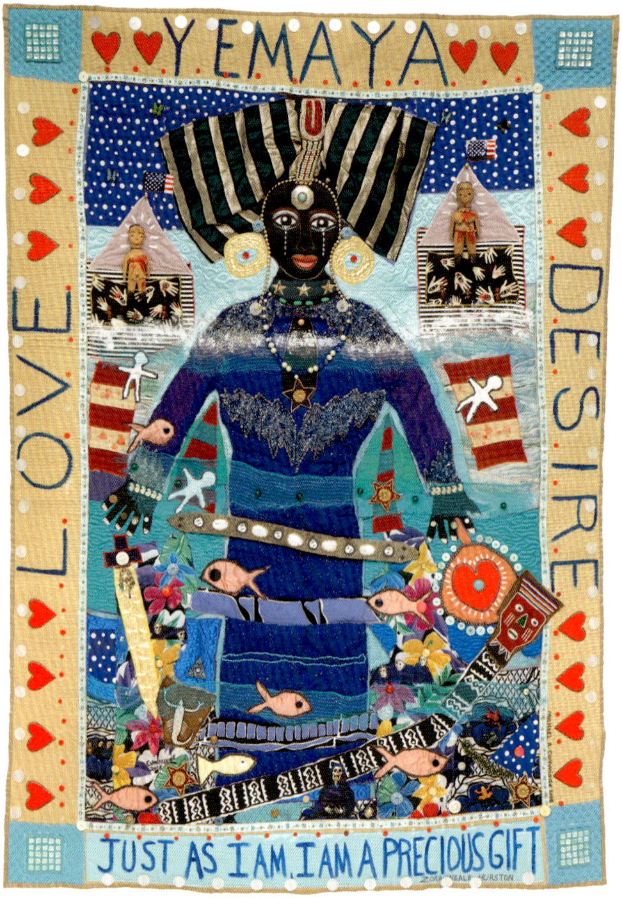

Yemaya, Michael Cummings, 2018

MICHAEL CUMMINGS

Michael Cummings's narrative quilts are embedded with iconography that reflects his passion for cultural heritage. As a National Endowment for the Arts Heritage Fellow and one of the most notable male quilters in the country, Cummings has spent over thirty years archiving histories that span the African diaspora. After relocating to New York in the 1970s to start a career with the Department of Cultural Affairs for New York City, he quickly became embedded within the city's cultural landscape. He was inspired by Romare Bearden, a beloved mentor, to work in collage along with painting, and in 1973 he experimented with fabric for a banner workshop at his job, which sparked a newfound appreciation for fabric.[104]

Cummings is known for his densely layered quilts that center Black historical figures and musicians as well as diasporic themes. His works often blur realism and abstraction, drawing from both African American folk traditions and global Black cultural references. Rather than following conventional quilt block patterns, he treats each quilt like a canvas, using fabric to construct scenes that tell stories about resilience, identity, and the fullness of Black life. His quilts aren't assembled by following detailed sketches or hyper-specific measurements. Instead, he sketches his designs using chalk, then follows the sketch by pinning and sewing fabric. He views fabric as a palette that he pulls from to create balance between color and texture.[105]

His *Yemaya* quilt is one example of his unmistakable style of appliqué. It pulls together text, other embellishments, and contrasting colors to reflect a story as layered as the piece itself. *Yemaya* is inspired by the Yoruba orisha who is the goddess of the ocean and considered mother of all. The quilt features her most noted symbolism, including the color blue, a sword that wards off evil, and a fan to calm the waters that she rules. Cummings also incorporates beads, paint, shells, and sculptural elements to create dimension and depth, along with a quote by Zora Neale Hurston: "Just as I am, I am a precious gift." He describes this quilt as portraying Yemaya weeping for her children who are held captive on two slave ships, *Love* and *Desire*, headed to America during the transatlantic slave trade. In the ocean are three white figures representing spirits of the dead in Yoruba mythology. These forms tell the story of those who jumped into ocean rather than suffer the pain and torture of enslavement. His coded symbolism amplifies connections between West African spirituality and Black American history.[106]

YVONNE WELLS

Yvonne Wells is a self-taught quilter whose pictorial works are inspired by a range of subjects, from biblical characters and civil rights to personal memories. Wells didn't begin quilting until 1979, at the age of forty, and she originally focused on warmth over beauty. Using what she had learned from watching her mother sew, she started making quilts with any materials she could find. That sparked an interest that still burns brightly today. In a 2024 interview she described the moment that quilting became her practice, saying, "Something was burning inside me. It made me say, *Yvonne, don't turn this loose. This is something that has to come out*."[107] After returning home from her job as a physical education teacher, Wells would immediately pivot to quilting. She would work late into the evening and rise early in the morning to return to her machine. Between 1979 and 2020 Wells made over five hundred quilts, which fall into five thematic categories that she has described: religious emphasis, potluck, children's moment, traditional, and sociopolitical.[108]

Wells refers to *Yesterday: The Civil Rights Movement in the South III* as one of the most "touching" and "colorful" pieces she's ever made.[109] It is her representation of the political climate of the 1950s through 1970s and the conditions that led to those critical years. Through simple shapes and strong color choices, Wells tells the story of the *Mayflower*, slavery, Jim Crow, and lynching. She specifically chose a red background to mark the brutality of the time. Also memorialized in the quilt are activists such as James Chaney, Michael Schwerner, and Andrew Goodman, as well as the victims of the 16th Street Baptist Church bombing of 1963: Addie

Mae Collins, Denise McNair, Carole Robertson, and Cynthia Wesley. Wells felt it equally important to depict the hope that existed during the civil rights movement, as shown by the multicultural figures united in a circle. They surround a representation of Martin Luther King Jr., who, according to Wells, is in the sunshine because he offered a ray of hope that was able to elicit change.[110]

ANNA WILLIAMS

Anna Williams, known for her bold and colorful approach to quilt-making, broke away from convention to create vivid and memorable designs. Born in 1927 in Baton Rouge, Louisiana, Williams learned the basics of quilting from her mother and grandmother. It wouldn't be until years later that her distinct style emerged. Williams once explained her intuitive and spontaneous process, saying, "I'll think of something and when I get home, I'll fool with it to see how it comes together. If I like it, I work with it."[111] Using only scissors and measuring by eye, she constructed hundreds of one-of-a-kind quilts.

She was committed to her practice; her bedroom also served as her studio. She quilted to forget her troubles, saying, "If I didn't have anything else to do, I would just sew."[112] Drawing only from memory, she would spend her nights working on multiple quilts at once. In addition to making strip quilts, she reworked traditional patterns to reflect more of her personal aesthetic, as seen in *LIX: Log Cabin*. Williams was also the first known Black maker to have a quilt become part of the Brooklyn Museum's collection.

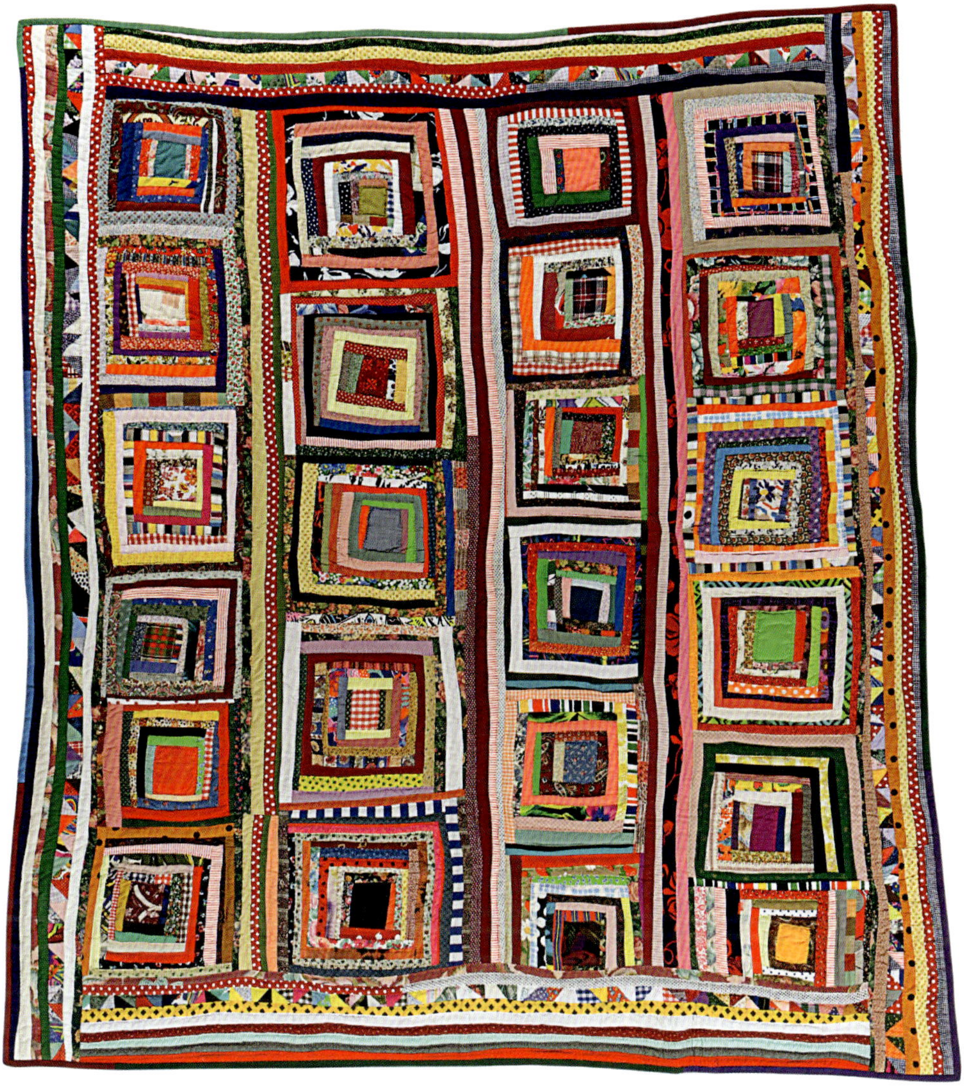

LIX: Log Cabin, Anna Williams, 1993

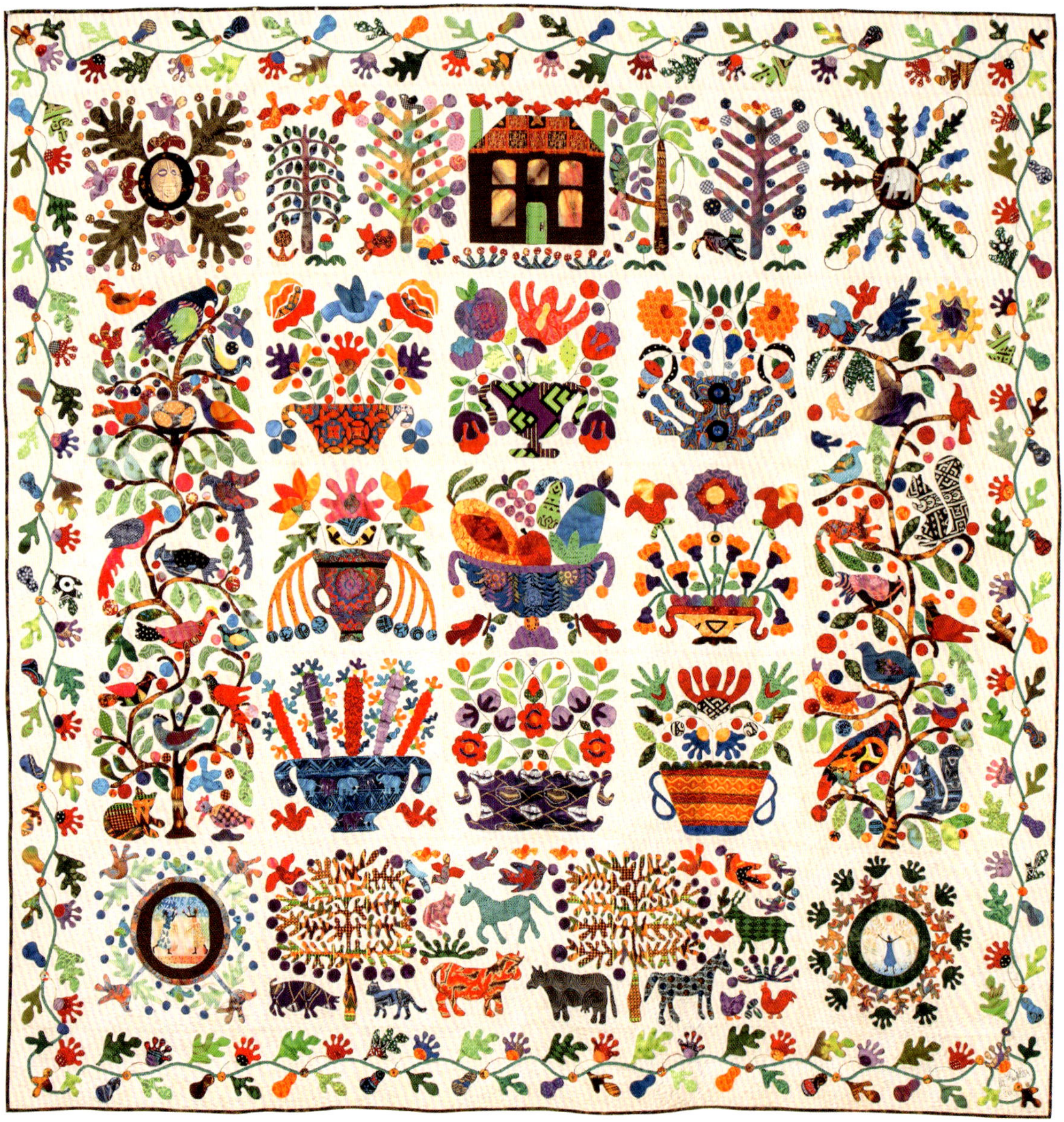

Choose to Bloom, O. V. Brantley, 2013

O. V. BRANTLEY

O. V. Brantley's journey as a quilter is just as colorful as her life. She was among the first wave of Black students to attend the University of Arkansas at Fayetteville. Her academic path led to Vanderbilt Law School and a successful legal career, including a tenure as the highest-ranking civil lawyer in Fulton County, Georgia. Brantley began quilting midway through her career, seeking an outlet for balance and joy. As she put it, "Quilting became that for me . . . my happy place, my calm down place, my place where I go to solve problems."[113]

She learned to quilt using the book *Teach Yourself to Quilt* and completing a sampler quilt that still hangs in her studio as a reminder of her humble beginnings. Her quilts are often autobiographical, incorporating African fabrics, political messaging, and connections to her sorority, Delta Sigma Theta. Handwork, for Brantley, is an act of self-care. "I try to end every day in my bedroom in my rocking chair with a quilt in my hoop," she describes, "taking a few stitches. . . . It helps my health, my happiness, and my general well-being."[114]

Beyond her personal practice, Brantley has cultivated space for others to stitch, share, and shine. She has served as president of the Brown Sugar Stitchers Quilt Guild and she cofounded the Atlanta Quilt Festival, a vibrant platform that celebrates African American quilting traditions with an emphasis on inclusion and visibility. Her *Choose to Bloom* is an award-winning quilt in the style of an album quilt, which is made to resemble "the popular autograph albums of the 1800s, similar to the scrapbooks of today[,] in which young ladies collected signatures and mementos from friends and family."[115] Quilters historically followed this design by placing signatures and other motifs in the center of quilt blocks to show off their handwork and even commemorate significant life events. Brantley incorporates African fabrics to add her own touch to the flora and fauna in each block. "I believe life is about choices," she says. "We can choose to accept our circumstances or we can get busy changing them. We all bloom in different ways. How will you bloom?"[116]

KEWON HUNTER

Kewon Hunter approaches quilting as a personal and cultural process, one that honors Black traditions while also reflecting a path of individual discovery. Hunter started as a photographer before expanding his practice to quiltmaking. He quilts to connect with his heritage and express himself and says, "I quilt to honor Black traditions and Black people, keeping that vital tradition alive."[117] He sees the act of quilting as intricately tied to the notion of self-sufficiency. "If you can quilt, you can make clothes, and that skill, sewing, is incredibly important," he says.[118]

For Hunter, the practice of quilting has been profoundly restorative, offering him an intentional space to slow down and engage with his emotions. He describes it as a "space for positive self-talk," and says that quiltmaking has made him more "patient and positive." He did not learn the skill from his mother or grandmothers in the usual way but instead forged his own way through research, online tutorials, and community engagement. "It's been a journey of self-discovery," he reflects, emphasizing that his craft is as much about personal growth as it is about artistic creation.

Hunter's quilting is a vibrant celebration of both heritage and resourcefulness, and he is intentional about the materials he uses. "Every piece is made with completely recycled fabric—whatever catches my eye, really," he explains.[119] His use of recycled materials and his focus on vivid colors reflect a deep reverence for the resourcefulness of his ancestors, who made do with what was available to them. His creations, which he describes as "improved sunshine," fuse resourcefulness with a personal aesthetic that meets in the middle of boldness and simplicity. He sees every quilt he creates as a living tribute to the Black quilters and makers whose legacy guides his craft. "Every single piece I create, I think of them," he says, "and I just let their spirit guide my hands, my heart, and my mind."[120]

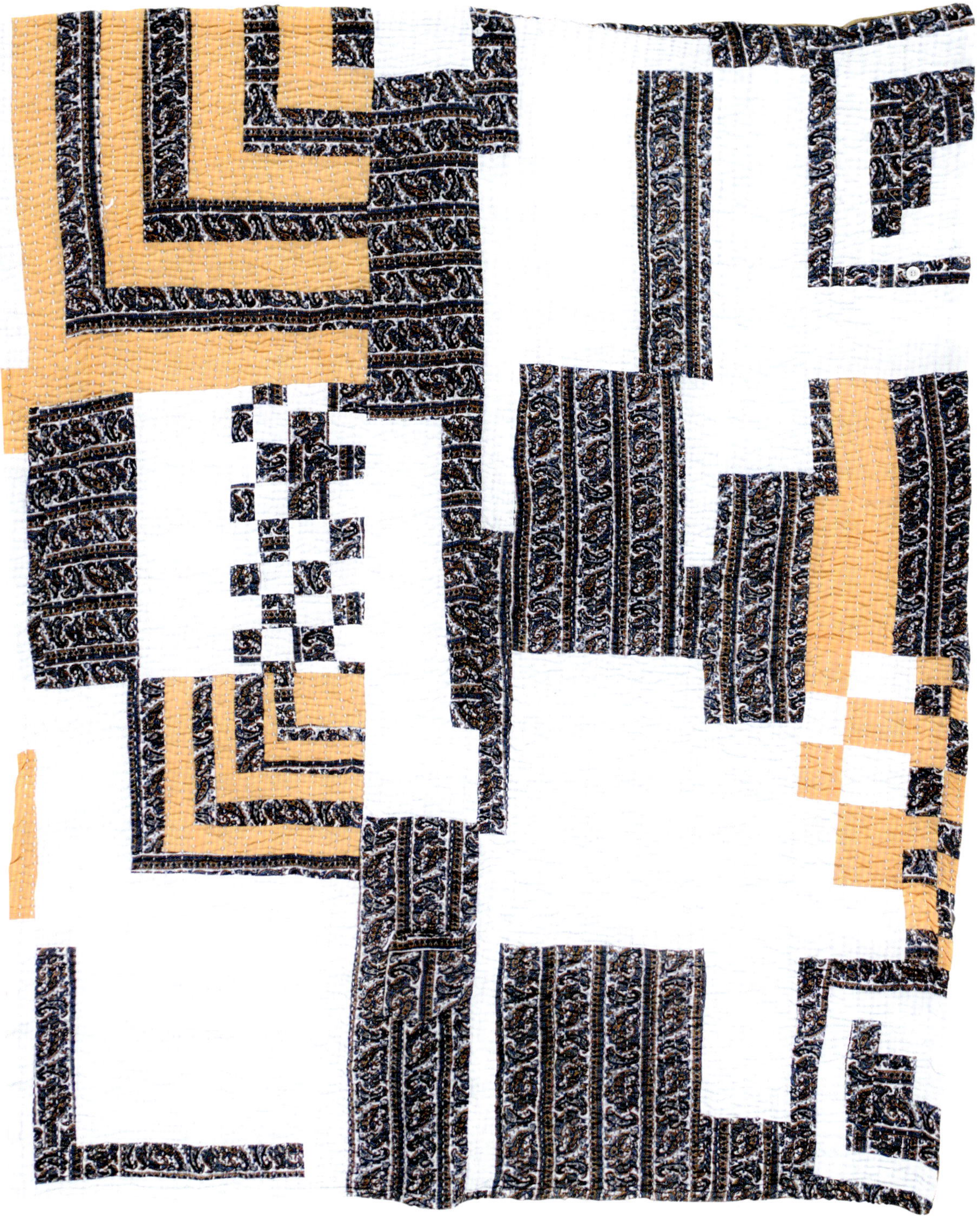

Out in the Open, Kewon Hunter, date unknown

PART III

MEDICINE

There is something about quilts that compels us to soften and exhale.

In their warmth we find comfort, rest, and a reprieve from the heaviness of the world around us. If you speak to anyone about quilts, they are likely to recall a moment when a quilt left them feeling held or restored. This section brings together the people who understand quilting as a remedy. In particular, I trace how Black quilters have made healing visible and accessible to others, found meaning, and shaped community through the work of their hands.

"Soft Altars" explores quilts as spaces where grief, memory, and spiritual care live collectively. In our homes, our dressers, tables, and walls often act as spaces for remembrance through the careful arrangement of personal items, and quilts can serve a similar role. Quilts for fallen fathers, for lost brothers, for children taken too soon allow loved ones to speak their names and remain connected in spirit. Traveling from Vivian Lucille McCullin's memorial to her Tuskegee Airman brother to Hystercine Rankin's testimony about her father's murder, this chapter describes the role quilts play in relieving burdens.

In "Sacred Space" I reframe the act of quilting itself as an embodied practice that gives Black women the space to breathe and renew. This chapter highlights the thoughts and concerns of Black quilters that often make their way into cloth. The works featured speak to granny midwives layering quilts beneath birthing chairs and celebrate artists like Rosemary Ollison and Cookie Washington who transmute trauma into fabric. Most importantly, it amplifies how quilters can find the sacred within the everyday and use that energy to inspire and uplift others.

"Stitched Sovereignty" closes out this section by discussing the role of self-governance in personal well-being. Here we examine how quilts aid their makers in exercising their authority and freedom. When Black women have been met with denial or exclusion, they have created systems of support through collective making. Cooperatives like the Freedom Quilting Bee and modern guilds like the Brown Sugar Stitchers and Princeton Sankofa Stitchers are all examples of how quilting creates space for Black women to determine the terms of their creative, economic, and emotional lives. These three journeys remind us of just how nuanced Black quilters' inner lives are and how, if we sit with their work, we can give them the consideration they so rightfully deserve.

Soft Altars

Ancestor veneration and the creation of altars hold deep significance for Black people. They are acts of remembrance, resistance, and relationship. This practice links the present to the past, honoring those who endured slavery, segregation, and systemic oppression while preserving cultural and spiritual traditions disrupted by the transatlantic slave trade. Altars dedicated to ancestors are spaces of both memory and power, where people can connect with those who came before them, seek guidance, and find the strength to continue. By centering photographs, personal items, notes, and other artifacts that recall loved ones, they link an earthly life to an unending spiritual relationship.

Black feminist scholars have emphasized the significance of ancestral veneration as a pathway toward reclaiming history and healing. The role of spirituality in Black life and its connection to survival and empowerment is a common theme in the writing of bell hooks. She asserts that honoring ancestors allows for a reconnection to self and community and resists the erasure of Black identities in dominant historical narratives.[121] Similarly, Saidiya Hartman's concept of "critical fabulation" suggests that engaging with ancestral memory—particularly for those whose histories were violently disrupted—becomes an act of creative resistance.[122] Through altars, African Americans piece together fragmented histories, making room for mourning and spiritual reclamation.

For Black women in particular, ancestral veneration is a deep cultural practice. Patricia Hill Collins's concept of the "motherline" highlights the transmission of knowledge, strength, and cultural traditions through generations of Black women.[123] Altars often honor maternal ancestors, reinforcing the centrality of Black women in sustaining community and survival.

A quilt, especially in the hands of Black makers, is not *just* a quilt. It can be seen as a soft altar—layered, intentional, and filled with spirit. Makers embed each stitch and seam with love, hope, and intention, using items and visual references connected to the recipient or a loved one who has passed on. Like the assemblages found on a grandmother's dresser—adorned with family photos, prayer cards, and bits of earth from long-gone places—quilts hold space for what refuses to be forgotten. In African diasporic history, where so much has been fractured and displaced, the quilt becomes a means of remembering, stitching back together kin and story.

Just as the altar invites reverence and ritual, so does the quilt. Whether draped on a bed, hung on a wall, or laid across a casket, it holds warmth and intention. It asks us to sit with what has been handed down, to honor the labor and love embedded in every thread. To envelop oneself into a quilt is to invoke a sense of reverence for all that went into its creation. Memory becomes tactile—something you can touch, fold, pass on. Like the altar, the quilt tells us: *We were here, we loved, we grieved, and we channeled those emotions into something beautiful.*

HONORING SECOND LIEUTENANT JAMES MCCULLIN

Memorial Quilt for Tuskegee Airman 2d Lt. James McCullin is a loving tribute to both his personal sacrifice and the achievements of the Tuskegee Airmen. Crafted by his sister, Vivian Lucille McCullin, this quilt not only commemorates her brother's life but also embodies the enduring legacy of African American military service during World War II.[124]

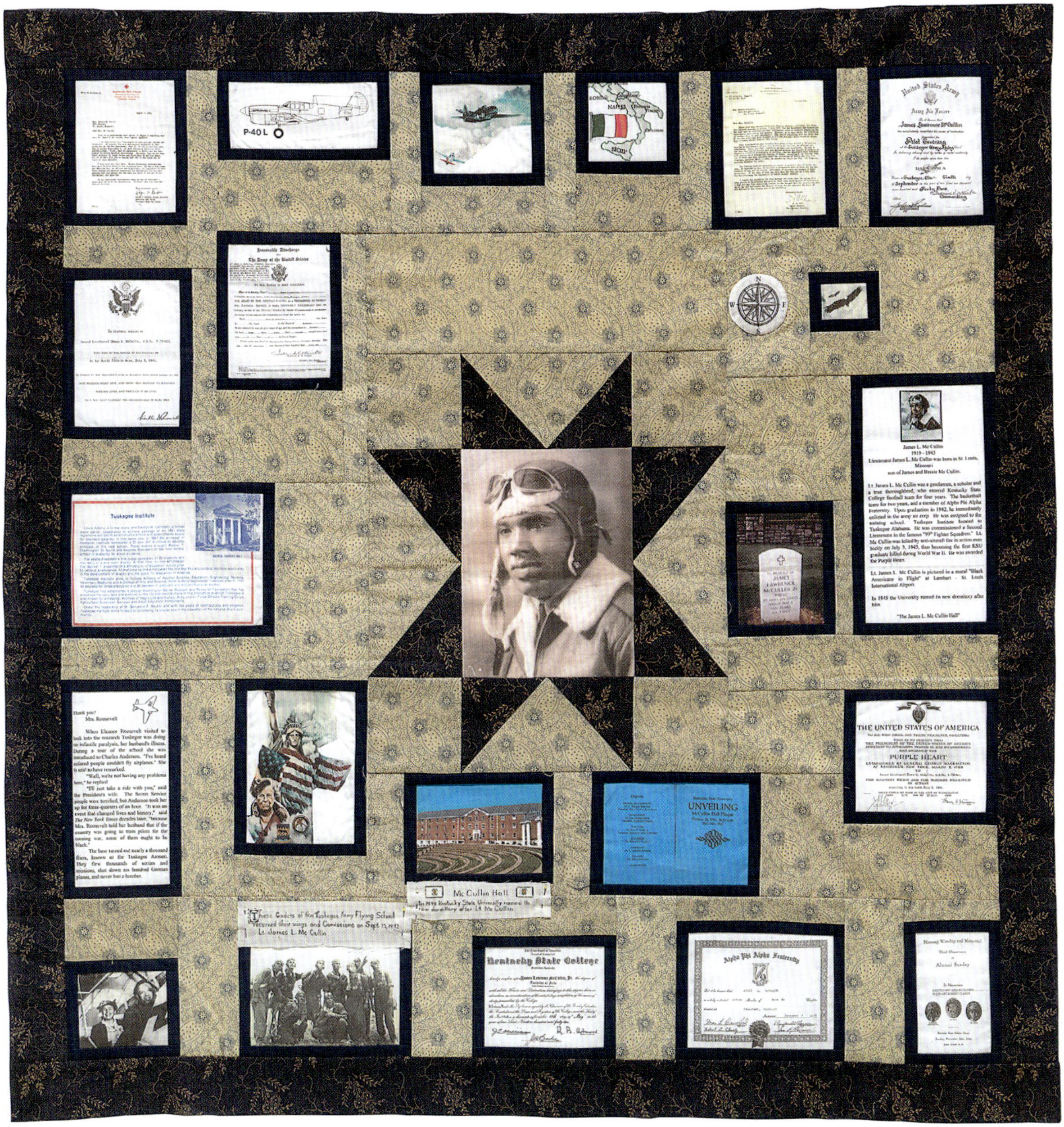

Memorial Quilt for Tuskegee Airman 2d Lt. James McCullin, Vivian Lucille McCullin, after 1943

The Tuskegee Airmen hold a significant place in American history as the first African American military aviators in the US Army Air Corps. Formed in 1941 at Tuskegee Army Air Field in Alabama, this group of pilots and support personnel shattered racial barriers and disproved the racist belief that African Americans were incapable of serving in combat roles. These aviators flew over fifteen thousand sorties during World War II and earned more than 150 Distinguished Flying Crosses for their exceptional performance in combat.

Despite their achievements, the Tuskegee Airmen faced discrimination both during and after the war. Often they were denied access to officers' clubs, faced segregation in military facilities, and were excluded from recognition for their service. However, their dedication and skill played a key role in the eventual desegregation of the US armed forces, culminating in President Harry S. Truman's Executive Order 9981 in 1948, which mandated the integration of all military branches.[125]

James L. McCullin Jr. was born into a family that valued education and service, leading him to attend Virginia State College, where he was an active member of the Reserve Officers' Training Corps (ROTC). His commitment to serving his country led him to join the Tuskegee Airmen.

On July 2, 1943, during a mission to escort B-25 bombers over Sicily, McCullin's plane was shot down, resulting in his death and making him one of the first Black pilots to lose his life in combat. In the aftermath of his passing, his sister Vivian sought a meaningful way to honor his memory. Drawing upon her cultural traditions, she created a memorial quilt that both honors his sacrifice and is a testament to the contributions of African American servicemen.

The quilt features a collection of personal and historical symbols that tell the story of McCullin's life and service. Prominently displayed at the center is a portrait of McCullin in uniform. Surrounding this image are military patches and insignia, including those from the US Army Air Corps, which emphasize his official service. Airplanes, including the P-40 Warhawk and P-51 Mustang—aircraft commonly flown by the Tuskegee Airmen—are also featured, highlighting the equipment that McCullin would have been trained to operate. Additionally, the quilt includes hand-stitched elements such as gold stars, which represent fallen soldiers, and a red, white, and blue color scheme, emphasizing McCullin's patriotic sacrifice. Vivian also incorporated letters and documents related to her brother's service, ensuring that his story would be preserved for future generations.[126]

HONORING DENVER GRAY

Hystercine Rankin's (1929–2010) quilts *Memories of My Father's Death* and *After My Father's Funeral* speak to the horrors of the Jim Crow South and show how quilting can be a deeply personal method of processing loss. Using narrative quilting as a form of storytelling, Rankin memorializes the trauma of losing her father at an early age and offers insight into the social hierarchy of her Mississippi hometown and its impact on Black residents. These quilts allowed Rankin to work through her sorrow and shed light on her family's story.

Rankin's father, Denver Gray, was tragically killed on October 1, 1943, in an act of racial violence. According to the text embroidered on *Memories of My Father's Death*, a white man named Farrel [sic] Humphrey shot and killed Gray for being "uppity." The quilt vividly depicts the murder scene, with Gray lying on the ground as a white figure stands over him with a gun. The background features a rural landscape, a small house, and trees, emphasizing the isolated roadway where the murder happened. Rankin, who heard the four fatal shots in the distance, recalled how her father was left to die on the side of the road in the quilt's text:

As I came back to the house Farrel [sic] *Humphrey's son was standing in front of the steps, he said Laula if you want Denver he is in the middle of the road. Mother said lord have mercy, she didn't have any one* [sic] *to go and pick him up. He stayed there until a log truck came and picked him up and brought him to the house. Mother buried him the next day. Blacks was afraid to come to the funeral.*[127]

Below his body, Rankin embroidered the names of the eight children he left behind, ranging in age from twelve years to six weeks old.

After My Father's Funeral picks up the story at a later point, showing the emotional burden that hovered over Rankin's family. The

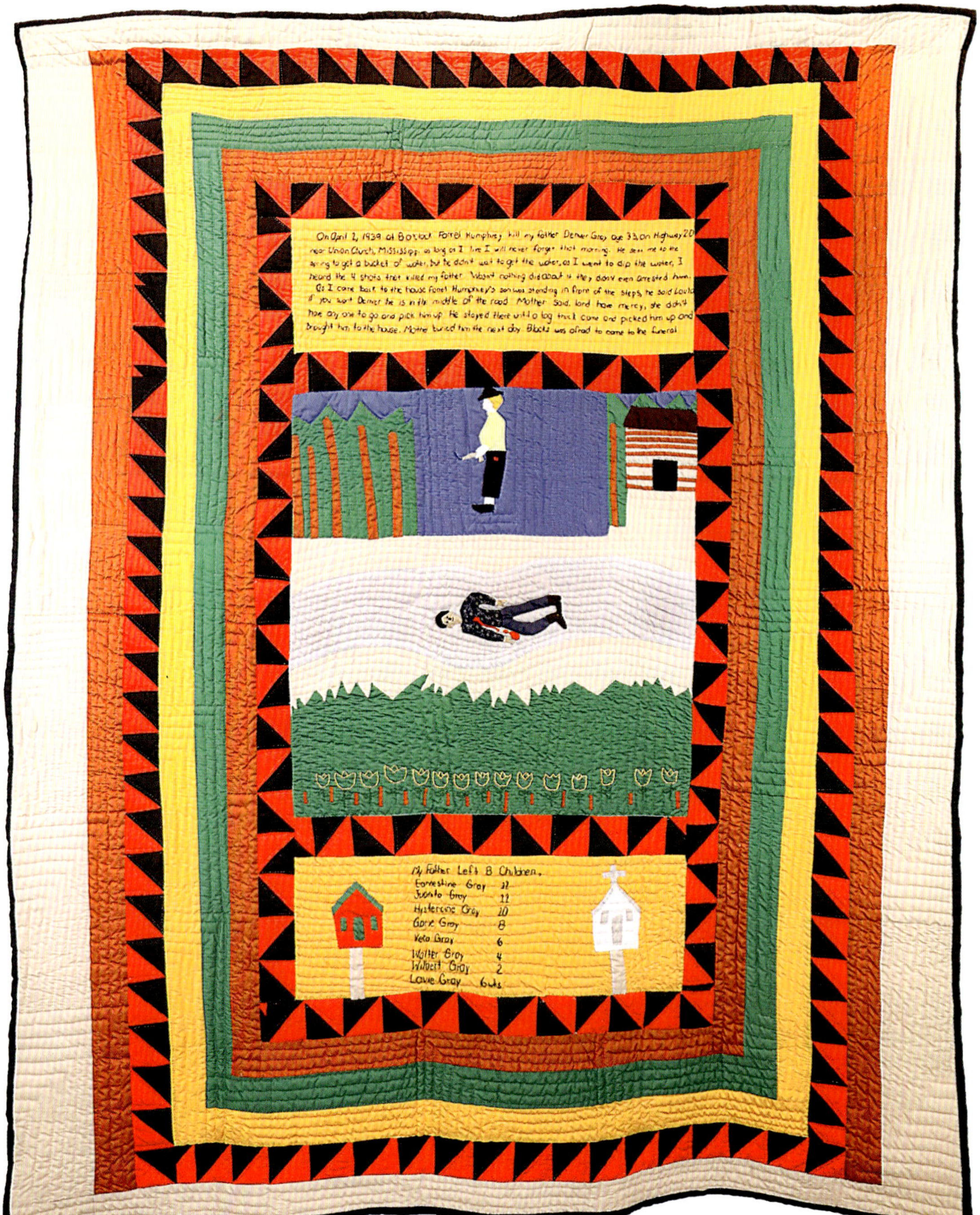

Memories of My Father's Death,
Hystercine Rankin, 1989

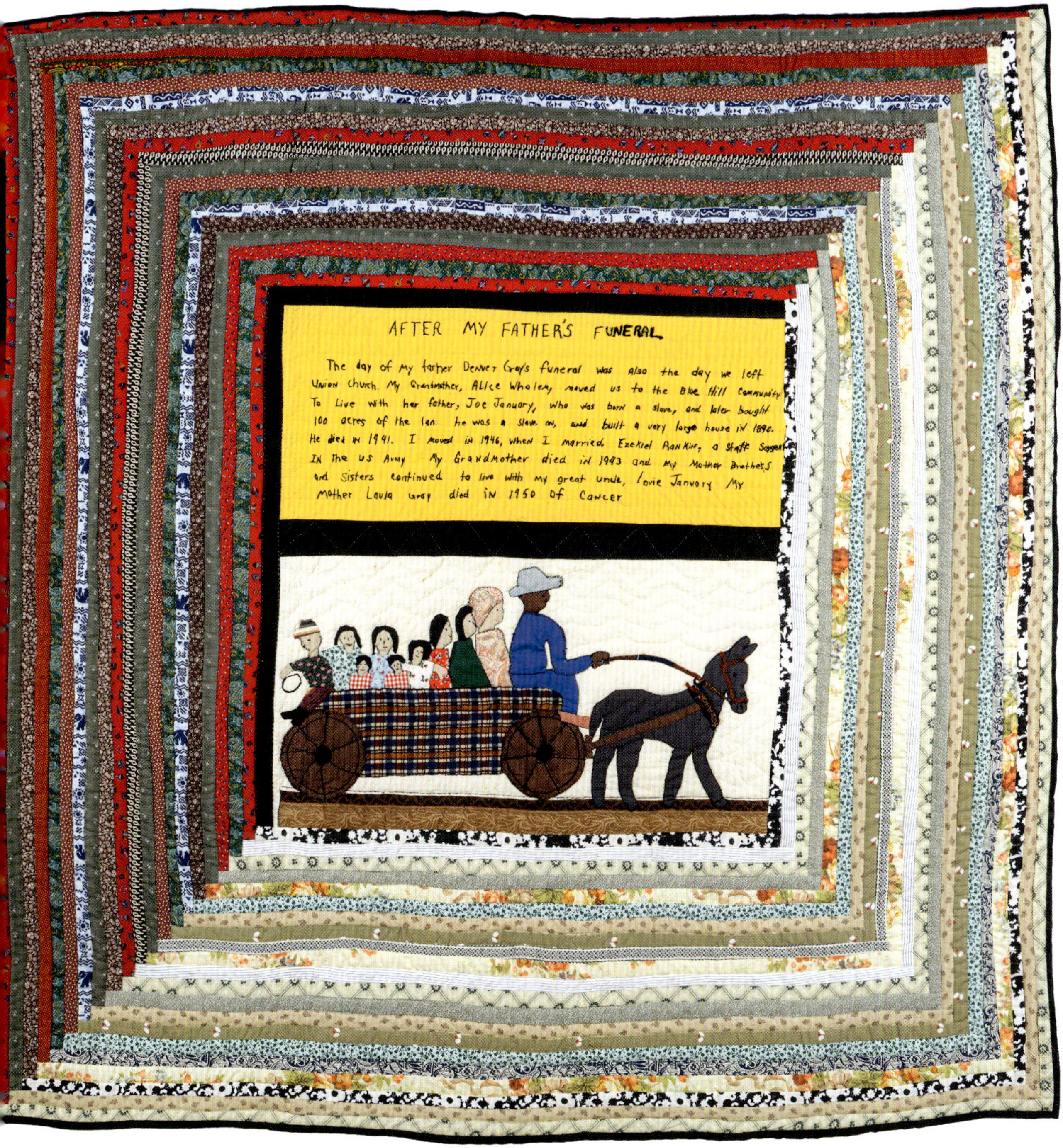

After My Father's Funeral, Hystercine Rankin, 1993

central image shows Rankin, her mother, and her siblings traveling to live with her grandmother the day of her father's funeral. Rankin surrounds her family with a log cabin motif, using color to mark the transition out of the shadows of grief into the light of the next chapter of their lives.[128]

Despite having quilted for decades, she had not considered creating quilts about her father's death until photographer Roland L. Freeman encouraged her to after learning about her story. Making the quilts allowed her to both liberate herself from the pain she had carried all those years and share her father's story in a direct way. In her book *A Communion of the Spirits*, she describes the feeling that washed over her after creating the quilt, writing, "To me it was a joy, knowing after all these years, something I had kept inside of me, I mean just how hurting that feeling was, it was now coming out in the open."[129] Later she shared that her father came to her in a dream, and she told him that people would finally know the truth about his killing, which allowed her to feel as though a burden had been lifted. Rankin's decision to create these quilts decades after her father's death shows how grief can be revisited and reshaped through artistic expression. By creating the quilt, she reclaimed agency in a world where historical narratives are often dictated by those in power. This altar for her father bears witness to his life and death on her own terms.

AIDS Memorial Quilt, block 5905. Names featured: Fela Kuti, Larry Stewart, Essex Hemphill, Gil Scott Heron, Thembi Ngubane, Marlon Riggs, Kenneth R. Robinson, Michael Morocco

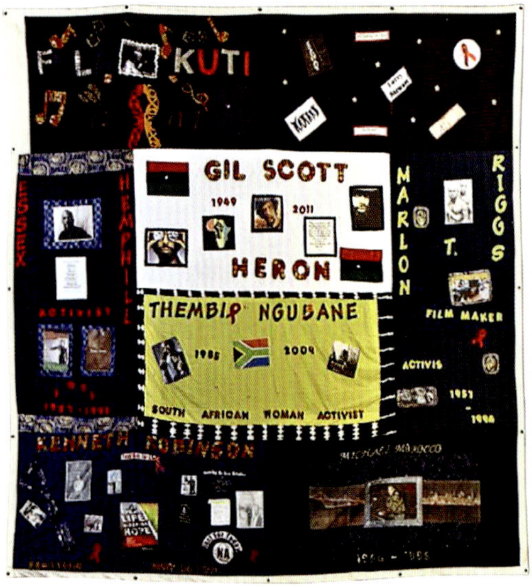

HONORING LIVES LOST TO HIV/AIDS

At the intersection of public health and social justice, few artifacts have captured the collective grief and resilience of a community quite like the *AIDS Memorial Quilt*. Conceived in 1985 by activist Cleve Jones in San Francisco, the quilt began as a response to the dehumanizing statistics of the AIDS epidemic. After founding the NAMES Project Foundation to preserve the quilts and their stories and inspire continued advocacy, Jones and several volunteers revealed the quilt during the National March on Washington for Lesbian and Gay Rights in 1987.[130] Composed of over fifty thousand individual panels, each measuring roughly the dimensions of a grave plot, the quilt translated grief into a raw and vulnerable form that showed the impact of AIDS and HIV. Although the disease's impact is not exclusive to Black people, it is impossible to discuss the *AIDS Memorial Quilt* without naming the fact that the AIDS epidemic has disproportionately impacted Black communities in the United States. Despite making up about 12 percent of the US population, Black people have accounted for nearly 40 percent of HIV diagnoses and deaths related to AIDS due to a variety of social and economic barriers.[131]

Many of the quilt's blocks commemorate Black lives and honor their stories. Just as items might be placed atop an altar or shrine, these blocks are adorned with elements that reflect the cultural and communal ties of the individuals they honor. For example, some panels incorporate African wax print and kente fabrics. Others feature words like *empathy*, *compassion*, and *acceptance*, symbolizing the care and love for a family member who may have been stigmatized by society because of their diagnosis. Some panels integrate religious symbols, family photos, and personal mementos. The quilt also honors monumental cultural producers such as Gil Scott-Heron and Fela Kuti, underscoring the gravity of the losses inflicted by the epidemic. Through the quilt, the loved ones who remain are able to transform statistics into stories and numbers into names.[132]

Today the *AIDS Memorial Quilt* has transcended its initial role as a memorial to become a tool for education and advocacy. It continues to be displayed worldwide, challenging the ongoing societal stigma and discrimination associated with AIDS, especially as it pertains to marginalized people. Bridging veneration and advocacy, the NAMES Project Foundation uses the quilt to foster spaces for healing and dialogue, pushing for changes in policy and the perception of the epidemic. Most importantly, the quilt provides a place for those who lost their lives to be remembered for the entirety of their lives rather than just their diagnosis.

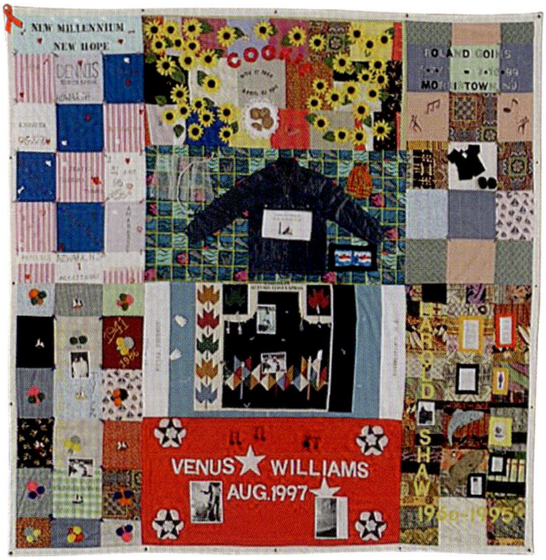

AIDS Memorial Quilt, block 5442. Names featured: Dennis Howarth, Cookie, Archie E. Friday, Roland Goins, Beatrice Tyler, Adrianne Tyler, Venus Williams, Harold Shaw

HONORING DOUGLASS TURNER

Lauren Austin uses images of her family in figurative quilting to capture the transition between life and death and to preserve her memories of a loved one in a peaceful way. Caring for her uncle, Douglass Turner, during his illness impacted her in a profound way, resulting in lingering sadness and hurt over how her uncle and their family were treated within the hospital system. She created drawings of her uncle and other loved ones while at the hospital to reduce her stress, and later was encouraged by a friend to translate them into large-scale quilts.[133] The resulting works, *Our Vision of His Transition* (2020) and *Paid for Pain* (2022), delve into the complexities of grief, dignity, and remembrance.

Our Vision of His Transition reimagines Austin's uncle's final moments, placing him not within the cold confines of a hospital but instead showing him resting peacefully amid the natural landscapes he cherished. Austin created the quilt to reframe her uncle's transition as one of serenity and unity with nature, free from the sterility and chaos of a medical facility. In contrast, *Paid for Pain* captures the stark reality of her uncle's hospital experience. Created as an accompanying piece to *Our Vision*, *Paid for Pain* portrays a clinical environment and the emotional toll of prolonged suffering. There is an absence of color, reflecting the harsh, cold feeling of his hospital room and the reality of what was to come. The juxtaposition of these two works offers two perspectives on the emotions around death, one that acknowledges the pain of a loved one's decline and another that seeks solace in reimagination and acceptance.

Rather than using specific items that belonged to her uncle, Austin combines hand-dyed, printed, and painted fabrics to reference his life. In *Our Vision*, her family is surrounded by live oak trees (an homage to his outdoorsmanship in the Florida forests) and birds (which speak to his bird-watching hobby). When describing her intentions, she reflected, "I wanted to envision what he would have wanted: resting in his beloved wild spaces with creatures and plants all around. The idea comforts me."[134] Austin's effort to reframe how she remembers her uncle is both an act of healing and a reclamation of joy while navigating loss.

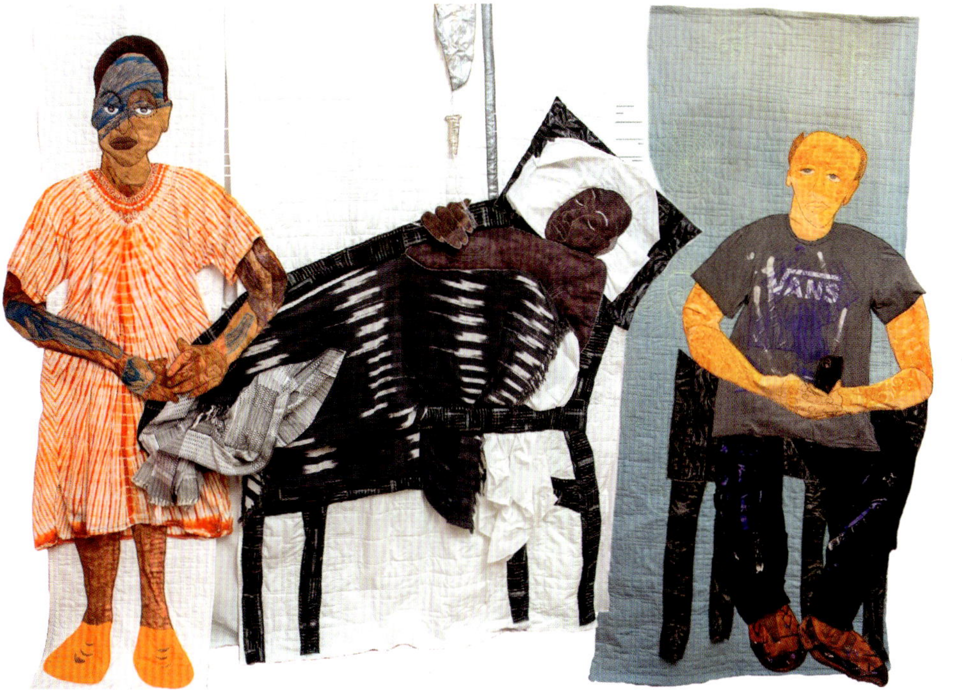

Paid for Pain,
Lauren Austin, 2022

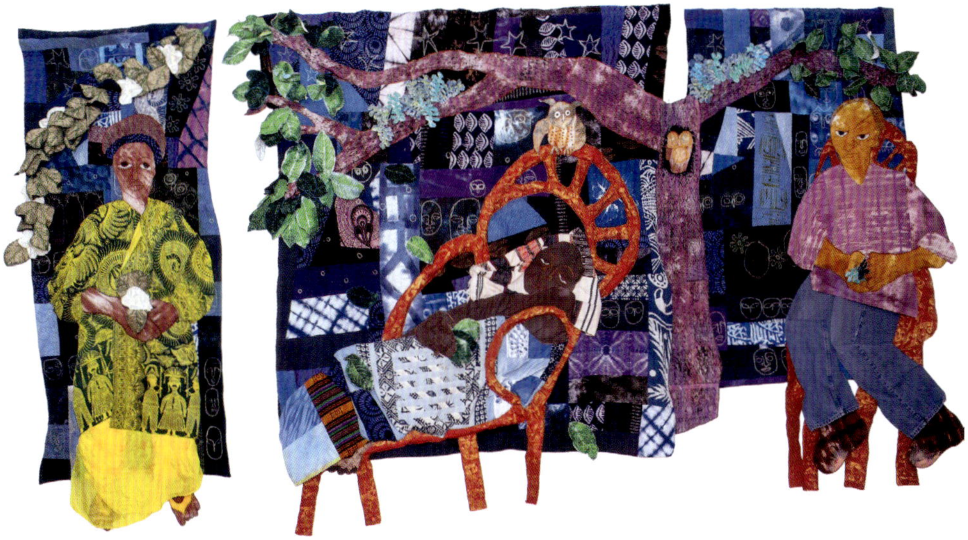

Our Vision of His Transition,
Lauren Austin, 2020

HONORING LAKE APOPKA FARMWORKERS

The *Lake Apopka Farmworker Memorial Quilt*, spearheaded by former farmworker Linda Lee, remembers Black agricultural laborers who faced health challenges and lost their lives due to pesticide exposure. Lake Apopka, in Florida, suffered damage to its ecosystem due to pollution, especially from the mid-twentieth century onward. In the 1940s, a levee was created to drain parts of the lake's wetlands, transforming twenty thousand acres into farmland. This led to the cultivation of crops and the application of pesticides such as DDT. The chemicals not only polluted the lake but also had serious health implications for the farmworkers laboring in the fields.[135]

Lake Apopka Farmworker Memorial Quilt, Lake Apopka Farmworkers, 2012

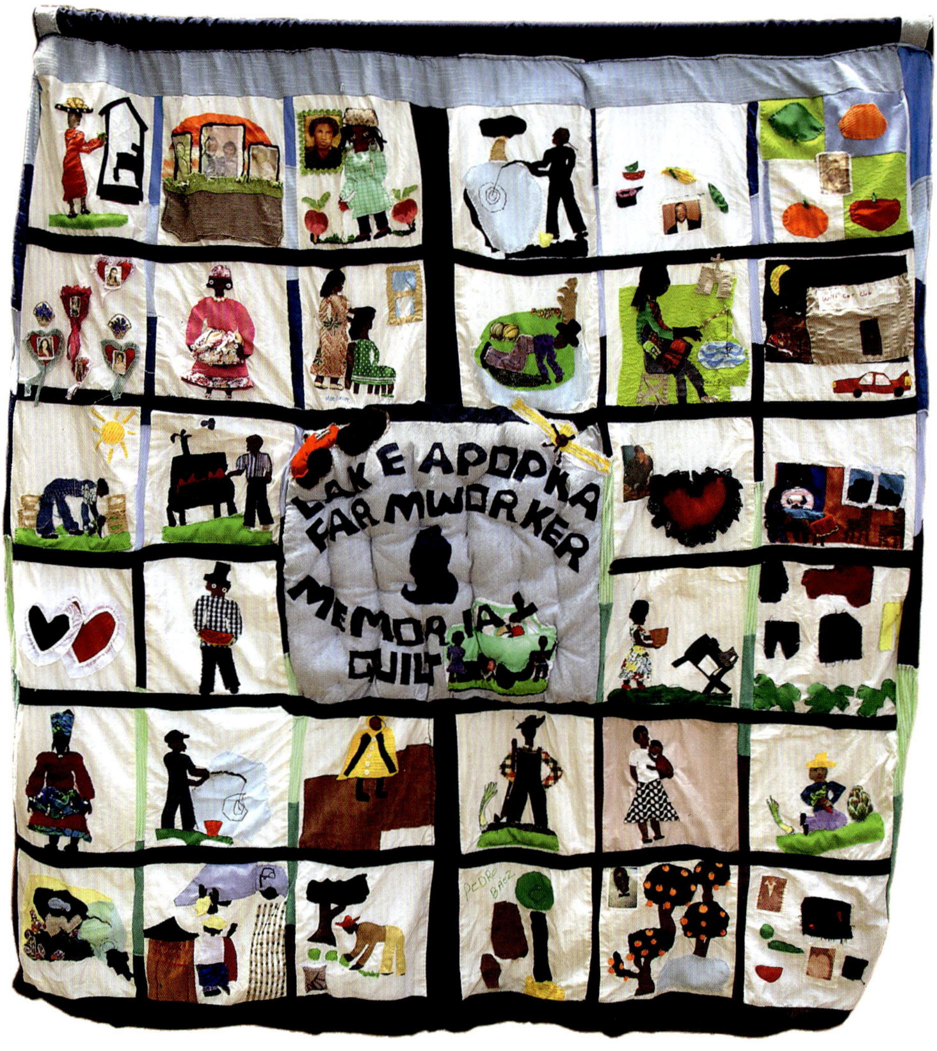

Over time, runoff from the fields carried toxins into the lake, and by the late 1990s the lake had become a wasteland. Following a government buyout, thousands of farmworkers—most from African American, Hispanic, and Haitian communities—faced economic hardship and significant health declines because of their prolonged exposure to hazardous pesticides. Reports indicated elevated incidents of illnesses such as lupus, cancer, and other chronic conditions among the group. Despite the evident connections between the polluted lake and their well-being, these communities received little attention and support, with most of the focus going to environmental restoration.[136]

The Farmworker Association of Florida (FWAF) chose to honor the affected farmworkers and raise public consciousness about their plight. This led to the creation of the *Lake Apopka Farmworker Memorial Quilt*, which narrates the workers' stories, featuring both their challenges and their triumphs. Lee, who started working on the farms when she was eight years old, has had multiple operations and still faces complications from kidney failure and lupus.[137] Despite having to tend to her own health, she has committed her life to ensuring that the deaths of her colleagues was not in vain. In a 2017 interview she described how the quilt came to be after the passing of her sister:

I decided to make sure—I promised the Lord—give me the strength to finish this quilt. It's to bring awareness of the chemicals that we have worked so hard in. . . . Because a lot of people who have worked in the fields were actually sick. Had headaches. A lot of pregnant women. A lot of people who were wracked in pain in the field, but yet still they worked to try to make a living. I try to get as many people that I knew in Apopka that lost a loved one, that worked on the farm. But I missed a lot of people because a lot of them had already died.[138]

Lee embedded her community members' stories in the quilt, ensuring the victims' sacrifices and struggles are neither forgotten nor overlooked. Despite facing environmental and medical neglect, the community continues to join together in support of the Memorial Quilt Project to voice its concern and honor its members.

HONORING VICTIMS OF LYNCHING AND RACIAL VIOLENCE

Strange Fruit: A Century of Lynching and Murder 1865–1965 is April Anue Shipp's call to never forget the thousands of Black lives taken by lynching during a dark chapter in American history. This monumental 10-by-10½-foot quilt meticulously lists the names of approximately five thousand Black individuals who were lynched between 1865 and 1965.[139] The inception of *Strange Fruit* was deeply personal and spiritual for Shipp. In 1999, while reading *The Face of Our Past*, a book featured on *The Oprah Winfrey Show*, she encountered a harrowing photograph of Laura Nelson and her son, Lawrence, who were lynched in Okemah, Oklahoma, in 1911. The image raised Shipp's awareness of the fact that women were also victims of lynching. She reflected on the horror she was faced with, thinking, "If an angry mob came after my boy, what would I do? Who do you turn to for help when the whole town is coming after your child?"[140]

This emotional encounter led Shipp to a moment of spiritual clarity. She recalls, "I believe I heard the spirit of God say to me, 'Find their names and make a quilt.'"[141] Despite her initial reservations about the magnitude of the task, she dedicated three years to researching and embroidering the names of lynching victims onto the quilt. She described her process: "I would get off work and come home and sew and make dinner and come back and sew and give the kids baths and come back and sew, for three years."[142] The quilt's title, *Strange Fruit*, refers to the haunting song recorded by Billie Holiday in 1939, which immortalizes the horror of lynching that African Americans faced in the South. The song itself is a protest against racial violence, and Shipp's quilt extends its legacy by providing a visual representation of the individuals who suffered this tragedy. In her dedication, Shipp also honors Ida B. Wells, who actively campaigned against lynching.

Beyond its role in capturing history, the quilt functions as an altar and a moment of repair for the departed. "The people on my quilt didn't get funerals," Shipp says. "No one brought them flowers. No one came

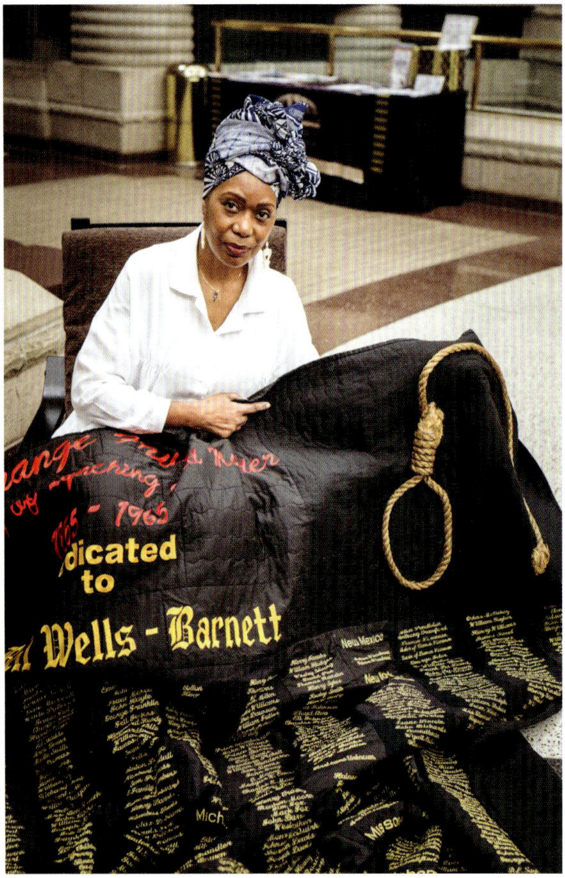

April Anue Shipp pictured with *Strange Fruit*

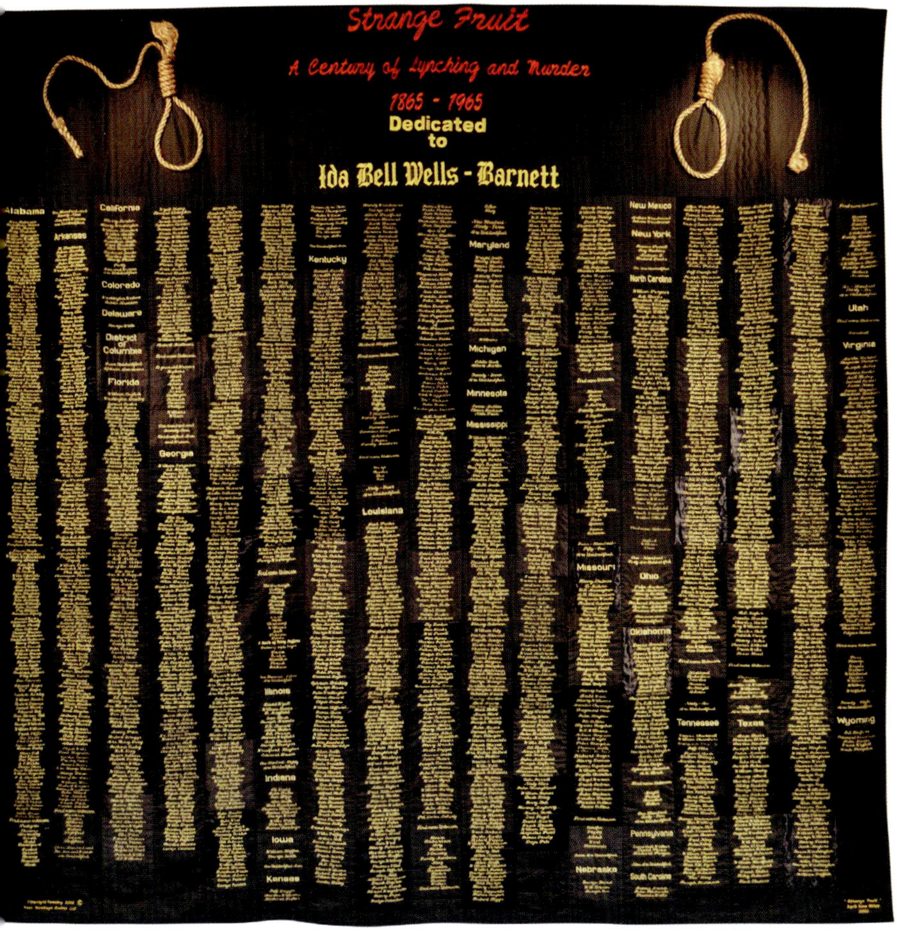

Strange Fruit: A Century of Lynching and Murder 1865–1965, April Anue Shipp, 2002

and sang any songs over their bodies."[143] By carefully stitching each name with gold thread on black fabric, she elevated these individuals, symbolizing the preciousness of their lives in a society that saw them as less than human. Shipp also used various shades of black fabric to represent the diversity within the African American community, as well as varied textures—ranging from silk to denim—to signify the social positions of the victims.[144]

Strange Fruit has elicited profound emotional responses from viewers. Shipp recalled an encounter at an exhibition where a woman discovered her grandfather's name on the quilt.[145] Reflecting on the quilt's significance, Shipp noted, "I cried every day I worked on it. . . . I still cry when I touch it. If no one else remembers their names, I remember them."

Sacred Space

I quilt to release the colors of my soul. Quilting has gotten me through heartaches, bad jobs, illness, and loss. In the darkest times, manipulating fabric and thread reminded me that bad times don't last forever. In a way, quilting is a metaphor for living. Life can shatter you but you have the choice to take all the pieces and put them together to make something beautiful.

—Angee Turner[146]

Quilts are one way that Black women show care for others, themselves, and moments that impact the world at large. Quilting has functioned not only as a domestic task but also as a healing practice, deeply connected to spiritual and emotional wellness. Through generations, quilting has offered a place to return to oneself. Sitting with a work in progress is an act of self-regulation, community building, and cultural continuity in the face of historical and ongoing harm. Many quilters will tell you that making quilts is a process grounded in intention. The combination of cutting, piecing, and stitching creates a meditative rhythm that quiets the mind and engages the body. In the act of quilting, women make space to process their thoughts. It opens up space to grieve, imagine, and heal. While quilting requires attention and presence, it also leaves room for the mind to wander, to return to the present, and to contemplate the future. In this way, quilting becomes an embodied mindfulness practice.

Black quilters have stitched while nursing the sick or recovering from life's many challenges—personal stress, illness, racial violence, and more. Midwives and caregivers have often quilted as part of their broader care practices. Some quilters have incorporated meaningful fabrics or symbols that held personal or shared significance. Others have quilted in groups, strengthening social ties while sharing wisdom and collective strategies for survival. In both solitary and communal settings, quilting has allowed women to weave themselves back into the world after loss, trauma, or exhaustion.

The physical act of stitching mirrors an emotional mending process that creates a sense of balance and restores order. To understand quilting as a healing practice is to understand how Black women have made space for themselves—psychologically, spiritually, and emotionally—in a world that too often demands their labor but denies their rest. On top of that, there is a long history of navigating the expectations of white traditionalism and a false sense of "correctness" that seeks to police what Black quilters produce. By understanding the sacredness of quilting, we learn how Black women have used quilts to heal, witness, liberate, and stitch the things that could not be easily spoken.

Crafting Care

The legacy of Black granny midwives in the American South is rooted in care and survival. These women, often elder figures in their communities, used ancestral knowledge to offer birthing support shaped by a spiritual calling.[147] Within this history, quilts were present not merely as domestic objects, but also as silent witnesses to birth, labor, and comfort. In rural Black communities, where medical segregation and poverty made institutional care inaccessible or untrustworthy, granny midwives filled the gap. Birth often took place in homes warmed by stoves, undoubtedly surrounded by quilts that bore witness to the transitions of life. Quilts served a practical use, providing warmth for laboring mothers and newborns. The midwife might place a quilt beneath the birthing woman, to protect both the bed and the sacredness of new life.

But quilts also held economic and symbolic value in midwifery. Cash was scarce and bartering was common. Oral histories reveal that some midwives were paid in chickens, vegetables, or handmade goods, including quilts.[148] In certain cases, the midwife herself might have been a quilter and might have used a quilting circle as an informal space for sharing knowledge. Though limited archival evidence exists linking specific granny midwives to quiltmaking, photographs and oral traditions

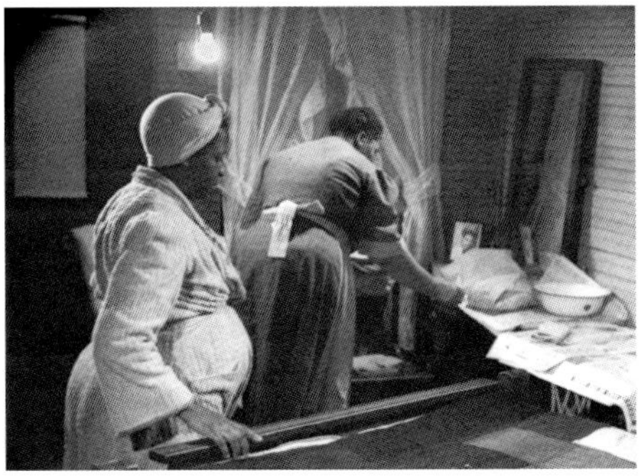

Image of Mary Francis Hill Coley and Expectant Mother Martha Butler Sapp, Robert Galbraith, 1952

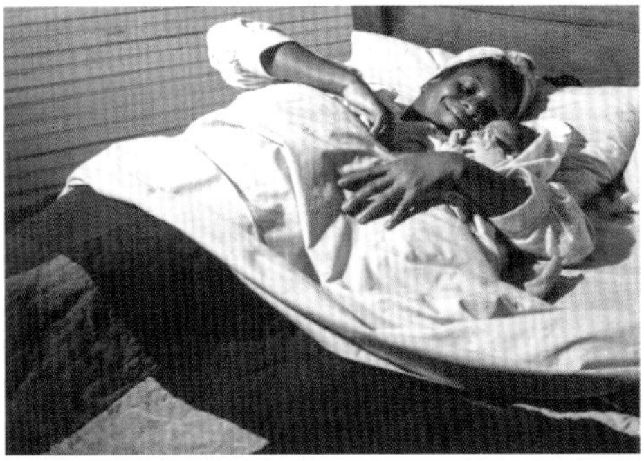

Sapp and Her Newborn at Rest, Robert Galbraith, 1952

hint at their proximity. In a still photograph from the renowned 1950s documentary *All My Babies*, a mother and newborn rest under a quilt shortly after a home birth, having been assisted by Georgia midwife Mary Francis Hill Coley.

The image captures a moment when fabric, family, and midwifery intersect. In her autobiography, *Listen to Me Good* (1996), midwife and quilter Margaret Smith discusses a multitude of uses for quilts, including menstrual cleanliness and labor preparation. She describes how quilts were incorporated into delivery in drafty homes, both as a way to keep out the cold and to manage contractions:

When it comes time to deliver, most of them want you to fold a quilt and put it down on the floor and turn down a straight back chair like that one yonder with the cane seat bottom. You put the pillows on the back of it. Turn it down where they can be halfway sitting up like, and their bottom part be scooted out. Somebody holds their bottom part and somebody holds their knees. You take this chair and turn it down

Witness: Honoring the Legacy of the Grand Midwives, Bekezela Mguni, 2020

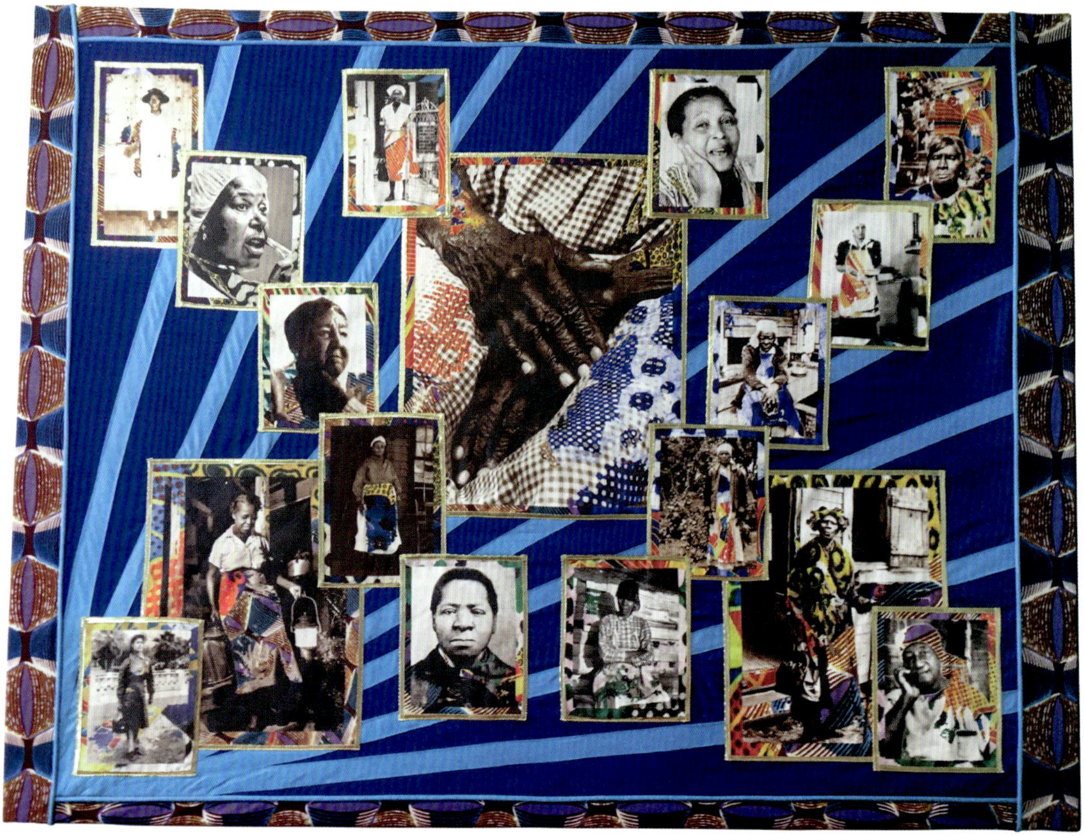

where she could feel the heat from the fireplace. The mother can't get cold, cause if she gets too cold, that's going to cut the pains down.[149]

The cultural resonance of the quilt in Black birthing spaces persists. In contemporary memorials to granny midwives such as *Witness: Honoring the Legacy of the Grand Midwives* by Bekezela Mguni, Black women's ways of knowing, which transcended scientific knowledge, are revered and celebrated. Granny midwives' sacred knowledge advanced reproductive health and ensured generations of Black babies were able to thrive.

Stitching the Spirit

The sacredness of quilts and quilting for Black women is not always easily discernible. There are times in which the act of making itself is seen as sacred. In other instances, the quilt is used as a tool for sharing stories of healing, growth, and repair.

ROSEMARY OLLISON

Rosemary Ollison talks about quilting as a lifeline. Born in 1942 and raised on a plantation in Arkansas until her grandfather died, she migrated to Milwaukee at age sixteen. It wasn't until 1994 that she started quiltmaking, in response to the trauma of an abusive marriage and years of depression. She describes the motivation to create as a sudden experience, "inspired by a passage of scripture and a desire to be healed."[150] Ollison says the prayer that anchored her was Psalm 139:23–24, which reads, "Search me, God, and know my heart; test me and know my anxious thoughts. See if there is any offensive way in me, and lead me in the way everlasting."[151] She began with drawings, creating over a thousand images in a few years, often portraying Black womanhood rooted in confidence and celebration.

From drawing, she transitioned to quilts and other textile works, using fabric scraps, leather, beads, costume jewelry, and other discarded materials in an intuitive way. Her use of found objects transcends thrift

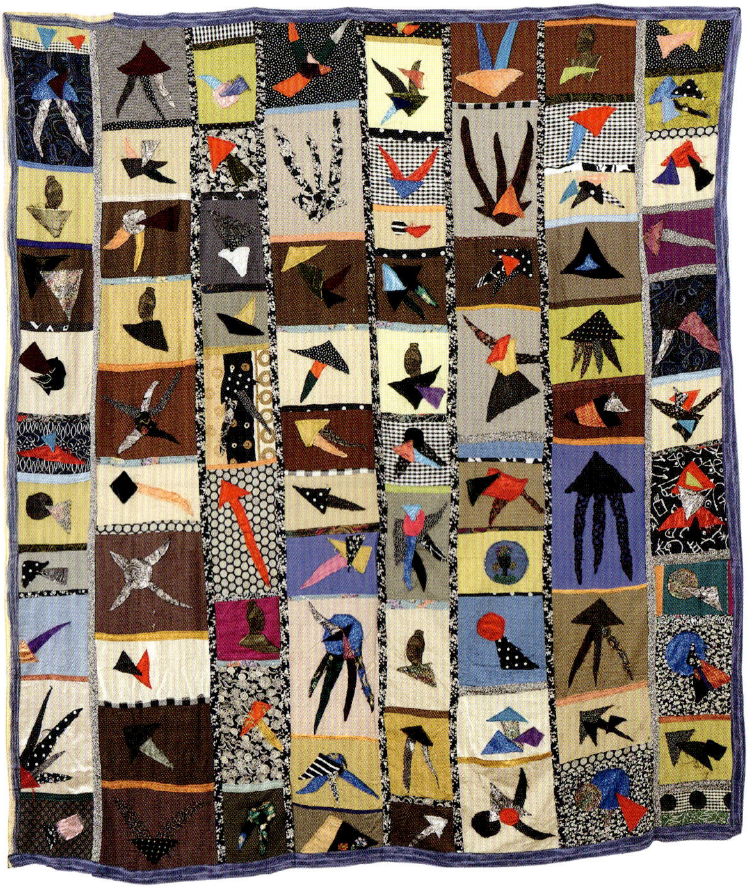

Comet Quilt, Rosemary Ollison, date unknown

and becomes a philosophical and spiritual act. She views her process as a way to commune with God, saying, "When I am creating I am satisfied, I am free! I no longer just exist, I am alive! I do not feel worthless, hopeless, alone, sad, afraid, ashamed, guilty, down hearted, unloved, uncared for, doubtful, and discontented and the like. . . . I can see the real me in my works."[152]

In quilting Ollison found a practice that stabilized her, giving structure to her emotions and an outlet for her stories. Her home is now an all-encompassing artistic shrine with stitched curtains, woven sculptures, and tiled walls that match the internal world she channels into her work. Her creative process is meditative and deeply embodied. Each finished quilt is an offering to herself and a mirror of the possibilities

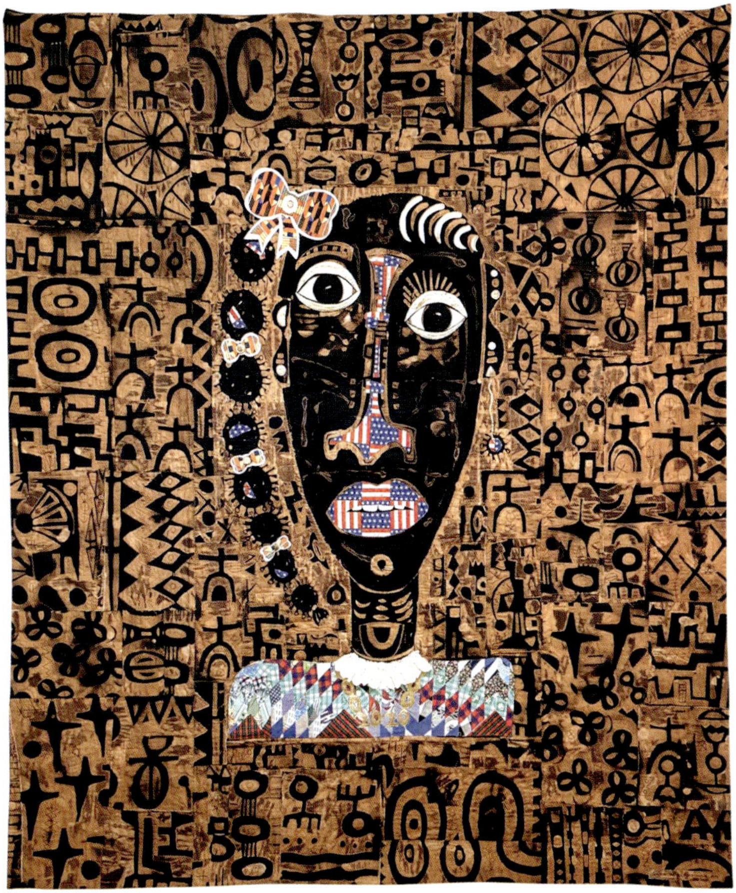

Portrait of Resilience, Sharon Kerry-Harlan, 2021

of who she can be. They have given her the ability to find meaning and wholeness. The *Comet Quilt* is one of her largest and most iconic works. A self-portrait of her personal evolution, it is composed of vivid colors and radiant bursts of patterns that speak to a life that collided with pain but has continued moving forward.

SHARON KERRY-HARLAN

Sharon Kerry-Harlan joins together the pain of the present and hope for the future in *Portrait of Resilience*. Using printed fabric and remnants of an antique quilt, she depicts a young Black girl as a symbol of persistence in the wake of national crisis. Created during the height of the COVID-19 pandemic, Harlan's quilt reflects that historical moment.[153]

The girl wears a bubble braided hairstyle adorned with African kente cloth bows. Each segment of her braid resembles a particle of the COVID-19 virus. A golden necklace with the year "2020" makes the reference clear. Her face is constructed from parts of the American flag, tying together a complicated relationship to national identity and belonging. Although the quilt seems playful and unassuming at first glance, deeper reflection reveals a commentary about the disproportionate effects of the virus on the Black community at the time, in addition to the heightened political climate.[154] Kerry-Harlan's use of an antique patchwork quilt as the girl's blouse adds another layer of meaning, showing how the past can still shape the present. Through this incorporation of older textiles into a new work, the artist gestures to the long history of Black women's creative labor and resourcefulness, particularly in times of upheaval.

Portrait of Resilience is not only about looking back. It also offers a way forward. Kerry-Harlan has personally described the work as a meditation on how African Americans and their allies continue to advocate for justice and a better future, even under extreme circumstances. Her quilt, then, is not simply about the COVID-19 pandemic; it's about how people respond to uncertainty with care and togetherness in order to strengthen those who are most vulnerable and least attended to.

DAWN WILLIAMS BOYD

Dawn Williams Boyd treats fabric as a site of refuge. In her cloth paintings—as she calls them—she quilts histories that are both personal and collective. Her subject matter spans a wide spectrum, primarily reckoning with violences of the past and exploring the levity found in everyday life. Boyd credits quilting with providing an important space for processing hard feelings. In a 2022 interview she described her practice as a cherished sanctuary, saying, "I get to work out all of the anger. All of my anger gets to come through my brain, through my fingers, into my artwork. I am happiest—and, at my age, I'm about making myself happy—when I am making artwork."[155] Early in her life, she was responsible for managing a busy home, raising children while also navigating a career, which took her away from creating. Now, she says, making art is "absolutely a sanctuary for me. It is where I am engaged. It's where I'm safe. It's where I am calm. That's not always true because

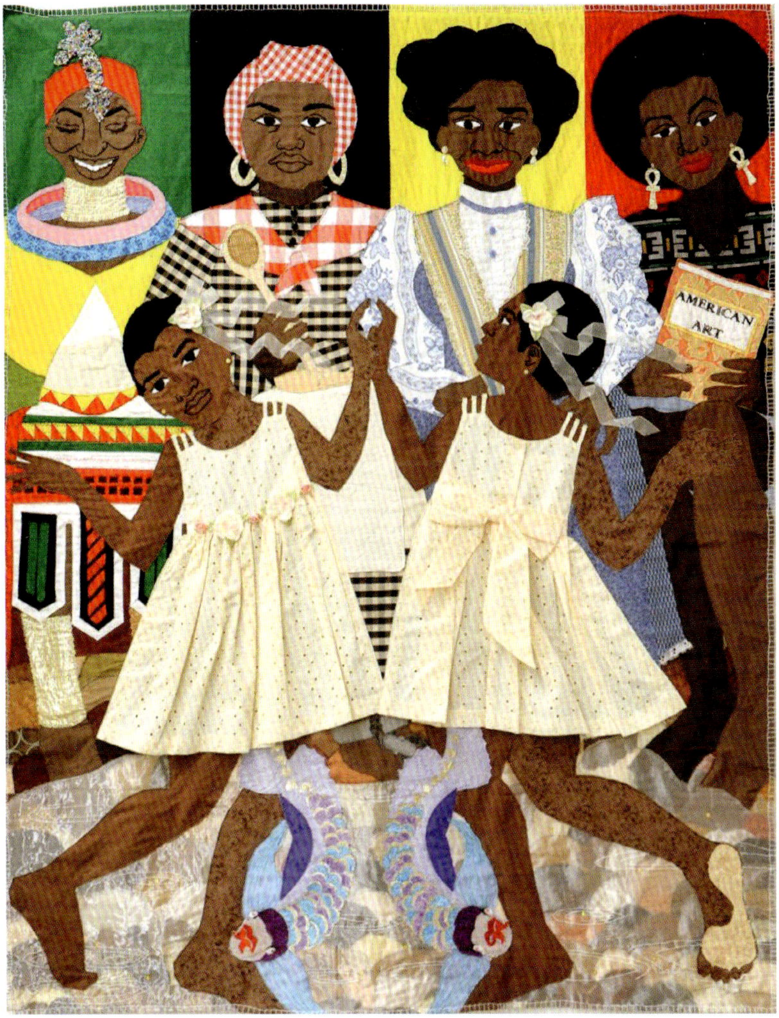

Piscean Dancer, Dawn Williams Boyd, 2016

sometimes I get overwrought because it's not happening the way I want it to happen. But 99 percent of the time I am a happy camper."[156]

Boyd's approach to constructing her work leans into experimentation and freedom. While instructing a class on the work of Faith Ringgold, she learned about Ringgold's practice of quilting onto canvas stretched over a wooden frame. The rectangular canvas structure provided a rigid working surface to assemble the top of the quilt. The completed composition was then removed from the four-sided frame to bind and finish it, leaving a piece that more closely resembles a traditional quilt structure. This inspired Boyd to explore making outside of her traditional painting practice, eventually shifting to fabric in place of paint. She is now able to "liberate" fabric from the bolt and herself from being pigeonholed into one mode of making.[157]

While some of Boyd's most notable works highlight racial terror, political injustice, and gendered trauma, *Piscean Dancer* offers something different. It is a personal statement about intergenerational love and the sacrifices that allowed generations of Black women to grow and become self-actualized. Boyd says, "I started thinking about the African American and Black women throughout history, all of the things that we have had to learn, the situations we have had to adapt to and the things that we have brought with us, from our ancestors through today, and the things that have been important for us."[158]

In the quilt, two young Black girls dance in a circle, representing the duality and fluidity of Pisces—a tribute to Boyd's zodiac sign. She continues to infuse references to her sun sign, using dragonfish as a nod to her birth year (1952, the Year of the Water Dragon) and her connection to the town of Neptune, New Jersey. The heart of the piece, however, is the women who surround the dancing girls. These figures are inspired by the Ndebele women of southern Africa, postslavery domestic workers, early twentieth-century Black women, and women of the 1970s, bold in their adornment and their politics.

Boyd sees all these foremothers as artists in their own right. Whether painting homes or repurposing cloth scraps into quilts, they alchemized what they had into something new. The four women stand in a stone-filled pond, representing the weight of the struggles they carried—yet the girls dance anyway. Their movement symbolizes the joy and possibility provided by those ancestors, even if they couldn't always experience it themselves.

Sophia Goddess of Wisdom I, Torreah "Cookie" Washington, 2012

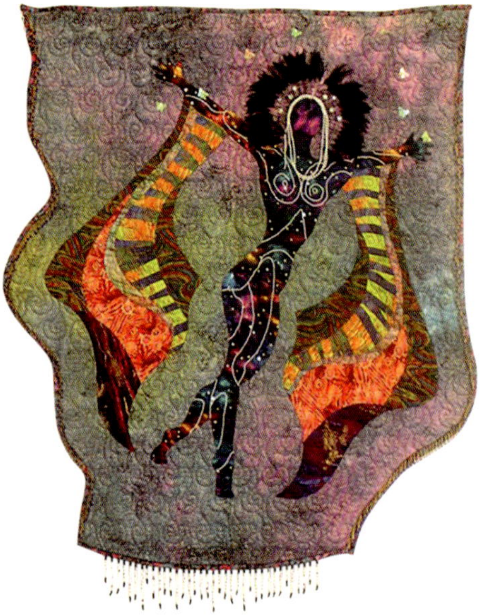

COOKIE WASHINGTON

The divine feminine intersects beautifully with African diasporic heritage in Cookie Washington's work, especially her goddess quilts. Her process is shaped by her belief in the transcendence of cloth; she says that textiles emit a kind of spirit or energy that separates them from other materials.[159] Washington uses the medium to honor the sacredness of womanhood across time and space, channeling the goddesses' strength, grace, and wisdom. She wants women like her to feel uplifted: "We Black women are not coming up

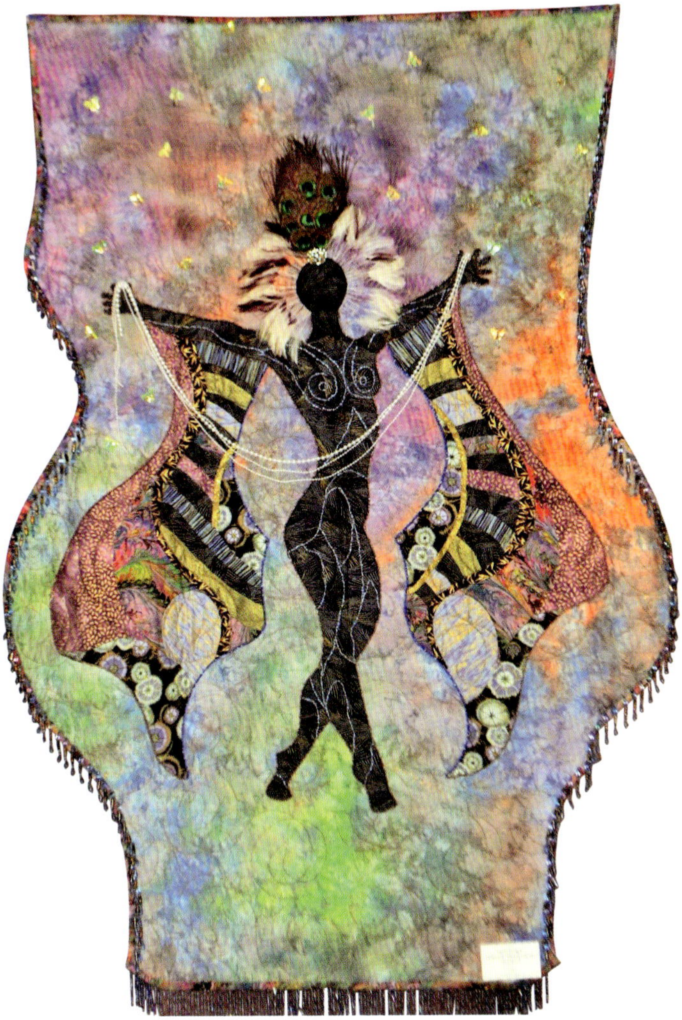

Sophia Goddess of Wisdom II, Torreah "Cookie" Washington, 2023

from slavery; we are coming down from being worshiped as deities. I want them to know that Black women were not just slaves and domestics, but also Amazonian goddesses, queens, and warriors."[160]

Sophia Goddess of Wisdom embodies this sentiment. Washington frames Sophia as "the Sacred Dark Feminine" who is able to hold space for people in the valleys of their lives. She describes Sophia as

the one who is with you in your darkest hour, who loves you at your worst, who faces disaster with you, and embraces you with her strong, loving arms. She knows the darkness and leads you out of it. To "live in the lap" of the Sacred Dark Feminine is to be in the embrace of the most complete love imaginable, to be safe, encouraged, and transformed in miraculous ways.[161]

With her arms outstretched, Sophia welcomes in all who seek her comfort. For Washington, that comfort was extended by so many real women who fit within Sophia's archetype. Through their guidance, prayers, and assistance, she was affirmed, supported, and able to grow into her fullness. As a result, she believes Sophia can exist in any woman, and she challenges viewers to engage with the sacred and the personal, determining how they see this femininity within themselves.

In 2022 Washington took her exploration of women's inner worlds a step further by curating *All That We Carry: The Epic Stitchers and Friends*. The show, which featured quilters along with dyers, basket weavers, and ceramicists, examined what Black people carry throughout their everyday lives and the journeys they have taken toward growth and healing. Inspired by the book *All That She Carried* by Tiya Miles, the show focused on a primary question: What is in the invisible emotional sack that Black women and men carry every day?[162]

Washington recognizes that acknowledging and sharing feelings has not always been safe for Black women. Whether dismissed at home or out in the world, they are often required to smother or compartmentalize certain emotions for the sake of progress. Eventually, Washington decided that she had a choice: to be defined by her pain or to start a journey toward personal happiness. She remains hopeful about the possibilities that emerge when you commit to healing. "When we heal," Washington says, "it unlocks all the joy that's held captive inside of us. So, can we carry joy alongside our pain? Joy in these times requires radical self-care. In the end, I am choosing to carry Joy in my sack. . . . So how will you show the public through your art, what's in your sack?"[163]

TINA WILLIAMS BREWER

Quilting is both a practice of mindfulness and an artistic outlet for Tina Williams Brewer. She began quilting in her mid-thirties, noting that material "became the purpose."[164] She believes in the connections between people and inanimate objects and believes quilts to be a safe space to process trauma. In her creative process, Brewer emphasizes the importance of listening over planning: "When I create a piece, I need silence to listen to the words inside myself."[165] She treats the process as a ritual, allowing space for intuition and spirit to guide her hands. She uses quilting to work through things internally, calling it her "own personal meditation and personal research" led by emotions and feelings.[166] With those emotions and the movement suggested by the shapes embedded in her quilts, she hopes to stir something up in the viewer.

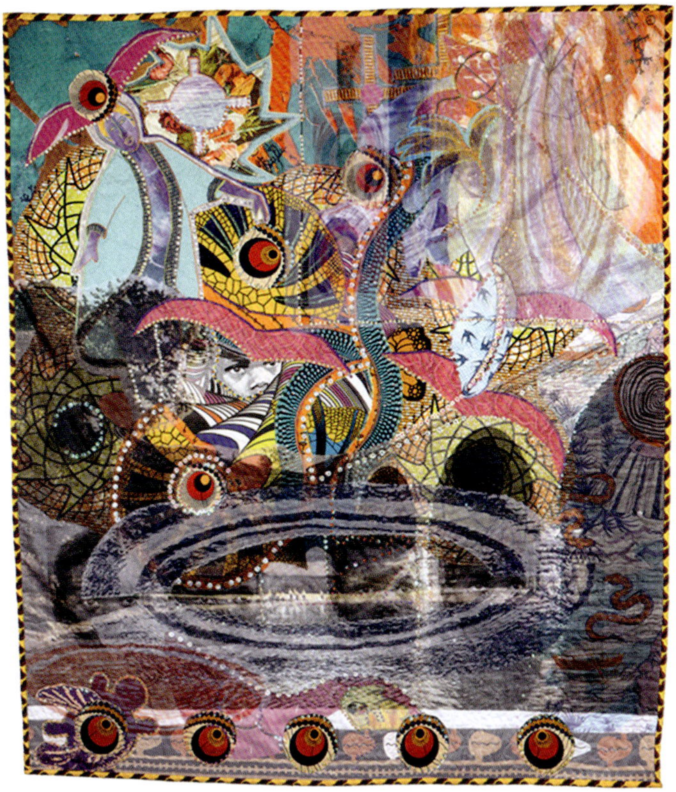

Sequences: Soul Spirit Heart from the *Oar Up or Down* series, Tina Williams Brewer, 2023

Brewer likens her quilts to sacred cloth and invokes ancestral connections through layered imagery. She incorporates symbolism like adinkra symbols, crossroads, rivers, and suns as a way to connect with spirit. The concept of *sankofa*—learning from the past in order to move toward a better future—is a guiding principle for her practice. This visual symbolism, deeply rooted in African cosmologies and African American spiritual traditions, recurs throughout her quilts. Her relationship to water also holds personal importance. "The theme of 'living waters' can be seen throughout my life's work," Brewer says. "They are cleansing, healing and refreshing to the soul."[167]

In her series *Oar Up or Down*, Brewer gives water new meaning. She uses this series to explore the choices we are faced with in life. From Brewer's perspective, we can either use the oar to actively paddle through the water toward a clear path, or we can remove the oar from the water and passively surrender to its spirit. In pieces like *Sequences: Soul Spirit Heart*, viewers are asked to "take on a more celestial way," to think about the crossroads of life and the symbolism that can be found if we are anchored enough to listen.[168] Rather than using clearly defined imagery, Brewer layers fabric and found objects in a way that invites you to use your own inner knowing and experience to receive the quilt's message. The water at the bottom of the piece acts as a portal that can carry you forward to your next destination.

Brewer uses quilts to elevate the beauty and joy found in togetherness and the fortitude found in spiritual connectedness. Her work, she says, "is an expression of the deep pain of racism and the pathways forward, the resilience of African American families and the light that lifts them up. My intention is to give dignity to human suffering, finding rhythms that are both mind-stirring and soul-soothing."[169]

SONJA HENDERSON

Sonja Henderson's practice sits at the crossroads of public memory and intimate repair. A sculptor, mixed-media artist, and community healer, she is perhaps best known for her monument to Mamie Till-Mobley and Emmett Till, yet her work with the Mothers Healing Circle in Chicago's Lawndale neighborhood offers an equally powerful form of memorial: a quilted practice of community care, created by and for mothers who have lost their children to violence.[170]

The genesis of the Mothers Healing Circle is inseparable from Henderson's own personal story. In 2019, she experienced a series of devastating losses—her brother, father, and grandmother passed within weeks of each other. While coping with personal grief, she started MHC with a group of bereaved mothers through a local clinic. Their children had died in public ways—through gun violence, vehicular accidents, or state-sanctioned harm—leaving families shattered and memories suspended in trauma. The Mothers Healing Circle emerged in response to that need for release, remembrance, and repair.

Before formally organizing the Mothers Healing Circle, Henderson led the mothers through the creation of a piece that was both a quilt and a structure, a 10-by-10-foot tent with story-quilt walls, each panel representing a child's life. "They were drawing, embroidering, appliquéing," Henderson recalls. "Each square told the story of a different child that was lost."[171] She and her mother then sewed the pieces together while grieving their own losses, literally stitching through sorrow. The tent's interior was hand dyed with indigo; it offered viewers a place to pause, reflect, and breathe after witnessing the weight of these stories. The finished piece, *Harbor for Mending Hearts*, laid the foundation for what would become a sustained communal practice, with the mothers meeting regularly to connect, heal, and create.

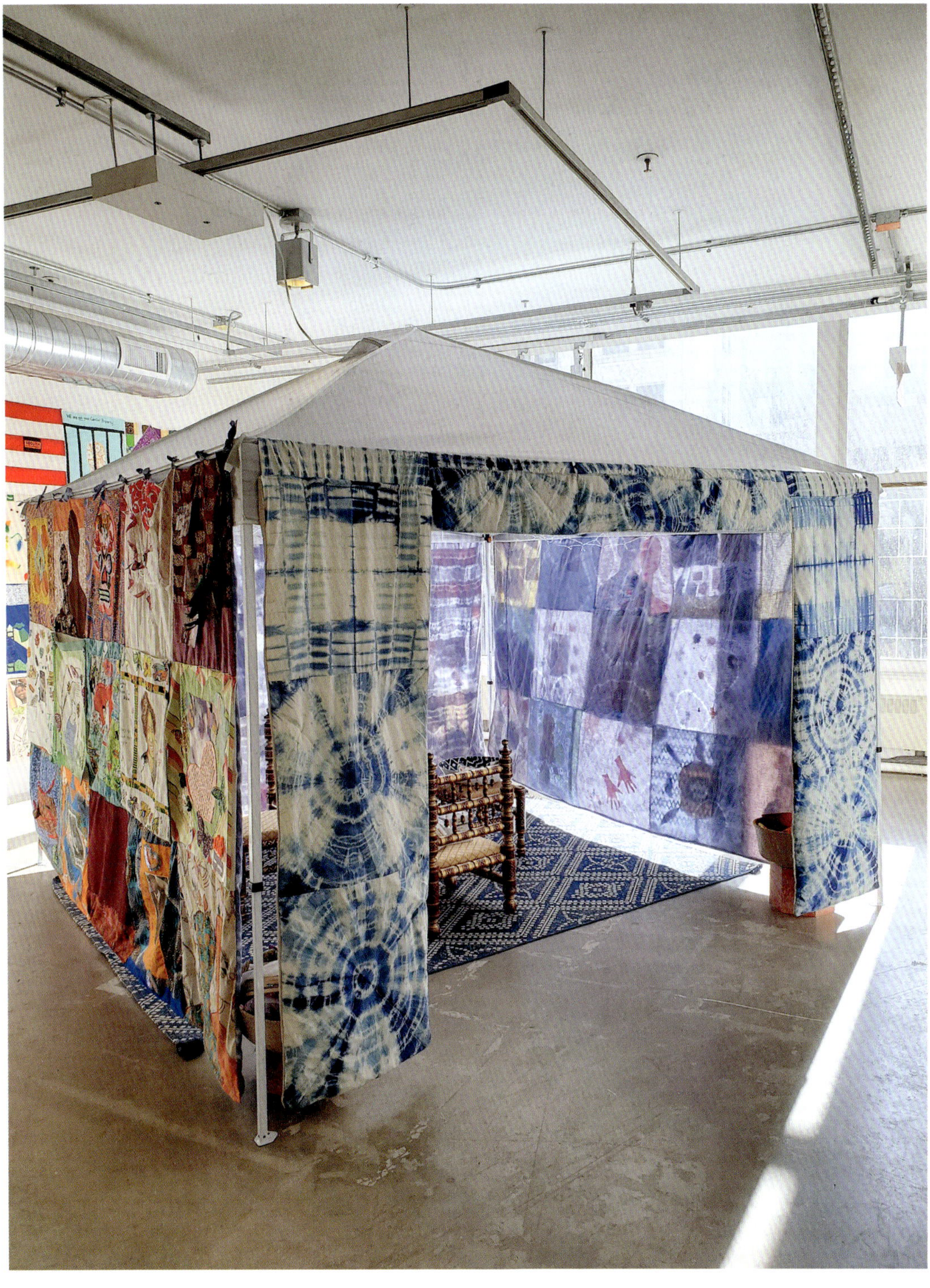

Harbor for Mending Hearts, Sonja Henderson and Mothers Healing Circle, 2019

Henderson describes quilting as a meditative technology. It is not just the act of making, but its repetition—one stitch at a time—that becomes a portal for healing. "The motion of stitching, pushing the needle in and pulling it out, grounds you. It's like touching the heavens and coming back to earth," she reflects.[172] Henderson sees sewing as a way to reconnect the frayed threads of body, memory, and spirit. The Mother's Healing Circle uses this process to stabilize the nervous system, to recenter the self in the present, and to allow space for storytelling that moves beyond photographs and obituaries.

The group's later project, *We Are Made from Stars*, draws on the rich history of the star quilt. Star quilts, traditionally composed of diamond shapes that are assembled into an eight-pointed star, are often gifted in Indigenous communities to mark births and deaths. Henderson sourced unfinished star quilt tops and invited mothers to choose colors and themes that honored their children. Combining appliqué with personal narrative, the quilt tops became intricate visual tributes. When we spoke, Henderson emphasized that these were still in progress, not yet quilted, and that she planned to complete them through communal quilting bees. It is her hope that the broader community can participate in the labor of caring for these mothers. "The mothers need that experience, too," she explains, "because it's in that collective stitching—when everyone adds their thread—that the energy transforms."[173]

Recognizing the intensity of the mothers' grief and their emotional attachment to the quilt tops, Henderson had them digitized and

Mothers Healing Circle gathering

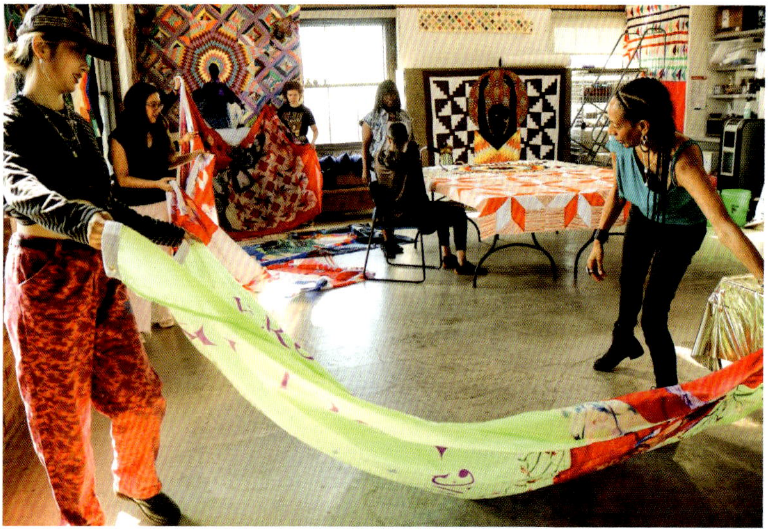

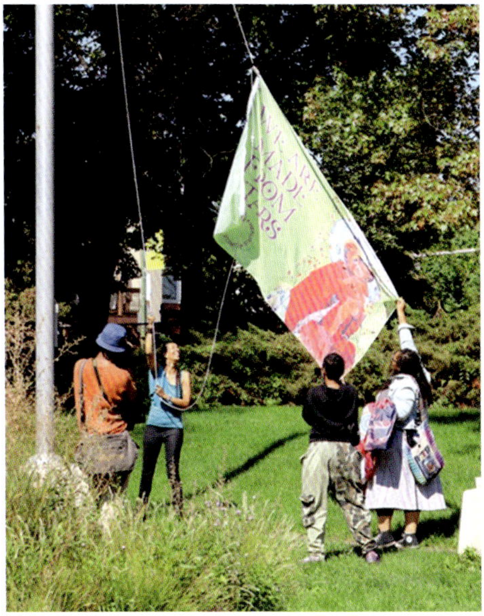

We Are Made from Stars installation, Sonja Henderson and Mothers Healing Circle, 2023

transformed into flags—5-by-8-foot banners that now fly in the historic Sears Sunken Garden in Lawndale. This act transformed private mourning into public memory. Where trauma had once left them avoiding street corners marked by loss, these mothers now visit the garden, take photos, and spend time with their children's presence. They will often share reflections, such as "My child is waving in the air today" or "There's no breeze—my child is resting."

The work of the Mother's Healing Circle is embodied and rooted in love. It pulls the power away from the spectacle of grief and toward the softness of fabric and communal support. Henderson describes composing something from fragments as its own kind of restoration. The process teaches presence, focus, and follow-through—skills that are often disrupted by the gravity of what the mothers have experienced. Over time, the quilting projects have shown the mothers that healing, while nonlinear, is possible—that they can begin something, stay with it, and witness its transformation alongside their own.

Stitched Sovereignty

Sovereignty is rooted in authority and self-governance. Across generations, quilting has been a form of sovereignty for Black women in the United States. While dealing with the realities of a marginalized identity, Black quilters have forged a path toward both creative and material support. What may appear as domestic labor or craft is better understood as cultivating economic possibility and artistic freedom in the face of exclusion. At the center of this tradition are quilting bees, cooperatives, and, more recently, guilds.

Broadly speaking, cooperatives in support of poor Black people emerged across the South in the mid-twentieth century as a grassroots response to economic disenfranchisement and racial segregation. Rooted in the cooperative traditions of Black mutual aid societies and land collectives, these co-ops offered a way for rural communities—and particularly Black people—to secure resources and agency outside of oppressive systems. As activist and scholar Jessica Gordon Nembhard notes, "cooperative economics has long been a part of Black resistance that allowed for collective survival."[174] In the 1960s and '70s, organizations like the Federation of Southern Cooperatives formalized these efforts, often supported by the Student Nonviolent Coordinating

Committee and local organizations. Co-ops became spaces for political education, collective empowerment, and freedom making.

In the years following emancipation and throughout the Jim Crow era, many Black women turned to quilting not just as a matter of necessity but as a means of survival on multiple fronts. While the quilts themselves were made for extensive use, the gatherings where they were made—quilting bees—became sites of mutual aid and intergenerational learning. These bees often started small, hosted in settings like neighborhoods and churches, but their impact was nonetheless significant. Through these gatherings, Black women pooled labor and developed local economies of support that stretched far beyond any one quilt.

Within these communal settings, artistic freedom also flourished. Unbound by the conventions of Euro-American quilting traditions, many Black women developed a distinctive aesthetic. The bee created space for this artistry to take shape, not in isolation but in dialogue with others. Through that process, quilting became a vehicle for Black women to articulate their perspectives, aesthetics, and values, even when the broader society denied their creative authority. This model challenged both economic and cultural hierarchies. By asserting that quilts could

Quilting Bee at Jane House, Good Hope Camp, Ridgeland, South Carolina, Albertype Co., 1916

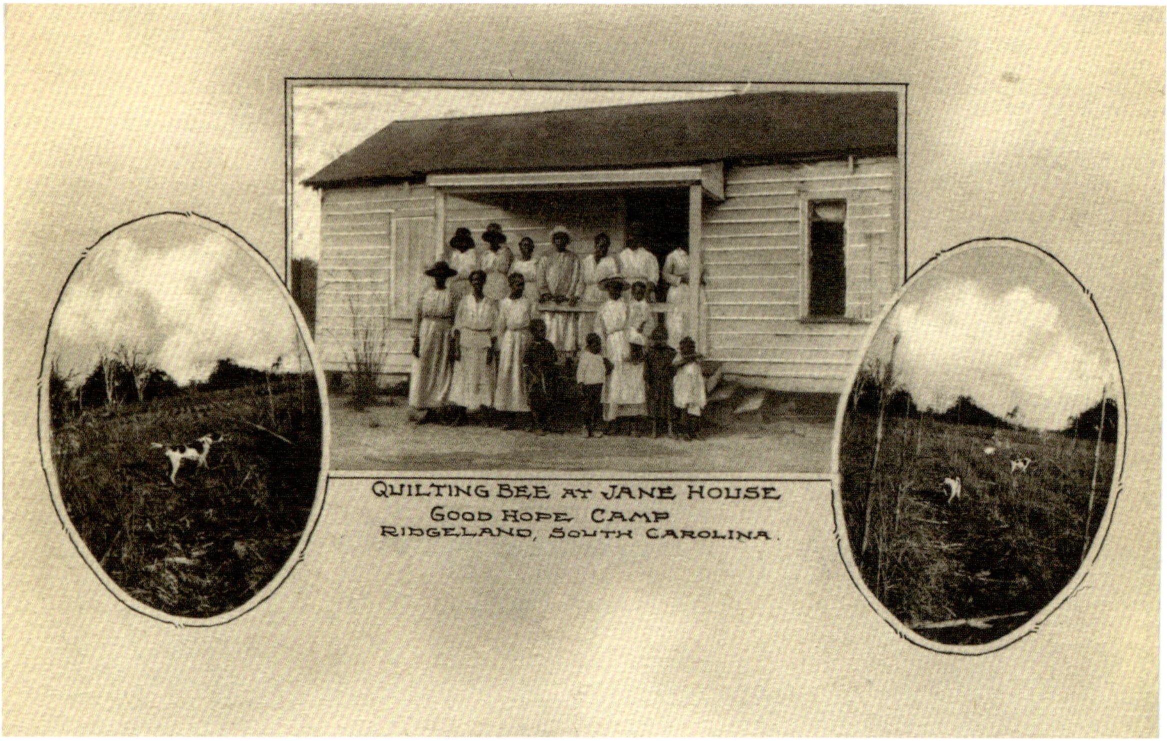

be both art and commodity, cooperatives redefined the value of Black women's work. They offered a structure where artistic choices were shaped by collective agency and input.

FREEDOM QUILTING BEE

The Freedom Quilting Bee remains one of the most notable examples of Black cooperative quiltmaking today. Founded in Alberta, Alabama, during the tumultuous civil rights era, the Freedom Quilting Bee was directly connected to broader struggles for racial justice and economic autonomy. Distinct from other quilting traditions, this collective bridged art with activism, advocating for self-sufficiency in the face of violent repercussions.[175]

By the mid-1960s, Wilcox County was representative of much of the rural Black South: impoverished and entrenched in racial inequality. Nearly half the local Black families earned roughly $1,000 annually (a little less than $11,000 today), and poverty was compounded by looming unemployment threats and both physical and economic retaliation against those who sought civil rights or participated in voting drives.[176] Quilting was an established practice in the community, often taking place individually or in informal gatherings on porches and in shared spaces. However, it was the potential for these quilts to transform economic realities that sparked the formal creation of the Freedom Quilting Bee.

As Nancy Callahan documents, the Freedom Quilting Bee emerged from both necessity and imagination, drawing upon a long tradition of collective Black labor and cooperative economics in the face of oppression. At the center of this transformation was Francis X. Walter, an Episcopal priest involved with the Selma Inter-religious Project. Seeing quilts hung casually on clotheslines during his visits to the area, he proposed organizing local quilters into a formal cooperative to sell their work. In doing so, they could leverage their skill to generate significant income while remaining determined in their political beliefs.

As a result of sustained organizing among the women themselves and support from Walker, more than sixty quilters met at Antioch Baptist Church to form the Freedom Quilting Bee in 1966. The bee's early meetings were spaces where women gathered not only to stitch but to strategize—navigating unfamiliar legal paperwork, discussing regulations, and conceptualizing possibilities. Their organizing was a radical act of refusal to let poverty, racism, or disenfranchisement define their futures.

From its inception, the bee established a dual mission: economic empowerment and political advocacy. Under the visionary leadership of Estelle Witherspoon, a local activist and one of the cooperative's long-term managers, the bee quickly scaled up its operation. It secured contracts with prominent national corporations and retailers, including Sears and Roebuck, and collaborated with interior design powerhouse Parish Hadley. Quilts from the bee graced the pages of *The New York Times* and *Life* magazine and were exhibited prominently at the Smithsonian Institution, underscoring the cultural value and skilled craftsmanship of these rural artisans.

This national attention translated directly into income and visibility for Black women whose labor had long been undervalued or exploited. The operational structure of the Freedom Quilting Bee was deliberately layered. Members were trained not only in quilt production but also in various aspects of business management, including bookkeeping, inventory control, marketing, and negotiating contracts. This strategic approach to skills development ensured some organizational sustainability, providing crucial economic stability in a region characterized by a lack of resources and limited employment opportunities.

Perhaps most crucially, the bee facilitated landownership. With proceeds from their work and through coordinated support, bee members purchased land along U.S. Route 80 where they built a sewing factory in 1969. This space functioned as both a production center and a community hub, anchoring the cooperative in physical and political space. Landownership, as Callahan notes, represented a form of Black sovereignty rarely achieved under the weight of Southern Jim Crow economics.

While financial success was central to their mission, the bee also embedded itself within the fabric of political advocacy. Through connections to civil rights groups like the Southern Christian Leadership Conference (SCLC), the bee provided financial and logistical support for voter registration drives, marches, and demonstrations. Estelle Witherspoon exemplified this intersection clearly, having been actively involved

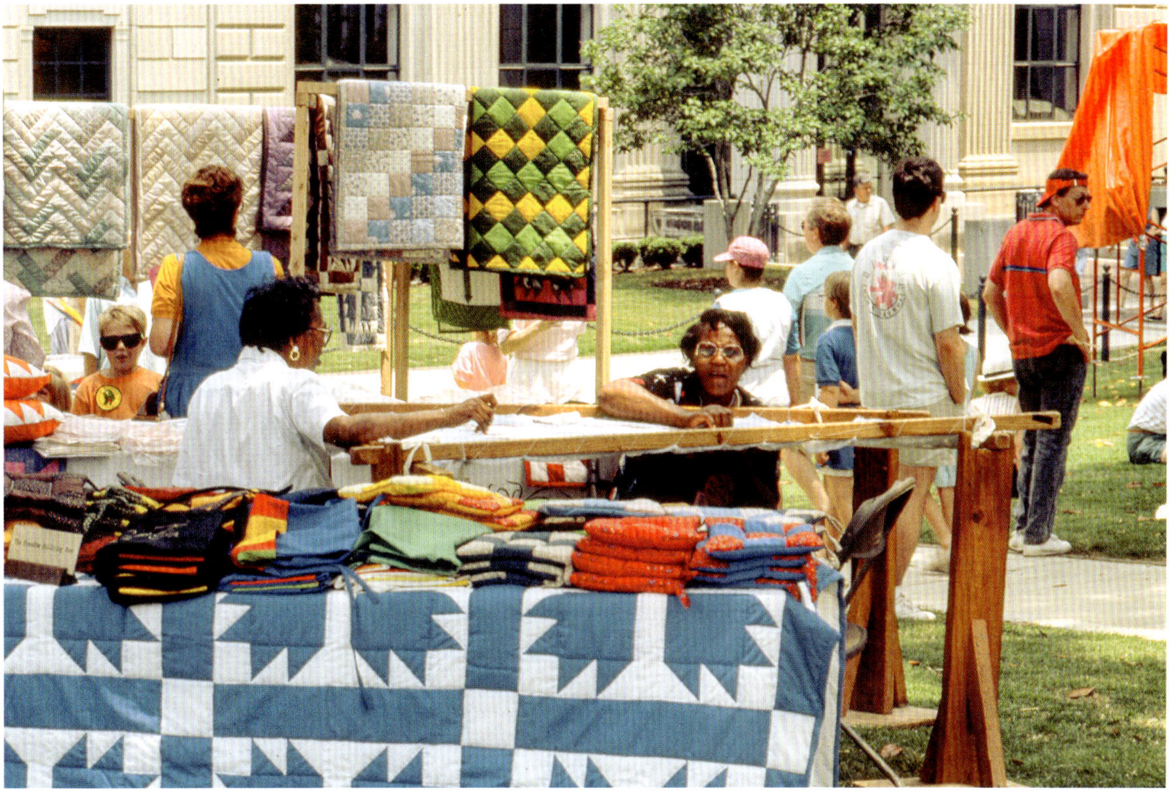

in local protests and arrested during demonstrations for civil rights. Her leadership emphasized economic independence as a key component of social empowerment.

Freedom Quilting Bee at the 1990 Alabama Folklife Festival in Birmingham, Alabama, Kim Appel, 1990

This integrated approach allowed members of the Freedom Quilting Bee to resist systemic oppression, providing a financial safety net should they want to engage in direct political action. As Callahan observed, the very structure of the cooperative encouraged civic participation. The bee's internal governance required collective decision-making, and meetings often included political updates and strategy discussions. Through the bee, women moved from the margins to the center of public life, claiming space not only as artisans but as leaders and organizers.[177]

Though the Freedom Quilting Bee's formal operations ceased in 2012, its impact is still felt today through the work of its descendants. The Freedom Quilting Bee Legacy is a contemporary initiative spearheaded by quilters like Fannie "Pearl" Etheridge, daughter of an original

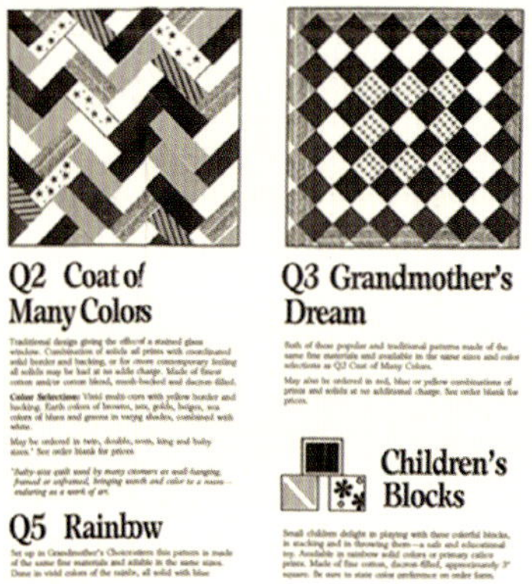

Freedom Quilting Bee brochure, Freedom Quilting Bee, 1980

bee member. This organization strives to preserve the original group's model of empowerment. Etheridge, who joined the original bee following her layoff from a local sewing factory in 1996, emphasizes the transformative impact it had on local women. She vividly remembers how the cooperative provided women with professional skills and economic opportunities that were previously nonexistent. The Freedom Quilting Bee Legacy continues to advocate for the same principles that inspired its predecessor, emphasizing economic sovereignty and self-determination as essential to community resilience and cultural continuity. This ongoing effort ensures that the story and lessons of the Freedom Quilting Bee remain available for future generations.[178]

LIBERTY HOUSE

Liberty House also emerged from the Federation of Southern Cooperatives. Under the umbrella of the Poor People's Corporation (PPC), Liberty House was founded in 1965 as a marketing and retail cooperative. A bridge between Mississippi's Black artisans and a larger national market, Liberty House offered training, supplies, and platforms for selling handcrafted goods, including quilts, dolls, rugs, and clothing. This support enabled artisans, particularly women, to achieve financial stability.[179]

Liberty House's headquarters were in Jackson, Mississippi, with additional stores in cities like New York and Washington, DC. These outlets connected Southern Black makers with Northern consumers eager to support civil rights through ethical commerce. The cooperative also organized workshops and training programs, equipping individuals with skills in craft making, business management, and marketing.

Liberty House's impact extended beyond economic benefits. It offered a national platform for Black Southern makers to showcase their work, fostered cultural pride, and highlighted the rich heritage

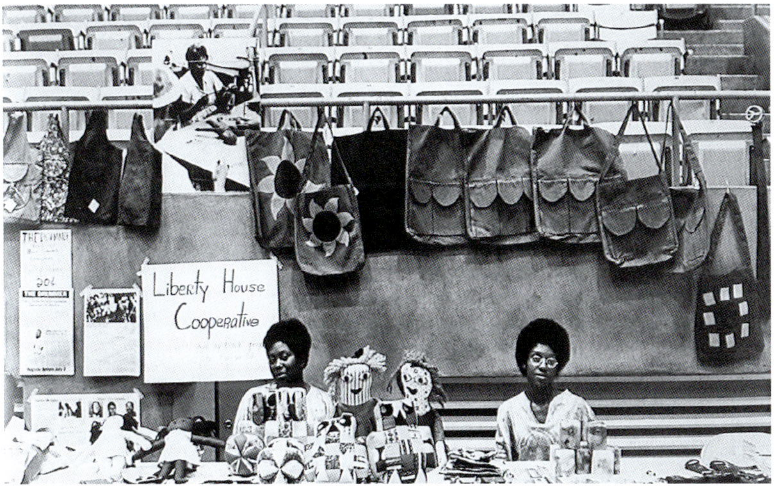

Annie and Vertilla Evans, Local Sales for Liberty House Handcraft Cooperative, photographed by Dr. Doris Derby

of Black craft traditions like patchwork quilting and doll making. Despite facing challenges, including financial constraints and external opposition, Liberty House and the PPC exemplified the civil rights movement's commitment to economic justice and cultural affirmation. Their legacy underscores the importance of supporting community-driven initiatives that empower marginalized groups and preserve cultural heritage.[180]

Guilds and collectives—past and present—carry forward the spirit of mutual aid and the cultural pride of their predecessors. These groups continue to support Black women as artists, cultural workers, and economic stewards. They offer artistic mentorship and, at times, opportunities to generate income. Whereas cooperatives have a stronger focus on economic empowerment, guilds are often committed to extending mutual aid and volunteerism while honoring and promoting the ancestral legacy of the quilting tradition.

TUTWILER QUILTERS

Present-day groups like the Tutwiler Quilters of Mississippi blend camaraderie with financial advancement. Founded in 1988 through the Tutwiler Community Education Center (TCEC), the group was established as a way to help local women generate steady income in an area impacted by hardship and limited job opportunities. The initiative was started by Sister Maureen Delaney, who recognized

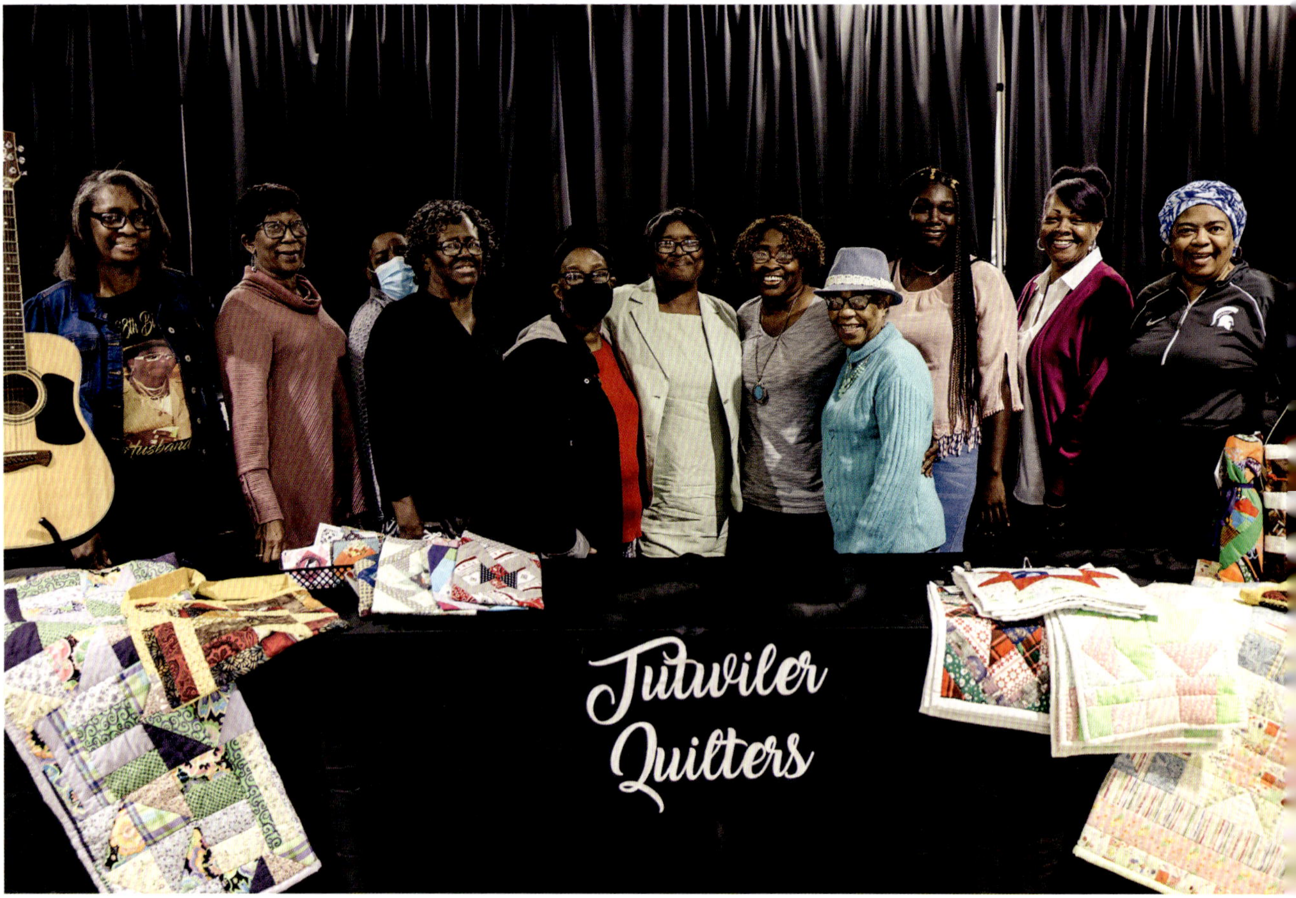

Tutwiler Quilters, Azuree Holloway, 2023

quilting as a skill many women already had and saw its potential for economic development.[181]

The members of the collective produce a range of products, including full-size quilts, baby quilts, pot holders, and tote bags. Each item is handmade, often using traditional quilting patterns and techniques. The quilters primarily work from their homes and bring completed items to the TCEC for quality control, pricing, and packaging.[182] Products are available for purchase at the TCEC in Tutwiler, through the organization's website, and at craft fairs and events around the country. A significant portion of the sale price goes directly to the individual quilter, offering a reliable stream of supplemental income for participants, many of whom are older women who have fixed incomes. Since 1988, the collective has sold over thirty thousand items.

In addition to providing income, the Tutwiler Quilters help preserve the region's quilting heritage. By continuing to practice and share quilting traditions, the group sustains cultural memory in the Mississippi Delta. In 2021 it received a Governor's Arts Award from the Mississippi Arts Commission, which recognized its contributions to community development through the arts.[183]

BROWN SUGAR STITCHERS QUILT GUILD

The Brown Sugar Stitchers Quilt Guild (BSSQG) is a collective based in Atlanta, Georgia, dedicated to preserving and celebrating African American quilting traditions. Conceptualized by Jocelyn Carter and Nancy Franklin and incorporated with the support of Doris Wells, the guild has grown to include 150 members from the metro Atlanta area and thirteen other states. From its inception, the BSSQG has been committed to community service and mutual aid. One of their signature initiatives is the annual donation of handmade quilts to children

Brown Sugar Stitchers Quilt Guild, Azuree Holloway, 2024

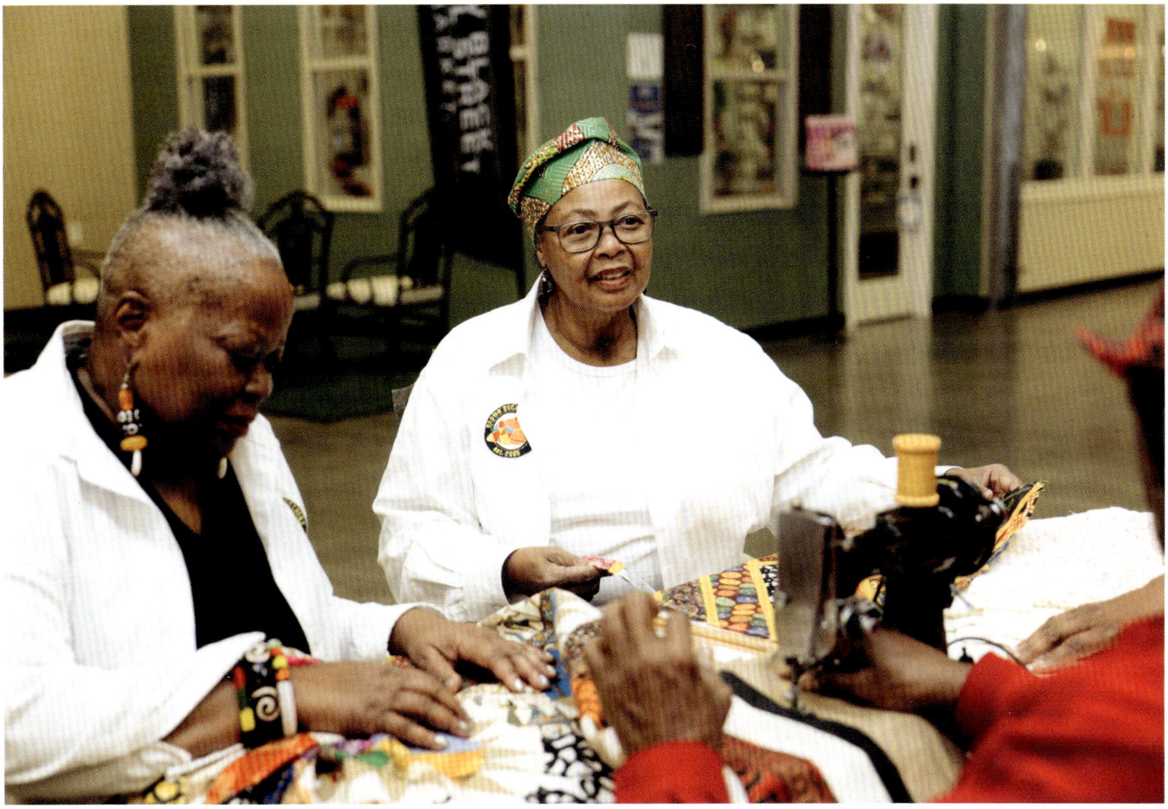

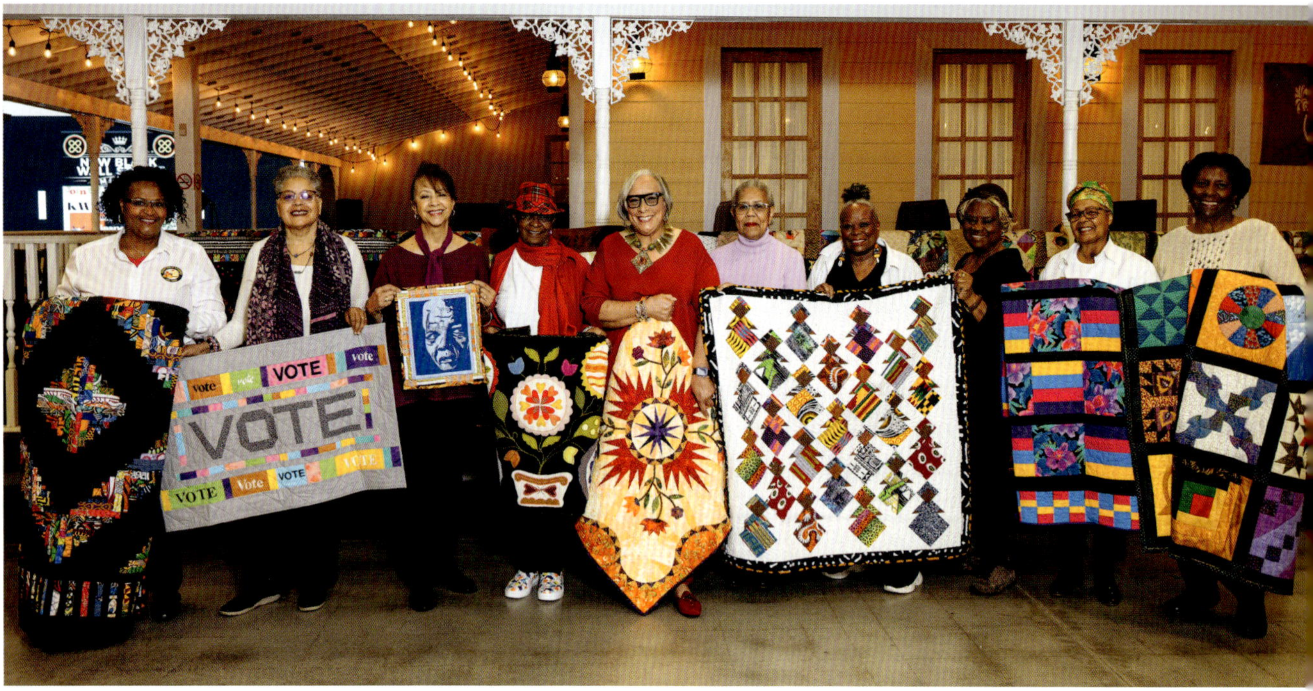

Brown Sugar Stitchers Quilt Guild, Azuree Holloway, 2024

residing at the Carrie Steele-Pitts Home, a foster care facility in southwest Atlanta. These quilts are crafted to provide the children with warmth, comfort, and a feeling of belonging. Additionally, the guild supports children suffering from sickle cell anemia by donating quilts and pillows to patients at Children's Healthcare of Atlanta–Hughes Spalding Hospital.[184]

The guild's philanthropic efforts extend beyond local initiatives. They have provided quilted purses to young individuals in Zambia for menstrual supplies and created tribute quilts for families of local victims of violence. With an added focus on education and outreach, the guild offers programs and quilting lessons led by experienced members, aiming to share the art and history of quilting with people of all ages. They have been involved in enrichment programs at local public schools, the High Museum of Art, the Atlanta History Center, Atlanta's National Black Arts Festival, the Girl Scouts, and Quilts of Valor.[185]

THE PRINCETON SANKOFA STITCHERS MODERN QUILT GUILD

The Princeton Sankofa Stitchers Modern Quilt Guild (PSSMQG) emerged from a need as personal as it was political. Initially born out of informal "sewing playdates" in the home of president and founder Juandamarie Gikandi, it was shaped by the desire to quilt in community with Black women who shared a cultural sensibility, aesthetic fluency, and sense of purpose. The guild's early members threaded together fabric and fellowship, creating a haven for affirmation, laughter, and shared learning in the shadow of predominantly white quilting spaces.

Their chosen name, Sankofa Stitchers, draws from the Akan concept of retrieving what is valuable from the past. It is a fitting name for a guild that centers historical memory and Black cultural expression while actively shaping a vibrant present. As Gikandi notes, "We always wanted to give back to our community," and that ethos is evident in their expansive programming—from MLK Day sewing sessions in living rooms to philanthropy projects benefiting women's shelters, children's homes, and veteran centers.[186]

While their charitable efforts speak volumes, the guild also nurtures deep internal growth. Membership is capped at thirty-five, ensuring intimacy and intergenerational dialogue among quilters who are artists, educators, attorneys, pastors, and poets. Members share skills through a variety of workshops and

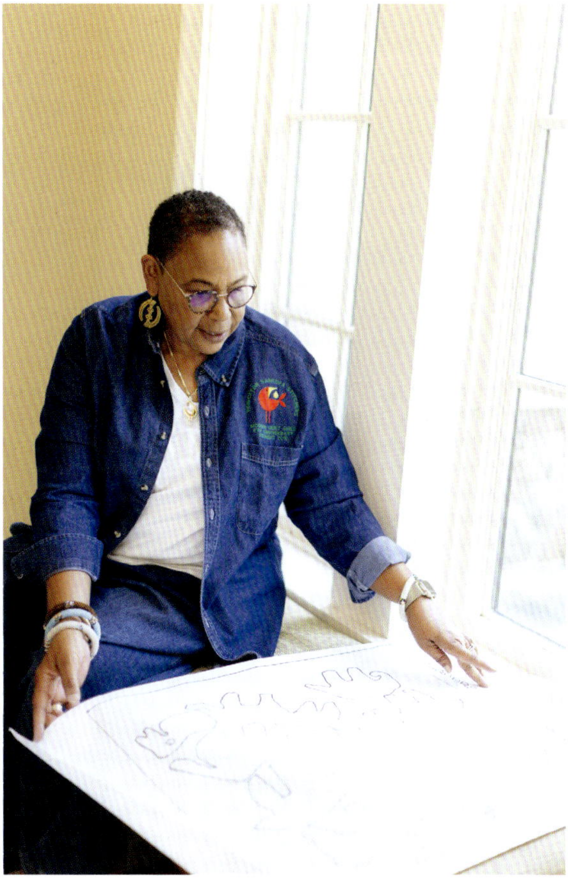

PSSMQG President Juandamarie Gikandi,
Azuree Holloway, 2023

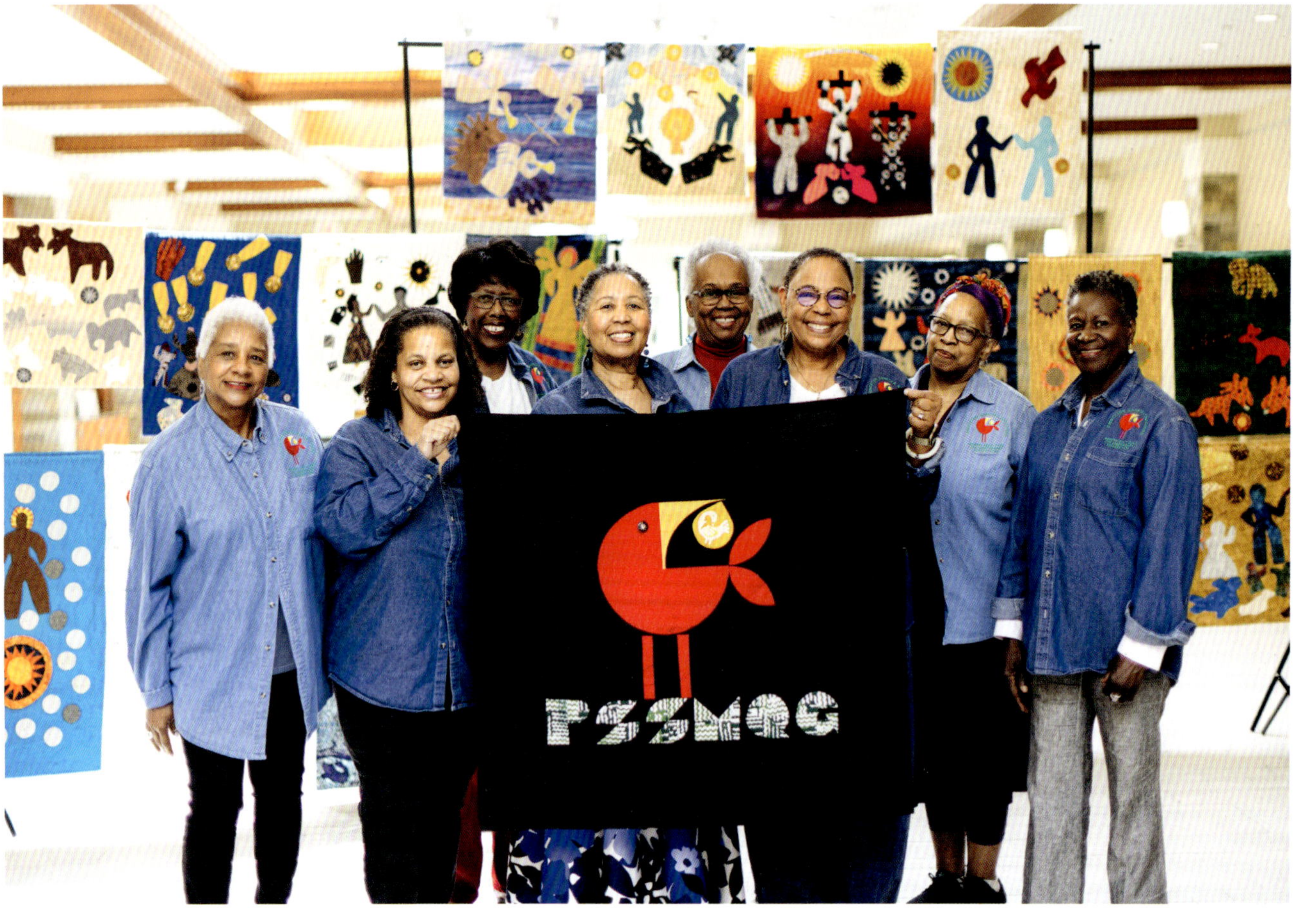

Princeton Sankofa Stitchers Modern Quilt Guild, Azuree Holloway, 2023

participate in creative challenges that explore African American history and diasporic aesthetics—such as their ongoing project re-creating Harriet Powers's biblical quilts as smaller replicas.

Gikandi is a strong believer in the power of guilds to support self-determination and artistic expression for Black quilters:

What unites us is our deep love for the craft. Our guild fosters creative freedom and celebrates all forms of artistic expression. At our core, self-determination drives us. We are intentional in supporting philanthropic efforts that uplift the women and children within our community. We define our identities and our work on our own terms—unrestricted by outside influences. Guided by the principle "Each one teach one," we are committed to a culture of shared learning and growth. Every member contributes to the collective knowledge and skills of the guild, ensuring that we evolve together.[187]

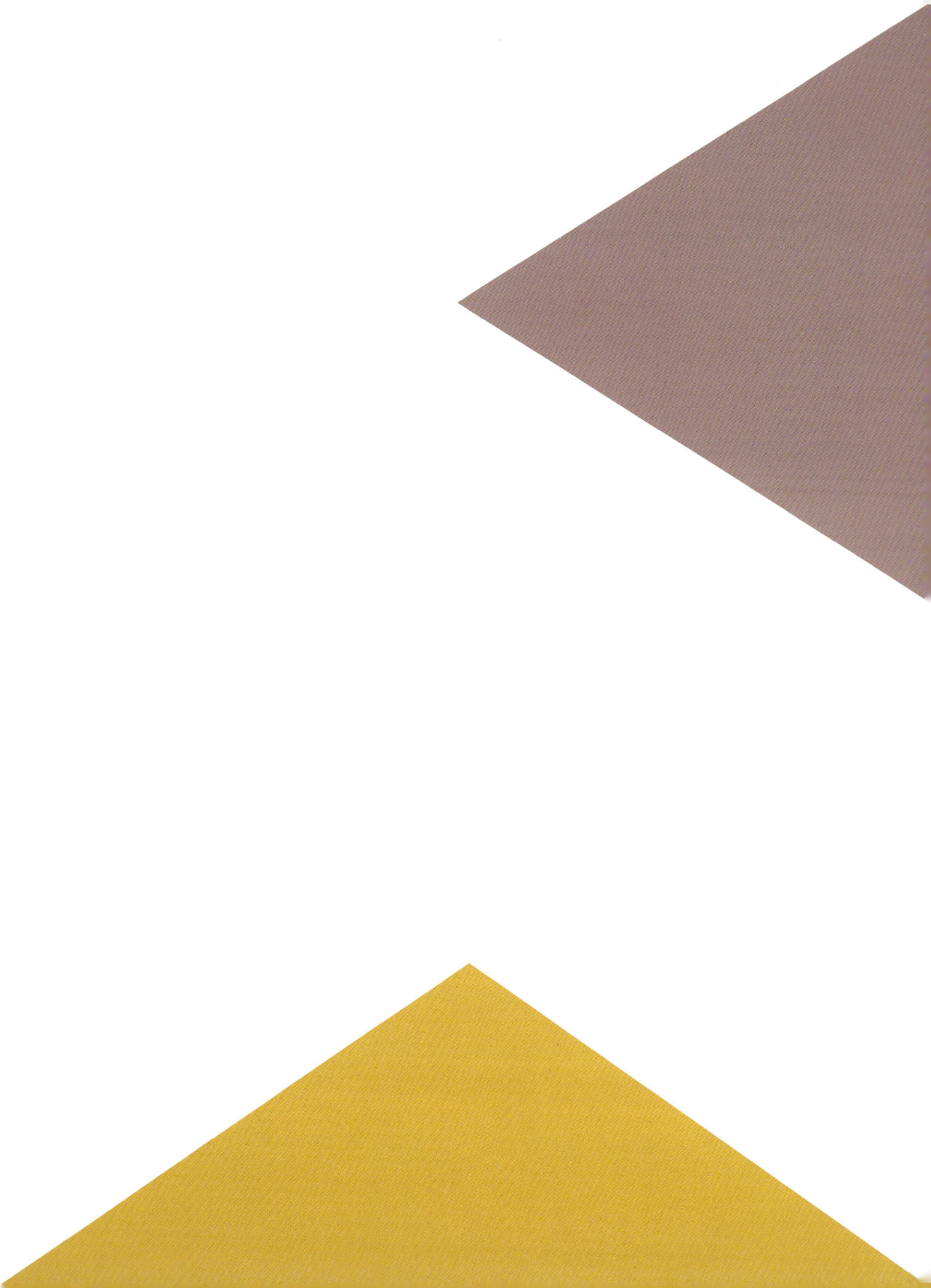

CONCLUSION

Take a moment to hold all that you've read. Do you feel the power and reverence embedded in each quilt? I don't see how you couldn't. I hope the previous chapters have offered a new perspective on or a refreshed understanding of the significance of Black quilters and their creativity. In these quilts, Black life is held tenderly, fiercely, eternally. Every piece is a representation of the centuries of resistance and networks of care that have sustained Black creative expression. I encourage you to consider your role in the preservation of these works as an archive of the past, inspiration for the present, and guide for the future. Archiving Black life and history through quilts is more than mere documentation. It is a gesture of reclamation and radical affirmation. When the stories and experiences of our most vulnerable communities are impacted by systemic violence and erasure, quilts remain a home for them to narrate their existence on their own terms. We should treat quilts as generational bridges that can reach back to inspire those behind us and touch lives yet unborn. Each stitch is imbued with love and protection for those who will inherit these textiles.

By protecting and supporting the creation and preservation of these works, you affirm that Black quilt history is invaluable for the development of our social fabric. As we safeguard these textiles and the lives they represent, we should commit ourselves to future making—a deliberate and hopeful crafting of worlds where Black self-expression thrives unbounded. What role will you play in ensuring that what was once conceptualized and created in love continues to inspire and fortify generations to come?

ENDNOTES

1 Karen Hampton, "African American Women: Plantation Textile Production from 1750 to 1830," *Surface Design Journal* 38, no. 2 (Winter 2014): 24–29.

2 Luisa Cazorla Torrado, *Black Stitches: African American Women's Quilting and Storytelling*, PhD diss., Universidade de Vigo, 2020.

3 Monticello, "Textile Shop," *Thomas Jefferson Encyclopedia*, https://www.monticello.org/research-education/thomas-jefferson-encyclopedia/textile-shop/.

4 Eugene R. Dattel, *Cotton and Race in the Making of America: The Human Costs of Economic Power* (Chicago: Ivan R. Dee, 2009).

5 Gene Dattel, "King Cotton," *New Criterion* 33, no. 2 (October 2014): 16–21.

6 Mississippi Department of Archives and History, "Stories Unfolded," https://proficioweb.mdah.ms.gov/mDetail.aspx?rID=1962.145.5&db=objects&dir=MDAHWEB&list=ex&exID=Stories%20Unfolded.

7 Gladys-Marie Fry, *Stitched from the Soul: Slave Quilts from the Antebellum South* (New York: Dutton Studio Books, 1990), 71.

8 Fry, *Stitched from the Soul*, 75.

9 "Federal Writers' Project, Slave Narrative Project, Vol. 4, Georgia, Part 2, Garey-Jones (1936)," Library of Congress, https://www.loc.gov/item/mesn042/.

10 "Federal Writers' Project, Slave Narrative Project, Vol. 4, Georgia, Part 1, Adams-Furr (1936)," Library of Congress, https://www.loc.gov/item/mesn041/.

11 Gladys-Marie Fry, "Harriet Powers: Portrait of a Black Quilter," *Sage: A Scholarly Journal on Black Women* 4, no. 1 (Spring 1987): 11–16.

12 Museum of Fine Arts, Boston, *Album Quilt*, https://collections.mfa.org/objects/116166.

13 Laurel Thatcher Ulrich, "'A Quilt Unlike Any Other': Rediscovering the Work of Harriet Powers," in Elizabeth Anne Payne, ed., *Writing Women's History: A Tribute to Anne Firor Scott* (Jackson, MS: 2011; online edition, Mississippi Scholarship Online, March 20, 2014), https://doi.org/10.14325/mississippi/9781617031731.003.0004.

14 Janneken Smucker, *A New Deal for Quilts* (Lincoln: University of Nebraska Press, 2023).

15 Smucker, *A New Deal for Quilts*.

16 Smucker, *A New Deal for Quilts*.

17 "Handicraft Projects," World Quilts: The Great Depression Story, n.d., https://worldquilts.quiltstudy.org/greatdepressionstory/unskilledwomen/handicraft.

18 "Unskilled Women," World Quilts: The Great Depression Story, n.d., https://worldquilts.quiltstudy.org/greatdepressionstory/unskilledwomen.

19 "Gee's Bend Quilters' Collective," *Encyclopedia of Alabama*, https://encyclopediaofalabama.org/article/gees-bend-quilters-collective.

20 "Tennessee Valley Authority Act (1933)," National Archives, February 8, 2022, https://www.archives.gov/milestone-documents/tennessee-valley-authority-act.

21 Alice Rawsthorn, “Ruth Clement Bond and the TVA Quilts,” *Maharam*, 2024, https://www.maharam.com/stories/rawsthorn_ruth-clement-bond-and-the-tva-quilts.

22 Angelik Vizcarrondo-Laboy, “Fabric of Change: The Quilt Art of Ruth Clement Bond,” Museum of Arts and Design, February 22, 2017, https://madmuseum.org/views/fabric-change-quilt-art-ruth-clement-bond.

23 James N. Gregory, *The Southern Diaspora: How the Great Migrations of Black and White Southerners Transformed America* (Chapel Hill: University of North Carolina Press, 2005).

24 “Grandmother’s Quilt,” Anacostia Community Museum, Smithsonian Institution, https://anacostia.si.edu/collection/object/acm_2017.10.1.

25 Elaine Velie, “The Incredible Synergy of Toni Morrison and Alison Saar,” *Hyperallergic*, April 13, 2023, https://hyperallergic.com/813895/the-incredible-synergy-of-toni-morrison-and-alison-saar/.

26 Black Women of Print (@blackwomenofprint), Instagram photo, October 25, 2023, https://www.instagram.com/blackwomenofprint/p/Cy1DjVYLaZK/.

27 “Sedrick Huckaby,” Huckaby Studios, https://huckabystudios.com/about/sedrick/.

28 Vicky Waltz, “Big Love,” *BU Today*, September 15, 2010, https://www.bu.edu/articles/2010/big-love/.

29 “Lovie Olivia, “COMFORTER Lovie Olivia Artist Assistant: Preetika Rajgariah Gate D4 Bush Intercontinental Airport,” accessed October 23, 2025.

30 Sandra K. German, “Surfacing: The Inevitable Rise of the Women of Color Quilters’ Network,” *Uncoverings* 14 (1993): 137–68.

31 “Cuesta Benberry—Quilt Treasures Interview,” MTAP Videos, https://www.youtube.com/watch?v=qiB5--YsoUc.

32 Cuesta Benberry, “Afro-American Women and Quilts,” *Uncoverings* 1 (1980): 64–67.

33 *A Tribute to Cuesta Benberry*, October 2, 2004, 2.3.b1.k1, Cuesta Benberry African and African American Quilt and Quilt History Collection, Michigan State University, Lansing, MI.

34 Cuesta Benberry, *Always There: The African-American Presence in American Quilts* (Louisville, KY: Kentucky Quilt Project, 1992).

35 “Curated Conversation with Roland L. Freeman (Part I),” Ogden Museum of Art, https://www.youtube.com/watch?v=LtGrYnP4N_o.

36 “Roland L. Freeman Oral History,” John F. Kennedy Presidential Library and Museum, https://www.jfk.org/collections-archive/roland-l-freeman-oral-history/.

37 Roland L. Freeman, *A Communion of the Spirits: African-American Quilters, Preservers, and Their Stories* (Nashville, TN: Rutledge Hill Press, 1996).

38 Freeman, *A Communion of the Spirits,* 115.

39 German, “Surfacing,” 152.

40 Ibid.

41 German, “Surfacing,” 158.

42 Oral history interview with Carolyn Mazloomi, September 17–30, 2002, Archives of American Art, Smithsonian Institution.

43 bell hooks, *Yearning: Race, Gender, and Cultural Politics* (Boston: South End Press, 1990).

44 Freeman, *A Communion of the Spirits*, 37.

45 Roland L. Freeman, “Folkroots: Images of Mississippi Black Folklife (1974–1976),” *Southern Exposure* 5, no. 2 (September 1, 1977), https://www.facingsouth.org/folkroots-images-mississippi-black-folklife-1974-1976.

46 Freeman, *A Communion of the Spirits.*

47 Celine Romano, “These Quilts Are Richly Stitched with the Stories of the Women Who Made

Them," *Smithsonian Institution Office of Academic Appointments and Internships* (blog), August 12, 2020, https://www.smithsonianmag.com/blogs/smithsonian-institution-office-fellowships-and-int/2020/08/12/these-quilts-are-richly-stitched-stories-women-who-made-them/.

48 Joyce Cauthen, *Presenting Mississippi's Traditional Artists: A Handbook for Local Arts Agencies* (Jackson: Mississippi Arts Commission, 1993).

49 Sharbreon Plummer, ed., *Of Salt and Spirit: Black Quilters in the American South* (Jackson: University Press of Mississippi, 2024).

50 Mary Elizabeth Johnson, *Mississippi Quilts* (Jackson: University Press of Mississippi, 2001).

51 "Hystercine Rankin on What Quilting Means to Her," *Craft in America*, June 27, 2012, https://www.youtube.com/watch?v=GJCxy-1qMKU.

52 Faith Ringgold, *We Flew over the Bridge: The Memoirs of Faith Ringgold* (Durham, NC: Duke University Press, 2005), 67.

53 Ringgold, *We Flew over the Bridge*, 71.

54 Faith Ringgold, *Echoes of Harlem*, 1980, hand-painted cotton, 80½ x 89½ in., Studio Museum in Harlem, https://www.studiomuseum.org/artworks/echoes-of-harlem.

55 Joyce J. Scott, *Walk a Mile in My Dreams*, exhibition catalog (Baltimore, MD: Baltimore Museum of Art; Seattle, WA: Seattle Art Museum, 2024).

56 "Transcending Tradition: The Art of Elizabeth Talford Scott and the MICA Quilt Group," Maryland Institute College of Art, https://www.mica.edu/events-exhibitions/current-upcoming-exhibitions/details/transcending-tradition-the-art-of-elizabeth-talford-scott-and-the-mica-quilt-group/.

57 Carl A. Schoettler, "The Scotts Preserve Heritage in Stitches," *Evening Sun*, April 13, 1981, https://quiltindex.org/view/view/view/?type=publications&kid=62-186-26.

58 "Stitches and Stories: The Quilts and Fiber Art of Elizabeth Talford Scott," streamed live on July 30, 2021, https://www.youtube.com/live/hhSN741ZAxA.

59 Philip Barcio, "Basil Kincaid Discusses Meaning and Symbolism in His New Quilts," *Kavi Gupta* (blog), June 29, 2021, https://kavigupta.com/blog/99-basil-kincaid-discusses-meaning-and-symbolism-in-his/.

60 Osman Can Yerebakan, "Made in His Accra Studio, Basil Kincaid's Quilts Tie Together Histories of Black Quilters, Including His Own Family," *Cultured Magazine*, September 15, 2022.

61 Barcio, "Basil Kincaid Discusses Meaning and Symbolism."

62 Sarah Shelton, "8 Finds Inspired by One Artist's Storied Quilt Creations," *Luxe Interiors + Design*, January 30, 2021.

63 Colony Little, "Kindred Spirits: Aliyah Bonnette's Unexpected Quilt Work," *WALTER Magazine*, January 30, 2025.

64 Aliyah Bonnette, "About," *Aliyah Bonnette*, https://www.aliyahbonnette.com/about.

65 Ibid.

66 Jane Benson and Nancy Olsen, eds., *The Power of Cloth: Political Quilts, 1845–1986* (Cupertino, CA: Euphrat Gallery, De Anza College, 1987).

67 L'Merchie Frazier, "1963–2013: A Civil Rights Retrospective: Introduction," *About Place Journal*, https://aboutplacejournal.org.

68 Frazier, "1963–2013."

69 Stacy C. Hollander, "African-American Quilts: Two Perspectives," *Folk Art* 18, no. 1 (Spring 1993).

70 Jerry Cohen and William S. Murphy, *Burn, Baby, Burn! The Los Angeles Race Riot, August, 1965* (New York: Dutton, 1966).

71 "Watts Riots," Civil Rights Digital Library (CRDL), https://crdl.usg.edu/events/watts_riots.

72 "Generations Later, a Remedy to Destroying Black Neighborhoods Is Fulfilled in Michigan," Associated Press, February 8, 2025, https://apnews.com/article/hamtramck-michigan-black-housing-discrimination-df0a849d251071c30f00955f4a8a02f3.

73 *Garrett v. City of Hamtramck*, 357 F. Supp. 925 (E.D. Mich. 1973), https://law.justia.com/cases/federal/district-courts/FSupp/357/925/2155027/.

74 Sharon Ray, "Hamtramck, My Home," Michigan State University Museum (Michigan Quilt Project; Michigan State University Museum Collection; Black Diaspora Quilt History Project), published in *The Quilt Index*, https://quiltindex.org/view/?type=fullrec&kid=12-8-10561.

75 Peter Granitz, "Senate Passes AntiLynching Bill and Sends Federal Hate Crimes Legislation to Biden," NPR, March 8, 2022, https://www.npr.org/2022/03/08/1085094040/senate-passes-anti-lynching-bill-and-sends-federal-hate-crimes-legislation-to-bi.

76 Leah Donnella, "On Flag Day, Remembering the Red, Black and Green," NPR, June 14, 2017, https://www.npr.org/sections/codeswitch/2017/06/14/532667081/on-flag-day-remembering-the-red-black-and-green.

77 Betty Leacraft, *Nation Time 2020: Power and Protection from Racial Terrorism*, https://bettyleacraft.com/work/contemporary-art-quilts/nation-time-2020-power-and-protection-from-racial-terrorism.

78 Leah Donnella, "On Flag Day, Remembering the Red, Black and Green," *NPR Code Switch*, June 14, 2017, https://www.youtube.com/watch?v=PfjchliUEWA.

79 Katie Neitz, "Beautiful and Powerful," *Lafayette Magazine*, July 11, 2018, Lafayette College.

80 Neitz, "Beautiful and Powerful."

81 Dindga McCannon and Lowery Sims, "In Conversation: Dindga McCannon and Lowery Sims," *Phillips X Presents: Dindga McCannon*, November 16, 2020, https://www.phillips.com/article/65959655/dindga-mccannon-lowery-sims-exhibition-phillips-presents.

82 Ksenia Soboleva, "Highlights from the Collection: Betye Saar—*Extreme Times Call for Extreme Heroines*," *New York Historical Society* (blog), February 28, 2023, https://www.nyhistory.org/blogs/betye-saar-extreme-times-call-for-extreme-heroines.

83 Marion Coleman, *Tender Gardens*, 2014, cotton fabric and batt, 72½ × 72⅛ in. (184.2 × 183.2 cm), Smithsonian American Art Museum, Gift of Michael Humphreys, object no. 2023.41, https://americanart.si.edu/artwork/tender-gardens-120775.

84 Tenderloin People's Garden, "About the Garden," https://www.tenderloinpeoplesgarden.com/about.

85 Leslie King-Hammond, ed., *Gumbo Ya Ya: An Anthology of Contemporary African-American Women Artists* (Baltimore, MD: Midmarch Arts Press, 1995), vii.

86 Hammond, ed., *Gumbo Ya Ya*, viii.

87 Nancy Callahan, *The Freedom Quilting Bee: Folk Art and the Civil Rights Movement* (Tuscaloosa: University of Alabama Press, 2005).

88 Betty Ford-Smith, *Pinecone Quilts: Keeping Tradition Alive, Learn to Make Your Own Heirloom* (Concord, CA: C&T Publishing, 2023).

89 "Let's Talk About Pinecone Quilts with Betty Ford-Smith—Karen Quilt Circle," 2023, https://www.youtube.com/watch?v=ErDw6wxOH6w.

90 "Alabama Folk Heritage Award: Nora Ezell," Alabama State Council on the Arts, https://arts.alabama.gov/Traditional_Culture/heritageaward/Nora_Ezell.aspx.

91 Ibid.

92 "Nora Ezell: African-American Quilter," National Endowment for the Arts, https://www.arts.gov/honors/heritage/nora-ezell.

93 Viola Canady, *Cathedral Window Quilt* (object no. ACM 1995.5009.0003), Anacostia Community Museum, Smithsonian Institution (Washington, DC).

94 "Interview with Viola Williams Canady, July 6, 2004," Quilt Alliance, https://quiltalliance.net/ohms-viewer-master/viewer.php?cachefile=2019oh0386_qsosdd0002.xml.

95 "Quilts of Wendy Kendrick, Music by Starlit Ways," *Broad and High* (aired November 19, 2020), PBS, https://video.kpbs.org/video/quilts-of-wendy-kendrick-music-by-starlift-way-tse0yr/.

96 Wendy Kendrick, "About the Artist," *Art by WEPA*, https://www.artbywepa.net/.

97 Wendy Kendrick, "Queen Mother," Artwork Archive, https://www.artworkarchive.com/profile/wendy-kendrick/artwork/queen-mother-wendy-kendrick.

98 Leslie King-Hammond, Carole Miller Genshaft, Ramona Austin, and Annegreth Nil, eds., *Symphonic Poem: The Art of Aminah Brenda Lynn Robinson* (New York: Harry N. Abrams, 2003).

99 "Aminah Brenda Lynn Robinson Legacy Project," Columbus Museum of Art, https://www.columbusmuseum.org/aminah-robinson-legacy-project/.

100 "The Raggonnon," National Underground Railroad Freedom Center, https://freedomcenter.org/wp-content/uploads/2022/06/Activity_PreK_Raggonnon_210310.pdf.

101 "The Legacy Quilt," Museum of Food and Drink, https://www.mofad.org/the-legacy-quilt.

102 "The Legacy Quilt."

103 "The Legacy Quilt."

104 Michael A. Cummings, "African-American Quilter, 2023 NEA National Heritage Fellow," National Endowment for the Arts, https://www.youtube.com/watch?v=p4-oMvKXFmg.

105 "QUILTS: Learn About Contemporary Quilters from Diverse Traditions," *Craft in America: QUILTS*, December 27, 2019, https://www.youtube.com/watch?v=uDfDIMUi4Fs.

106 *Michael A. Cummings Walks Us Through Yemaya, 2018*, Hunter Dunbar Projects, https://www.instagram.com/hunterdunbarprojects/reel/CyjTgSERKcj/.

107 Ella Martin-Gachot, "Yvonne Wells Doesn't Care If You Call Her Art 'Folk or Fine.' She Just Wants to Keep Creating," *Cultured Magazine*, September 13, 2024, https://www.culturedmag.com/article/2024/09/13/yvonne-wells-quilt-artist-fort-gansevoort.

108 Stacy I. Morgan and Yvonne Thomas Wells, *The Story Quilts of Yvonne Wells* (Tuscaloosa: University of Alabama Press, 2024).

109 Yvonne Wells, *Yesterday: Civil Rights in the South III*, quilt (1976–99), Quilt Index KID 8-5-491, https://quiltindex.org//view/?type=fullrec&kid=8-5-491.

110 Wells, *Yesterday*.

111 Morgan and Wells, *The Story Quilts of Yvonne Wells*, 7.

112 Morgan and Wells, *The Story Quilts of Yvonne Wells*, 6.

113 Author interview with O. V. Brantley, December 18, 2023.

114 Author interview with O. V. Brantley.

115 "Album Quilt—Minneapolis Institute of Art," Artsmia.org, 2024, https://new.artsmia.org/programs/teachers-and-students/teaching-the-arts/artwork-in-focus/album-quilt.

116 "Choose to Bloom by O. V. Brantley," Artwork Archive, 2025, https://www.artworkarchive.com/profile/o-v-brantley/artwork/choose-to-bloom.

117 Author interview with Kewon Hunter, March 15, 2025.

118 Author interview with Kewon Hunter.

119 Kewon Hunter, "About Kewon Hunter," n.d., https://kewonhunter.com/about-3#:~:text=Kewon%20Hunter%2C%20raised%20in%20Mississippi,Black%20lives%20and%20Black%20Culture.

120 Hunter, "About Kewon Hunter."

121 bell hooks, *Belonging: A Culture of Place* (New York: Routledge, 2009).

122 Saidiya Hartman, "Venus in Two Acts," *Small Axe* 12, no. 2 (2008): 1–14.

123 Patricia Hill Collins, *Black Feminist Thought: Knowledge, Consciousness, and the Politics of Empowerment* (New York: Routledge, 2000).

124 *Memorial Quilt for Tuskegee Airman 2d Lt. James McCullin*, National Museum of African American History & Culture, https://nmaahc.si.edu/object/nmaahc_2013.52.2.

125 Charles River Editors, *The Tuskegee Airmen: The History and Legacy of America's First Black Fighter Pilots in World War II* (Boston: Charles River Editors, 2015).

126 "Lt. James L. McCullin Jr.: A Memorial to a Fallen Hero," Google Arts & Culture, Smithsonian National Museum of African American History and Culture, https://artsandculture.google.com/story/lt-james-l-mccullin-jr-a-memorial-to-a-fallen-hero-national-museum-of-african-american-history-and-culture/MAUhp_pZIHtIKw?hl=en.

127 "Quilt, 'Memories of My Father's Death'; 1989," by Hystercine Gray Rankin, Mississippi Department of Archives and Humanities, https://www.dh-mdah.org/rankin-nash-quilts/memories-of-my-fathers-death.

128 "Quilt, 'After My Father's Funeral'; 1993," by Hystercine Gray Rankin, Mississippi Department of Archives and Humanities, https://proficioweb.mdah.ms.gov/mDetail.aspx?rID=2016.20.1&db=objects&dir=MDAHWEB&osearch=hystercine&list=res&rname=&rimage=&page=1.

129 Freeman, *A Communion of the Spirits*, 98.

130 Cameron R. Sandlin, "The AIDS Memorial Quilt on the National Mall," *Smithsonian Institution Archives* (blog), December 17, 2020, https://siarchives.si.edu/blog/aids-memorial-quilt-national-mall.

131 "The Impact of HIV on Black People in the United States," Henry J. Kaiser Family Foundation, September 9, 2024, https://www.kff.org/hivaids/fact-sheet/the-impact-of-hiv-on-black-people-in-the-united-states/.

132 "Interactive AIDS Quilt," National AIDS Memorial, https://www.aidsmemorial.org/interactive-aids-quilt.

133 Lauren Austin, "Gallery Perspectives," Ashley Gibson Barnett Museum of Art, January 12, 2023, https://agbmuseum.org/media/2023/1/12/watch-lauren-austin-gallery-perspectives.

134 Emily Lee Stehle, "Life in Quilts," *Creative Pinellas Magazine*, March 15, 2023, https://creativepinellas.org/magazine/life-in-quilts/.

135 Lake Apopka Farmworker Memorial Quilt Project, "Event in Showcasing Linda Lee's Quilt Pieces," February 26, 2024, https://apopkaquiltproject.blogspot.com/.

136 "Blog: Lake Apopka Farmworker Memorial Quilt," Farmworker Association of Florida, August 24, 2021, https://floridafarmworkers.org/resources/blog-lake-apopka-farmworker-memorial-quilt.

137 Becky Wilson, "Linda Lee: A Voice for Lake Apopka Farmworkers," *Gainesville Iguana*, October 15, 2015, https://gainesvilleiguana.org/2015/articles/linda-lee-a-voice-for-lake-apopka-farmworkers/.

138 Wilson, "Linda Lee."

139 April Shipp, "Strange Fruit Quilt: A Loving Ancestral Remembrance," *Riverwise Magazine,*

April 24, 2019, https://riverwisedetroit.org/article/strange-fruit-quilt-a-loving-ancestral-remembrance/.

140 "April Thomas-Shipp," Space One Eleven Arts Center, October 28, 2021, https://spaceoneeleven.org/exhibition-archive/just-injust/april-thomas-shipp.

141 "Detroiter, Interactive Artist Hails the Black Quilting Tradition Ahead of Juneteenth Workshop at WSU," *Wayne Today*, June 13, 2024, https://today.wayne.edu/news/2024/06/13/detroiter-interactive-artist-hails-the-black-quilting-tradition-ahead-of-juneteenth-workshop-at-wsu-62877.

142 "The People on My Quilt Didn't Get Funerals: 10-ft. Quilt at ArtPrize Honors Victims of Lynching," *Fox 17 Online*, September 30, 2021, https://www.fox17online.com/homepage-showcase/the-people-on-my-quilt-didnt-get-funerals-10-ft-quilt-honors-victims-of-lynching-during-artprize.

143 "The People on My Quilt Didn't Get Funerals."

144 Shipp, "Strange Fruit Quilt."

145 Liv Furman, "Interview with April Anue Shipp," Black Diaspora Quilt History Project, Quilt Index, August 22, 2023, https://quiltindex.org/view/?kid=62-186-75&type=stories&utm.

146 Furman, "Interview with April Anue Shipp."

147 George C. Stonedy, dir., "All My Babies . . . A Midwife's Own Story," Library of Congress, www.loc.gov/item/2017604960/.

148 Maida Owens, "Waiting for Babies: Lay Midwives in Louisiana," Louisiana Folklife Program, https://www.louisianafolklife.org/lt/articles_essays/main_misc_wait_babies.html.

149 Margaret Charles Smith and Linda Janet Holmes, *Listen to Me Good: The Life Story of an Alabama Midwife* (Columbus: Ohio State University Press, 1996), 92.

150 *Learning to Live with Abundance*, solo exhibition by Rosemary Ollison, Portrait Society Gallery, https://www.portraitsocietygallery.com/rosemary-ollison-learning-to-live.

151 Mary Louise Schumacher, "Gallery Night & Day: Rosemary Ollison's Healing Quilts," *Milwaukee Journal Sentinel*, April 14, 2016, https://archive.jsonline.com/entertainment/arts/gallery-night-day-rosemary-ollisons-healing-quilts-b99696831z1-375715521.html.

152 *Learning to Live with Abundance.*

153 "Contemporary Craft in Focus: *Portrait of Resilience*," *Smithsonian American Art Museum* (blog), July 8, 2022, https://americanart.si.edu/blog/portrait-of-resilience.

154 James D. Balestrieri, "New Universes: *This Present Moment: Crafting A Better World*," *Antiques & The Arts Weekly*, August 9, 2022, https://www.antiquesandthearts.com/new-universes-this-present-moment-crafting-a-better-world/.

155 Dawn Williams Boyd and Margaret T. McGehee, "A Place to Sigh: Dawn Williams Boyd in Conversation with Margaret T. McGehee," *Southern Cultures* 28, no. 2 (2022): 48–65, https://www.jstor.org/stable/27179791.

156 Boyd and McGehee, "A Place to Sigh."

157 Rose Corteau, "Dawn Williams Boyd Stitches Together a New American Story," *Cultured Magazine*, November 18, 2022, https://www.culturedmag.com/article/2022/11/18/dawn-williams-boyd-quilt-art.

158 Boyd and McGehee, "A Place to Sigh."

159 "Cookie Washington," Quilters' S.O.S.—Save Our Stories, https://qsos.quiltalliance.org/items/show/2576.

160 Sterling Eason, "Black Mermaids and Goddesses Tell Empowering Stories on Cookie Washington's Quilts," *Charleston Magazine*, June 2021, https://charlestonmag.com/features/

black_mermaids_and_goddesses_tell_empowering_stories_on_cookie_washington_s_quilts.

161 Torreah "Cookie" Washington, "Sophia Goddess of Wisdom by Cookie Washington," Cookie Sews Quilts, https://www.cookiesewsquilts.com/copy-of-califia-goddess-of-california.

162 "All That We Carry: The Epic Stitchers and Friends," Sumter County Gallery of Art, https://sumtergallery.com/cookie-washington-all-that-we-carry-the-epic-stitchers-and-friends/.

163 "All That We Carry."

164 "Celebration for Tina Williams Brewer: Stories of Grace," Columbia Museum of Art, https://www.youtube.com/watch?v=tnD8zlghwcs&t=904s.

165 "Cultivation: Journey of the Work," Westmoreland Museum of American Art, https://thewestmoreland.org/exhibitions/tina-williams-brewer-cultivation-journey-of-the-work/.

166 "Tina Williams Brewer: Stories of Grace," Columbia Museum of Art, https://www.youtube.com/watch?v=wZdlWwSr0mQ.

167 "Cultivation: Journey of the Work."

168 "Tina Williams Brewer: Stories of Grace."

169 Tina Williams Brewer, artist profile, De Buck Gallery, https://www.debuckgallery.com/artist/tina-williams-brewer/.

170 Sonja Henderson, artist portfolio, https://sonja-henderson.format.com/.

171 Author interview with Sonja Henderson, January 29, 2025.

172 Author interview with Sonja Henderson.

173 Author interview with Sonja Henderson.

174 Jessica Gordon Nembhard, *Collective Courage: A History of African American Cooperative Economic Thought and Practice* (University Park, PA: Penn State University Press, 2014).

175 Nancy Callahan, *The Freedom Quilting Bee: Folk Art and the Civil Rights Movement* (Tuscaloosa: University of Alabama Press, 2005).

176 Callahan, *The Freedom Quilting Bee*, 21.

177 Callahan, *The Freedom Quilting Bee*, 21.

178 Sharbreon Plummer, "Come Together: Stitching for a Better Future," *Love and Patchwork Magazine*, December 2023.

179 Elizabeth Rodriguez Fielder, *The Revolution Will Be Improvised: The Intimacy of Cultural Activism* (Ann Arbor: University of Michigan Press, October 22, 2024).

180 "Liberty House and Craft Cooperatives," *Margaret Walker Center* (blog), June 21, 2022, https://www.jsums.edu/margaretwalkercenter/liberty-house-and-craft-cooperatives/.

181 "Tutwiler Quilters," *Mississippi Encyclopedia*, April 15, 2018, https://mississippiencyclopedia.org/entries/tutwiler-quilters/.

182 "Tutwiler Quilters: Building Community Through the Arts," *Mississippi Arts Commission* (blog), January 27, 2021, https://arts.ms.gov/tutwiler-quilters-building-community-through-the-arts/.

183 Sarah Fowler, "Tutwiler Quilters," *Delta Magazine*, May 4, 2021, https://deltamagazine.com/tutwiler-quilters/.

184 Beth Ward, "The Sisterhood of Stitchers: Sewing, Crochet & Craftivism," *Bitter Southerner*, February 2019, https://bittersoutherner.com/the-sisterhood-of-stitchers-sewing-crochet-craftivism.

185 Brown Sugar Stitchers Quilt Guild, http://bssquiltguild.com/.

186 Author interview with Juandamarie Gikandi, October 22, 2023.

187 Author interview with Juandamarie Gikandi.

IMAGE CREDITS

Page 17: Collection of the Museum Division, Mississippi Department of Archives and History

Page 18: Robert E. Williams Photographic Collection, Hargrett Rare Book and Manuscript Library, University of Georgia Libraries, as presented in the Digital Library of Georgia

Page 20: Photograph copyright 2026 Museum of Fine Arts, Boston

Page 22: Courtesy of the Alabama Department of Archives and History

Page 23: Collection of the Museum Division, Mississippi Department of Archives and History

Page 25, top: Library of Congress, Prints & Photographs Division, FSA/OWI Collection, LC-USF34-051612-D [P&P] LOT 1541 (corresponding photographic print)

Page 25, bottom: Library of Congress, Prints & Photographs Division, FSA/OWI Collection, LC-USF33-021233-M1 [P&P] LOT 1248 (Possible associated group of images)

Page 27: Courtesy of the Museum of Arts and Design, NY

Page 29: Courtesy of the Newark Art Museum, copyright Bisa Butler

Page 30: Bequest of the Eli Leon Living Trust, University of California, Berkeley Art Museum and Pacific Film Archive

Page 32: Anacostia Community Museum, Smithsonian Institution, Gift of Dianne Dale

Page 36: The Phillips Collection, Washington, DC, Acquired 1942; copyright 2022 the Jacob and Gwendolyn Knight Lawrence Foundation, Seattle / Artists Rights Society (ARS), New York

Page 38: Digital image the Museum of Modern Art/ Licensed by SCALA / Art Resource, NY

Page 39: Detroit Institute of Arts, copyright Detroit Institute of Arts/Bridgeman Images

Page 41: Copyright Alison Saar. Courtesy of L.A. Louver, Venice, CA

Page 42: Courtesy of Tanekeya Word Harris

Pages 43–45: Courtesy of Sedrick Huckaby

Pages 46–48: Courtesy of Lovie Olivia

Page 50: Roland L. Freeman Photographic Collection (70147), Southern Folklife Collection at Wilson Special Collections Library, UNC-Chapel Hill

Page 52: Alice Walker papers, circa 1930–2014, Stuart A. Rose Manuscript, Archives, & Rare Book Library, Emory University

Page 58: Cuesta Benberry Quilt and Ephemera Collection, The Quilt Index, Michigan State University

Page 59: Collection of Michigan State University Museum #2008:119.1; Courtesy of the Cuesta Benberry Quilt and Ephemera Collection, The Quilt Index, Michigan State University

Page 61: Cuesta Benberry Quilt and Ephemera Collection, The Quilt Index, Michigan State University

Pages 63–66 and 91: Roland L. Freeman Photographic Collection (70147), Southern Folklife Collection at Wilson Special Collections Library, UNC-Chapel Hill

Page 68: Courtesy of Dr. Carolyn L. Mazloomi

Page 69: Women of Color Quilters Network Newsletter, Cuesta Benberry Ephemera Collection at the Michigan State University Museum, Container 1.1.b4, Section 1.1.b4.f7 9

Page 71: Cuesta Benberry Quilt and Ephemera Collection, The Quilt Index, Michigan State University

Pages 71 and 186–90: Courtesy of Quiltfolk Magazine

Page 79: Phoeba Johnson (1883–1984), Slave Chain, 1969. Cotton; hand pieced, hand quilted. 83½ x 70¾ in. Collection of the Mississippi Museum of Art, Jackson. Gift of the Kohler Foundation, Inc., 2022.9.103

Page 80: Phoeba Johnson (1883–1984), quilted by Annie Dennis (1904–1997), Honeycomb Quilt, 1976. Fabric; machine pieced, hand quilted. 71¼ x 64¾ in. Collection of the Mississippi Museum of Art, Jackson. Gift of the Kohler Foundation, Inc., 2022.9.93

Pages 81, 82, and 124: Anacostia Community Museum, Smithsonian Institution

Page 84: Courtesy of Mississippi Folklife

Pages 85 and 86: Copyright 2025 Anyone Can Fly Foundation / Artists Rights Society (ARS), New York

Page 90: Copyright Joyce J. Scott and the Estate of Elizabeth Talford Scott at Goya Contemporary, Courtesy of The Artist Legacy Project (TALP)

Page 92: Courtesy of Basil Kincaid and JPMorgan-Chase Art Collection. Copyright Basil Kincaid

Page 94: Courtesy of Aliyah Bonnette

Page 98: Courtesy of the Alabama Department of Archives and History

Page 100: Smithsonian American Art Museum, Gift of L'Merchie Frazier in memory of Watty and Alberta Frazier and James and Merchie Dooley (grandparents), 2002.41

Page 103: Collection of the Smithsonian National Museum of African American History and Culture Gift of Virginia Dwan

Page 104: Courtesy of Viola Burley Leak

Page 107: From Michigan State University Museum, Michigan Quilt Project; Michigan State University Museum Collection; Black Diaspora Quilt History Project. Published in The Quilt Index

Page 109: Courtesy of Betty Leacraft

Page 111: International Quilt Museum, University of Nebraska-Lincoln, 2021.050.0001

Page 112: Copyright Dindga McCannon and Fridman Gallery, New York

Page 115: Courtesy of Erin LeAnn Mitchell

Page 116: Smithsonian American Art Museum, Gift of Michael Humphreys, 2023.41

Page 121: Courtesy of Betty Ford-Smith; Photo taken by Karla Respress

Page 123: Collection of the Art Fund, Inc. at the Birmingham Museum of Art; Robert and Helen Cargo African American Quilt Collection; Gift of Caroline Cargo

Page 125: Courtesy of the Columbus Museum of Art

Page 127: Courtesy of the National Underground Railroad Freedom Center

Pages 129–31: Courtesy of the Museum of Food and Drink, Brooklyn, NY. Photo credit: Francis Dzikowski for the Museum of Food and Drink

Page 132: Collection of Michael Cummings

Page 135: International Quilt Museum, University of Nebraska-Lincoln, 1997.007.1104

Page 136: Courtesy of O. V. Brantley

Page 139: Courtesy of Kewon Hunter

Page 147: Collection of the Smithsonian National Museum of African American History and Culture, Gift from the McCullin Family, in memory of Second Lieutenant James L. McCullin

Pages 150–51: Collection of the Museum Division, Mississippi Department of Archives and History

Page 152–53: Courtesy of the AIDS Memorial Quilt/ The National AIDS Memorial

Page 155: Courtesy of Lauren Austin

Page 156: Courtesy of the Lake Apopka Farmworker Memorial Quilt Project

Pages 158 and 159: Courtesy of April Anue Shipp

Page 163: Courtesy of Galbraith Photo Arts

Page 164: Artist Bekezela Mguni, created with support from etta cetera and Emily Griz

Page 166: Courtesy of Rosemary Ollison and Portrait Society Gallery of Contemporary Art

Page 167: Smithsonian American Art Museum, Museum purchase through the Kenneth R. Trapp Acquisition Fund, 2021.35

Page 169: Courtesy of Wofford College Fine Arts Collection

Pages 170 and 171: Courtesy of Torreah "Cookie" Washington

Page 173: Courtesy of Tina Williams Brewer

Pages 175–77: Courtesy of Sonja Henderson and the Mothers Healing Circle

Page 180: From the South Caroliniana Library, University of South Carolina, Columbia, SC

Page 183: Courtesy of the Alabama Department of Archives and History

Page 185: International Quilt Museum, University of Nebraska-Lincoln

ACKNOWLEDGMENTS

I would first like to thank my Creator for the gifts of creativity and self-expression. This project was divinely guided at every turn.

This work would not have been possible without the love and care of my mother, Cheletta Plummer, grandparents Ermel and Orlanders Plummer, late great-grandparents Rebecca Northern and Herbert Wells, and extended family and friends who bring so much joy to my life. Thank you, and I love you dearly.

Thank you to Dr. Carolyn Mazloomi, whose mentorship, scholarship, humor, and dedication have been invaluable.

To Dr. Jess Bailey, thank you for your continued friendship and collaboration (and for reminding me that no idea is ever too big).

I am forever grateful to the entire Chronicle team for the time, commitment, excitement, and beauty that is threaded through every page of this publication. I would like to give an extra special thank you to my editor, Mirabelle Korn, and past editorial fellow Isabel Ngo for your advocacy and insight. Mirabelle, working with you has been nothing short of a joy. Thank you for understanding the significance this project holds not only to me, but also to our larger society.

Lastly, thank you to every single quilter/artist/maker who has ever responded to an email, text, call, or direct message since I started my journey as a researcher. You are such an important part of my practice and community, and your collaboration means the world to me. This book is for each of you!

INDEX

ABOUT THE AUTHOR

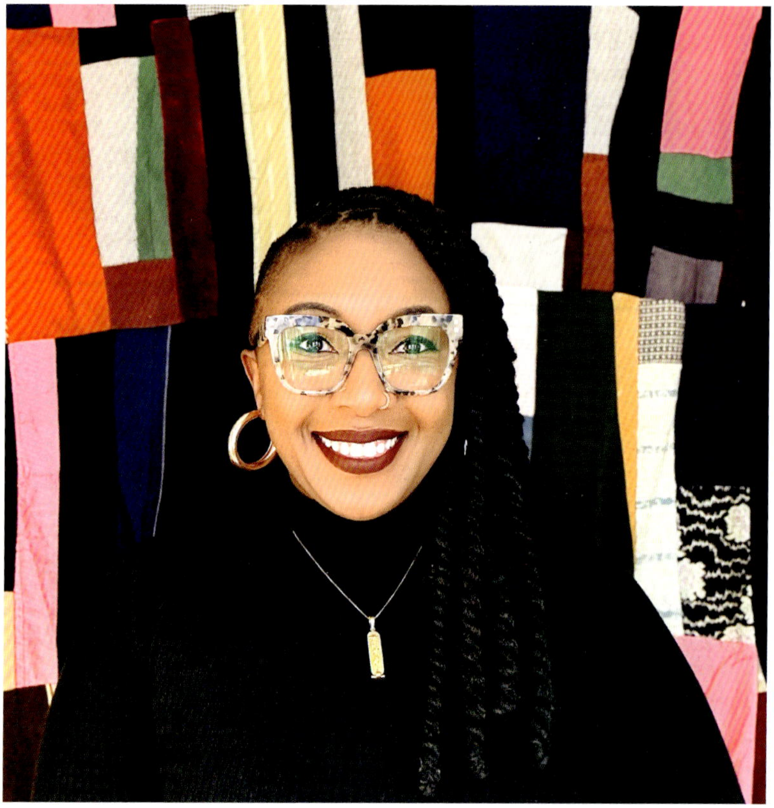

Dr. Sharbreon Plummer is an internationally distributed writer, public scholar, curator, and interdisciplinary artist. Her research and artistic practice have been shaped by her investigations into Black art history and cultural studies, craft and material studies, Southern folkways, and her lived experience as a native of south Louisiana. She is the author of *Diasporic Threads: Black Women, Fibre and Textiles* and editor of *Of Salt and Spirit: Black Quilts in the American South*. She is primarily based in New Orleans, Louisiana.